Date Due

DEC 1 0	2006		

CAPITALISM UNLEASHED

Capitalism Unleashed

FINANCE GLOBALIZATION AND
WELFARE

Andrew Glyn

OXFORD
UNIVERSITY PRESS

OXFORD
UNIVERSITY PRESS

Great Clarendon Street, Oxford OX2 6DP

Oxford University Press is a department of the University of Oxford.
It furthers the University's objective of excellence in research, scholarship,
and education by publishing worldwide in

Oxford New York

Auckland Cape Town Dar es Salaam Hong Kong Karachi
Kuala Lumpur Madrid Melbourne Mexico City Nairobi
New Delhi Shanghai Taipei Toronto

With offices in

Argentina Austria Brazil Chile Czech Republic France Greece
Guatemala Hungary Italy Japan Poland Portugal Singapore
South Korea Switzerland Thailand Turkey Ukraine Vietnam

Oxford is a registered trade mark of Oxford University Press
in the UK and in certain other countries

Published in the United States
by Oxford University Press Inc., New York

© Andrew Glyn, 2006

British Library Cataloguing in Publication Data

Data available

Library of Congress Cataloging in Publication Data

Data available

Typeset by Newgen Imaging Systems (P) Ltd., Chennai, India
Printed in Great Britain
on acid-free paper by
Biddles Ltd., King's Lynn, Norfolk

ISBN 0-19-929199-3   978-0-19-929199-1

1 3 5 7 9 10 8 6 4 2

To Miles, Lucy, Tessa and Jonathan

Preface

Low inflation, quiescent industrial relations, freedom for capital to chase profitable opportunities without restraint and the domination of market-based solutions have become familiar features of the economic landscape of the rich economies. When such a pattern becomes firmly established it soon acquires the status of business as usual. Yet 30 years ago inflation was rising, profits were squeezed, trades unions were bargaining aggressively and parties of the left were actively discussing ideas for deeper state intervention in industry. A huge shift in economic policies and behaviour was needed to launch our economies on their new trajectory. This book provides a short history of how this transformation was achieved and examines the impact on growth, stability and equality of letting free enterprise off the leash.

Authors of books like this one always hope that it will be widely accessible, in this case to anybody interested in the current debates on economics and economic policy. Some acquaintance with economic terminology and ideas is helpful, though I have tried to explain the less familiar concepts. I trust that it will be useful to students in a wide range of social sciences, not just economics, who would like to get a feel for the 'big picture' of how the economic system has been developing.

The focus is on the rich countries—Western Europe, North America, Japan and Australasia. The rest of the world features only when and where its economic development has a major effect on the most developed economies. Thus Africa barely figures, whilst China receives considerable attention. Those primarily interested in the 'South' should still find the book of interest. After all, economic trends in the rich 'North' have such important effects on the rest of the world that they are far from irrelevant to those whose primary concerns are with the poorer countries. Moreover, as Marx pointed out in 1867, '[T]he country that is more developed industrially only shows, to the less developed, the image of its own future' (Preface to first German edition of *Capital*, volume 1).

In previous work with co-authors[1] I have analysed the development of the rich economies from 1945 through the 1980s. The main focus was on profitability, growth and the labour market. The post-war story unfolds around a central theme of the relations between capital and labour, with the balance of economic power betweeen the USA, Europe and Japan an important sub-plot. It is often assumed that the great 'Golden Age' boom of the 1950s and 1960s only required the helping hand of Marshall Aid to emerge smoothly out of post-World War II devastation. This was far from the case. The period of reconstruction was one of social and political turmoil, illustrated in the following quotations from *The Economist* during the late 1940s[2]

The [French] bourgeoisie are not reconciled to the passing of a large measure of political and even economic power to the organised working class . . . Cold War in Italian Industry . . . With hoarse democratic shouts of 'Down with Communism' Japanese employers are rushing to . . . knock out the tottering Japanese trade union movement.

The boom only emerged after the restoration of employer authority in the factories and macroeconomic discipline—with government budgets balanced, modest increases in the money supply and low inflation.

The boom in turn brought a strengthening of labour, the weakening of the previously dominant position of the USA and the economic turmoil of the 1960s and 1970s—rising inflation, profits squeeze, unstable exchange rates, heightened industrial conflict. This turmoil posed severe challenges to the functioning of capitalism, as Chapter 1 of the present book recounts. The next two chapters deal with the response of governments—in terms of restoring macroeconomic discipline, privatization and the encouragement of market forces and the focus of business on 'shareholder value'.

Taking the story through from the 1970s up to the present day necessarily involves a widening of the perspective. Distributional conflict between capital and labour in the rich economies is for now not the most problematic element in their functioning. Thus *The Economist*, as ever the reliable weathervane for assessing the concerns of business, published 61 articles with a focus on trade unions, labour relations and industrial disputes in the period April–June 1979 and only ten in the corresponding months of 2005.

What then are the most significant new developments which have to be interwoven with the continuing themes of the position of the unions, the standing of the dollar, macroeconomic policy and the behaviour of profitability and capital accumulation? One has been the growth of the financial sector, in terms of its rising profitability, its widening sphere of operation and its growing influence on many aspects of economic life. This has important implications for the dynamism and stability of the advanced economies. Secondly, the expansion of manufacturing capacity by low wage producers in the South has undermined the competitive position of traditional industries in the North whilst bolstering the living standards of workers in other sectors. Thirdly, new technology is believed to be undermining the position of the less qualified workers in the rich countries. Thus the chapters which follow cover such issues as the drive for shareholder value, corporate scandals, the growth of China's exports, the New Economy boom in the USA, the impact of globalization on the welfare state, inequality and declining demand for unskilled labour.

Providing a coherent interpretation of such a wide range of issues posed a considerable challenge. Fortunately there is a mass of research now available on most contemporary economic trends and issues. Important surveys appear regularly in the *Journal of Economic Perspectives*, the *Oxford Review of Economic Policy* and the working papers of the National Bureau of Economic Research, for example. The references in the back of the book show how much I have drawn on all this work, which the internet makes instantly and freely available to those fortunate enough to have access to a good university library system. I have used endnotes collected after the text mainly to indicate sources used and in some cases to explain a calculation or to amplify a point. In constructing an argument from this material I have used direct quotations more often than is usual;

hopefully it is more convincing to hear directly from the horse's mouth. Of course I selected the quotes and I have interpreted the analyses contained in them to support my own line of argument. Readers can pursue these issues further using the material referenced. I have avoided lengthy discussion of alternative interpretations of the trends as this would break up the story and may be of limited interest to many readers. However I have tried to indicate where such debates can be pursued.

Much of the material in this book is inevitably quantitative in nature. It is often essential to know not just whether some indicator moved up or down but roughly by how much. As a result my other major source was statistical databases. Much of this material is available on the websites of the national statistical authorities and the international organizations such as the OECD and IMF. Wherever possible I have presented the numbers in graphs which I hope illustrate the argument in an accessible fashion. Since the main point is always covered in the text, the graphs can be skipped by readers who do not find them helpful. Notes on the sources and definitions for the data in the graphs and tables are collected in the Data Appendix. Where very standard variables are referred to—inflation, GDP growth, unemployment—I have used standard OECD series (as in OECD, *Economic Outlook*) without referencing the source.

When distributional conflict—inflation, the wage–price spiral and the profit squeeze—was such a central and destabilizing feature of many of the developed capitalist economies it seemed clear that a resolution one way or the other was inevitable. This is how Bob Sutcliffe and I saw the situation in 1971:

for British capitalism it looks as if this time the wolf is really at the door... From 1964 to 1969 there was a huge increase in the share of the national income taken by the working class... while economic measures and structural changes could bring some relief to capital they are unlikely to offer more than a partial way out... Capital's necessary counter-attack demands that the struggle assumes a more political character.' (Glyn and Sutcliffe 1971: 1)

We now know that the outcome of this struggle was the radical weakening of the labour movement, macroeconomic stabilization and domination of free market ideas[3]. This applied in varying degrees not only throughout the developed capitalist economies but took the form of a much more thoroughgoing, dramatic and wholly unexpected 'restoration of capitalism' in the planned economies of the USSR and the rest of the formerly communist world. This latter development has brought a huge crisis for socialists who, however critical of the communist system, could still look to the centrally planned economies as evidence that alternatives to capitalism could at least maintain themselves. Old certainties, which I shared, that economic problems would be readily solved once free market logic was supplanted by a planned economy operating according to production for need, now seem far too abstract to carry much conviction or political credibility.

However we are not at the 'end of economic history' to adapt a famous catchphrase. On the contrary new questions have been thrown up by the unleashing of capitalism in the 1980s. Will the ever more complex financial system implode in a major financial crisis and bring prolonged recession? Will the integration of the vast labour supplies of China and India into the world economy shift the balance of power even further in the direction of employers and bring a sustained shift in the distribution of income from labour to capital in the rich countries or a renewed outbreak of distributional conflict in the industrializing countries? Can the welfare states of Northern Europe survive the combined pressures of globalization and free market ideology and be developed in a way that meet the aspirations of egalitarians?

Some pointers to possible answers emerge from the analysis which follows. However it is useless to speculate about the next instalment of the history of capitalism before trying to understand the current episode. That is the primary focus of this book.

Corpus Christi College and the University of Oxford gave me a term's leave in the autumn of 2004 and the Oxford Economic Papers Research Fund provided financial support.

I am most grateful for help with references, access to the unpublished work or data from the following: Chris Allsopp, Philip Armstrong, Paul Auerbach, Pulapre Balakrishnan, Jo Blanden, Susan M. Collins,

Martin Conyon, Paul Ekins, Jerry Epstein, Jonathan Garner, John Grahl, Francis Green, Bob Hancke, Brian Harrison, Dieter Helm, Torben Iversen, John Kelly, Matthias Lang, John Knight, Anthony Maidment, William Nordhaus, Tao Ran, Kath Scanlon, Kathleen Thelen, Roberto Torrini and finally Phillipe Van Parijs whose long campaign in support of Basic Income eventually notched up one more adherent. Luca Nunziata was graciously unproprietorial about a key quotation which featured in his thesis. Makoto Itoh gave me the excellent advice that if I didn't want to write a long book I could try writing a short one.

I had very valuable comments on drafts from, Perry Anderson, Andrea Boltho, David Chambers, Andrew Charlton, Jonathan Garner, Francis Green, David Howell, Makoto Itoh, John Kelly, Harry Lee, John Quiggin, Terry Peach, David Soskice and anonymous publishers' readers. I have benefited enormously from collaborations over a long period and have drawn freely on joint work with Philip Armstrong, Dean Baker, V. Bhaskar, Esra Erdem, John Harrison, David Howell, Alan Hughes, Alain Lipietz, Steve Machin, Bob Rowthorn, John Schmitt, Ajit Singh, Wiemer Salverda and Bob Sutcliffe.

Mary Robertson provided great assistance and suggestions in the final stages of writing. Discussions on many of the issues over a long period with Bob Brenner, Bob Rowthorn, David Soskice and Lynn Walsh have been extremely helpful. The person who was most responsible for my involvement with political economy, Bob Sutcliffe, read and commented closely on the whole text, saved me from gaffes, and urged a positive approach to future prospects. Sarah Caro was a most encouraging and helpful editor. Finally, and above all, Wendy Carlin was hugely supportive throughout the whole enterprise and exceeded any possible obligation by reading and commenting in detail on the whole draft twice, despite having to complete a far weightier tome at the same time.

AJG

Contents

List of Figures   xiv
List of Tables   xvi

1 **Challenges to Capital**   I

2 **Austerity, Privatization and Deregulation**   24

3 **Finance and Ownership**   50

4 **Globalization and International Economic Relations**   77

5 **Labour's Retreats**   104

6 **Growth and Stability**   129

7 **Welfare and Income Inequality**   156

Data Appendix   184
Notes   195

References   209
Index   227

List of Figures

1.1 Strikes: Days on Strike per 1,000 Industrial Workers, 1953–2003   6

1.2 Inflation and Real Wage Increases, 1963–2003   6

1.3 Manufacturing Gross Profit Share of Value Added, 1960–2000   7

1.4 Real Commodity Prices, 1952–2004   10

1.5 Consumer Prices in Germany and Italy relative to USA, 1960–2003   12

1.6 Deutschemark and Lira Exchange Rates versus Dollar, 1950–1980   12

1.7 Growth in Labour Productivity, Whole Economy, 1960–2004   14

1.8 OECD Government Expenditure, 1952–2003   17

1.9 Share Prices compared to Average Wages, 1950–2002   22

2.1 Unemployment Rates, 1960–2004   26

2.2 US Short-Term Interest Rates, 1950–2004   26

2.3 Long-Term Real Interest Rates, 1850–2003   29

2.4 Unemployment 1990–1999 and Strikes, 1968–1979   32

2.5 Structural Unemployment and Unemployment Benefits, 1999   48

3.1 US Financial Sector Corporate Profits, 1950–2004   52

3.2 Real Exchange Rates, 1975–2004   68

4.1 Manufacturing Productivity relative to USA, 1979–2003   78

4.2 US$ Exchange Rate: Nominal and Real, 1975–2003   80

4.3 US Current Account and Domestic Investment, 1980–2003   82

4.4 Shares of World Output, 1950–2004   89

4.5 Catch-Up to USA in Asia—per capita GDP, 1950–2001   89

4.6 Shares of World Commodity Exports, 1948–2003   92

4.7 Manufacturing Wages during Catch-Up, 1950–2003   93

4.8 Trade as a Percentage of GDP, 1950–2000   97

5.1 Men's Employment Rate in Industry, 1970–2001   105

5.2 Women's Employment Rate in Services, 1970–2001   106

5.3 Employment Rates, Men and Women, 1970–2001   106

5.4 Employment Rate Changes by Skill Groups, 1980–2000   108

5.5 Unemployment Benefits: Ratio to Earnings, 1960–1999   115

5.6 Wage Differentials, 1980–2000   117

5.7 Minimum Wages—Ratio to Average Pay, 1964–2000   119

5.8 Trade Union Membership as a Percentage of
     Employees, 1960–2001   121

6.1 Growth of Output per Head of the Population, 1960–2004   131

6.2 Contributions to US GDP Growth: Three Long Expansions   132

6.3 US Capital Stock Growth: Private Business, 1950–2003   134

6.4 US Profit Rates: Non-financial Corporations, 1950–2004   136

6.5 Japan Profit Rates: Non-financial Corporations, 1952–2003   141

6.6 Europe Profit Rates: Non-financial Sector, 1950–2003   146

7.1 Correlation between Sons' and Fathers' Incomes, 2000   174

List of Tables

1.1 Labour Market Trends, 1960–1979   4

2.1 Budget Deficits, 1952–2004   33

2.2 Production and Incomes in UK Utilities, 1970–2002   40

4.1 Financing the US Balance of Payments Deficit, 1980–2004   85

4.2 Capital Accumulation: Growth Rates of Fixed Capital Stock,
    1960–2004   86

4.3 China's Exports, 1980–2003   91

4.4 Import Penetration of Domestic Markets for Manufactures,
    1913–2001   97

4.5 Foreign Direct Investment Flows, 1992–2003   100

6.1 Labour Productivity Growth in Business Sector, 1976–2003   143

6.2 Global Growth Volatility, 1954–2003   148

7.1 Corporation Tax Rates: OECD Countries, 1982–2001   165

7.2 Social Spending: OECD Countries, 1980–2001   166

7.3 Income Inequality: OECD Countries, 1980–2000   169

7.4 Poverty and Impact of the Benefit and Tax System, 2000   171

1

Challenges to Capital

We all had the feeling it could come apart in quite a serious way. As I saw it, it was a choice between Britain remaining in the liberal financial system of the West as opposed to a radical change of course because we were concerned about Tony Benn precipitating a policy decision by Britain to turn its back on the IMF. I think if that had happened the whole system would have begun to come apart. God knows what Italy might have done; then France might have taken a radical change in the same direction. It would not only have had consequences for economic recovery, it would have had great political consequences. So we tended to see it in cosmic terms.

(US State Department official recalling UK negotiations with the IMF in 1976, quoted in *Sunday Times*, 21 May 1978).

In the 1950s and 1960s the economies of the most developed capitalist countries (North America, Western Europe, Japan and Australasia)[1] enjoyed an unprecedented boom, combined with low unemployment, low inflation and rapidly growing living standards. This was soon to be designated the 'Golden Age', because in the second half of the 1960s and through the 1970s the whole structure of stable, profitable growth threatened to fall apart. As the comment at the top of the page indicates, the very stability of the capitalist system seemed to be under serious threat.

The rest of this chapter outlines the various strands of this story. The long boom of the 1950s and 1960s brought high employment and greatly strengthened the bargaining position of workers. This led to wage increases and a profits squeeze and powerful unions challenged the freedom of employers to run their businesses and invest as they pleased. The relatively orderly international economic system, presided over by the USA after World War II, was unravelling as Europe and Japan were closing the gap in productive efficiency with the USA. Combined with different degrees of wage pressure in different economies, this led to a splintering of the fixed exchange rate system. Inflationary pressure was exacerbated by the rise in food and raw material prices in the early 1970s, a response to high demand and topped up by speculation. More ominous was the fourfold increase in oil prices at the end of 1973, initiated by the OPEC producers and reflecting the much more assertive stance of some ex-colonial countries. A further underlying problem, though this only became clear with the benefit of several years' hindsight, was a severe decline in the rate of productivity growth from the mid-1970s. Since productivity growth is the basic source of increased living standards and improved public services, a slower rate of expansion was bound to exacerbate conflicts over the distribution of national output.

The common theme to these apparently disparate problems was that the very success of the 'Golden Age' seemed to have undermined its basis. It brought extended full employment and thus the strengthening of labour; high demand for energy and other materials was pressing against available supplies; Europe and Japan were catching up with the USA thus disrupting international economic relations; productivity growth appeared to be running out of steam as the potential of existing technologies was used up. Moreover, although the USSR and the other planned economies had deep economic problems of their own, their continued existence still held out the possibility of an alternative path for development to that offered by free market capitalism. Although particularly important as a model for developing countries, the apparent viability of planned economies also made more credible a range of proposals from the labour movements of the rich countries for radical constraints on free market capitalism. The sections which follow consider the various aspects of the turmoil of the 1970s in a little more detail. The origins and nature of this widely heralded 'crisis of capitalism' are hotly debated and different authors ascribe varying weights to the factors considered below.[2] The account given here follows the emphasis on profitability and capital-labour relations of Armstrong *et al.* (1991).

Organized Labour

The most striking employment trend in the highly developed economies during the long boom of the 1950s and 1960s was the decline in importance of agricultural employment and the corresponding rise in the number of wage workers in industry and services. Agricultural employment fell from 25% of total employment in OECD countries in 1950 to 9% in 1973[3] and the proportion of those working classified as self-employed fell from 31% in 1954 to 17% in 1973 as peasants shifted to the towns.[4]

In Europe the decline in agriculture was not quite as fast as in Japan but much greater than in the USA, which had far fewer farmers to start with. The exodus from agriculture contributed as much to the labour force available for work in industry and services as did the growing population of working age overall. Services employment rose more rapidly than industrial employment because of slower growth of labour productivity in services.[5] The proportion of men of working age (15–64) employed fell as more stayed on in education and fewer carried on working into retirement. This rise in 'inactivity' did not imply an overall shortage of jobs for men, however, as male unemployment was falling.

Women kept their rather small number of industrial jobs (14% of urban women worked in industry in 1950 and 1973 whilst 52% of urban men had industrial jobs in 1950 and 44% in 1973). However urban women's employment in Europe rose almost twice as fast as men's as large numbers moved from household work into jobs in services.[6]

Although net inward migration was significant, by the end of the 1960s and early 1970s, when labour markets had become very tight, it was only contributing 0.1% per year to the population of the highly industrialized economies or a tenth of the total increase in population of working age. In Europe net inward migration was only one-fifth as important as a source of additional labour as the shift out of agriculture.

The motor behind the expansion of jobs in the modern industrial and services sector was the rapid accumulation of capital. Businesses increased their stock of capital equipment by about 5 % a year in the 1960s and early 1970s.[7] Although capital per worker grew strongly, more workers were still required in the new factories and offices.

The great expansion of urban population brought with it a strengthening of trade unionism and legislative changes supporting labour's bargaining position. Table 1.1 shows a number of relevant indicators. The proportion of those at work who were union members increased in the average OECD country. The increase was modest since employment in services was expanding and service workers (apart from the growing group of public sector employees) tended to be much less unionized than industrial workers. However, with unemployment low over a prolonged period, union organization was strengthened. The table also shows that the level of unemployment benefits rose substantially compared to pay, and eligibility for benefit became more relaxed. Unemployment, as well as being less likely, was also less costly financially to those affected, thus reducing the pressure to take the first job that became available regardless of conditions. Employment protection legislation (EPL), against arbitrary dismissal and generally limiting employer prerogatives over hiring

Table 1.1 **Labour Market Trends, 1960–1979**

Average for 19 OECD countries	Union Membership % of employment	Employment protection legislation index	Unemployment benefit as % of average pay	Unemployment rate (%)
1960–4	38.8	0.79	28.0	2.1
1965–9	39.1	0.85	31.0	2.1
1970–4	41.4	0.99	34.6	2.5
1975–9	44.8	1.09	43.2	4.3

Sources: Baker *et al.* (2005). See Data Appendix.

and firing, was also extended in this period, as shown in the OECD's index. Another very significant gain for workers was a sharp fall in average hours worked from around 2000 per year in 1950 to 1750 in 1973—the equivalent of more than a half day less work per week.[8]

An important manifestation of labour's stronger position, and employers' resistance to workers' demands, was the high level of industrial conflict. The most spectacular examples of labour militancy were the strike waves of the late 1960s. Some 150 million days were taken in strikes in France in May–June 1968 as workers occupied the factories, initially in protest at the suppression of student demonstrations. Radical demands for workers' control were channelled by the trade union leadership into negotiations which settled for a 10% wage increase, an increase in the minimum wage, and some extension of trade union rights. In 1969 60 million days in Italy were taken by successive strike waves, originating on the shop floor. These culminated in another 10% pay increase, combined with reductions in working hours, parity of treatment when sick for blue and white-collar workers and eventually a major extension of trade union rights at the factory level. Nearly 25 million working days were given over to strikes in the UK during 1970/71 after a national incomes policy broke down.[9] Even normally peaceful German industrial relations were ruffled by a wave of unofficial strikes and the United States topped the OECD league table in days on strike per worker in 1970 (as it had done in 1954, 1955, 1959, 1960 and 1967).

Figure 1.1 shows the longer-run trend in strikes for OECD countries, with year to year fluctuations ironed out by using a five-year average. Strikes are measured as days on strike per 1,000 workers in industry. Strikes build up from the later 1960s to the mid-1970s and then decline dramatically through the 1980s and 1990s. The 1990s appear very quiet in terms of open industrial conflict even as compared to the golden years of the 1950s and 1960s.

In each of the European countries the rate of money wage increases more or less doubled after the major strike movements[10] and the trend of real wage increases rose steadily to reach over 4% per year in the early 1970s in the OECD countries (see Fig. 1.2). The sharp rise in money wages also contributed to the upward trend in inflation in the second part of the 1960s. Inflation rose more sharply in the early 1970s with the rise in oil and commodity prices (see below); when inflation reaches 12% a year the real value of pay packets is falling by 1% a month—fast enough to be very noticeable and a source of increased social tension. The rise in inflation reined in the rate of real wage increases, especially towards the end of the 1970s.

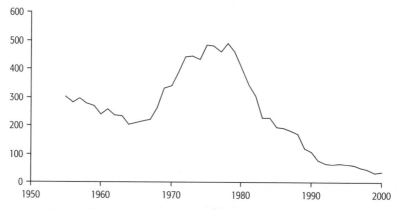

Fig. 1.1. **Strikes: Days on Strike per 1,000 Industrial Workers, 1953–2003**
Source: Office of National Statistics. See Data Appendix. 16 countries.

Fig. 1.2. **Inflation and Real Wage Increases, 1963–2003**
Source: IMF. See Data Appendix. 13 countries.

Wage pressure also contributed to a squeeze on profitability. By the mid-1970s the gross profit share in manufacturing, a sensitive and readily available indicator of returns on investment in the sector of the economy most exposed to the vicissitudes of industrial strife and competition, had sunk by more than one-quarter in a decade (see Fig. 1.3) having been pretty stable until the late 1960s. Gross profits are calculated before deduction of depreciation on capital employed. Depreciation was tending to rise as a share of value added, in part because more of the capital stock was machinery, which depreciates faster than factory building. Thus the fall in net profits was proportionately considerably greater than the fall in the gross share. Further, employers are most concerned with the rate of profits compared to their capital outlays rather than output produced, and these outlays were rising faster than output. Allowing for this, the net rate of profit on capital employed in manufacturing had fallen by nearly one-half by the end of the 1970s.[11] It was apparent that the profits squeeze was reflecting a combination of militant wage pressure pushing up earnings and international competition restraining price increases.[12] The rise in imported material costs and weakening of productivity growth (see below) further exacerbated the distributional struggle.

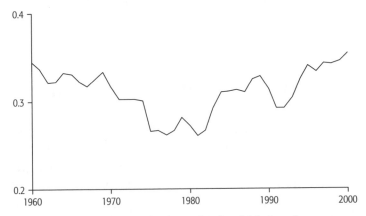

Fig. 1.3. **Manufacturing Gross Profit Share of Value Added, 1960–2000**
Source: OECD. See Data Appendix. 15 countries.

It is hard, 30 years or so later, to appreciate the sense of alarm engendered by the industrial strife and distributional conflict of the late 1960s and 1970s. In the UK the defeat of the Conservative government in early 1974, after a second successful miners' strike, provoked an article in *The Times* (5 Aug. 1974) headlined 'Could Britain be heading for a military takeover' by Lord Chalfont, a Defence Minister in a previous Labour government. In it he wrote of 'the massive power and often ruthless action of the great industrial trades unions' and noted that 'Large industrial concerns are beginning to talk in terms of a co-ordinated defence against industrial action or wholesale nationalisation'. A reply shortly thereafter (16 Aug. 1974) by the then Defence Correspondent of *The Times*, appeared under the headline 'It would not take a coup to bring British troops onto the streets', where he envisaged a scenario when 'an annual rate of inflation of 20 per cent would soon bring us to a point where there had to be a stabilization plan involving great hardship to most of the country or—even without a stabilization plan—the effects of rising prices and shortages had caused such chaos that conventional economic and social life was being overthrown'. He went on to discuss scenarios in which the forces would be called in to break strikes, which could escalate to a situation where 'normal legal administration is impossible and the only authority left is the military commander'. Such a scenario, he wrote is 'still *nearly* inconceivable' (his emphasis).

International Disorganization

At the end of World War II the USA was in an unrivalled position of economic and political leadership of the OECD countries. In 1950, with the bulk of post-war reconstruction completed, the USA still produced about 60% of the total output of the biggest seven capitalist countries, and its manufacturing industry was about twice as productive, per person employed, as that of the UK, three times as productive as German manufacturing and nine times as productive as Japanese manufacturing.[13] The economic power of the USA placed the dollar at the centre of the international financial system, and other countries fixed the value of their currencies to the dollar at rates which were competitive after devaluations in 1949.

The long boom of the 1950s and 1960s was much stronger in Japan and Europe than in the USA. Faster growth of the capital stock, encouraged by plentiful supplies of relatively cheap labour and taking advantage of new technologies and management practices developed in the USA over the previous decades, eroded the productivity gap of European and Japanese manufacturing whilst lower wage levels kept their exports highly competitive. Between 1955 and 1970 hourly labour productivity in manufacturing grew by 10.3% per year in Japan and 6.7% in Germany, as compared to 2.3% per year in the USA.[14] Although money (and real) wages grew more slowly in the USA this was not sufficient to maintain export competitiveness. The US share of world manufactured exports halved between 1950 and 1970 (from 33% to 16%). Japan, having excelled in heavy industry (basic metals including steel was estimated as 60% more productive per hour worked in Japan than in the USA by 1980), was rapidly developing world leadership in mass production industries. In electrical machinery and instruments Japanese productivity exceeded the US level by 1980.[15] The US trade account moved into deficit by the end of the 1960s compounding the weakness of the dollar caused by heavy outflows of 'direct investment' as US corporations expanded their production activities abroad, mainly in other OECD countries.

A second disorganizing influence on the international economic relations of the OECD countries was the rise in the cost of raw materials, food and energy imported from outside the OECD. Figure 1.4 shows oil and non-energy commodity prices in real terms, that is as compared to US domestic inflation. It shows the very sharp rise in all commodity prices in 1974, especially oil. The combined index for food, agricultural materials (like cotton) and metals has been on a pretty continuous slide since then. Oil prices, however, kept up with US inflation after 1974 before nearly doubling again in 1979/80 to a real level about seven times as high as during the 1960s and early 1970s.

The OPEC price increases at the end of 1973 were precipitated by political developments in the Middle East but the underlying factor was rapidly increasing demand for oil. Energy and metals consumption by the OECD countries were both growing at 5–6% per year over the period 1960–73 and the rapid price increases of the period seemed to confirm the message of the influential Club of Rome 1972 report, *Limits to Growth*.[16] This popularized the idea that the existing pattern of growth was unsustainable as the world was running out of non-renewable resources. It became commonplace to point out that the discovery of new reserves equivalent to Libya's production would be necessary every year to prevent the 'depletion horizon' for oil from shrinking inexorably.

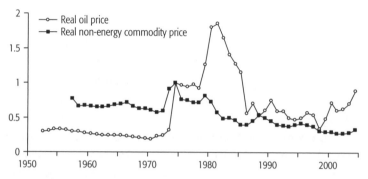

Fig. 1.4. **Real Commodity Prices, 1952–2004**
Source: IMF. See Data Appendix. 1974 = 1.

The rise in commodity prices, especially oil, added a vicious twist to the inflationary pressure which had been bubbling away since the mid-1960s. Workers found their real wage increases constrained (see Fig. 1.2), but were able to pass part of the burden of reduced real incomes onto the employers via the lower profit share (see Fig. 1.3).

The post-war international monetary system formulated at Bretton Woods was supposed to keep exchange rates between other currencies and the dollar fixed unless countries moved into 'fundamental disequilibrium' on the balance of payments. This did not rule out exchange rate changes but these were few and far between (devaluations of the French franc in 1958 and 1959; minor revaluations of the German mark and Swiss franc in the early 1960s). Somewhat surprisingly, countries were equally reluctant to devalue or revalue. Devaluation added more pressure to inflation as import prices rose and real wages were cut. In the case of the UK, forced to devalue in 1967, there were the added fears that this would undermine the reserve role of sterling and the position of the City of London as a financial centre, though in fact the City adapted by dealing in other currencies (notably Eurodollars). At the same time, countries with balance of payments surpluses were very reluctant to revalue as this reduced the profitability and thus the competitiveness of their powerful export industries.

However, differences in inflation rates tended to undermine the fixed exchange rate system. In the 1960s inflation was at relatively similar rates across the OECD countries and the desire to keep a fixed exchange rate against the dollar put pressure on countries with high inflation to cut demand and squeeze down on their economies. However, the combination of the wage explosions, at different times and intensities across the most industrialized countries, and the varying impacts of the commodity price increases, brought an increasing divergence of inflation rates in the 1970s. Over the period 1973–9 the degree of dispersion of inflation rates across the OECD more than trebled. Figure 1.5 illustrates this dispersion by comparing Germany, which established its anti-inflationary credentials in the 1970s, with Italy, the most notoriously inflation-prone of the larger OECD economies. In the 1960s neither of their inflation rates significantly diverged from that of the USA, which was the anchor of the system. In the 1970s faster inflation pushed the nominal price level in Italy higher and higher compared to the USA, whereas in Germany low inflation brought steady falls in the price level relative to that of the USA.

The combination of diverging productivity growth and inflation rates generated persistent payments imbalances which undermined the fixed exchange system. Exchange rate depreciations then reflected, but also perpetuated or even increased, inflation differentials. Figure 1.6 shows how the value of the mark and lira moved against the dollar; the mark appreciated strongly whilst the value of the lira declined, reflecting the relatively low inflation in Germany (relative to the USA) and the high inflation rate in Italy.

The broadly offsetting movements of inflation and exchange rates noted above for the examples of Italy, Germany and the USA did not mean that floating exchange rates painlessly eliminated all problems of international competitiveness. On the contrary, the *real* exchange rate of an average OECD country fluctuated by an average of 6% per year in the 1970s, twice the rate of fluctuation in the

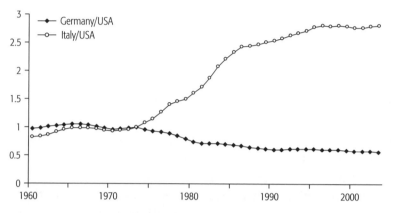

Fig. 1.5. **Consumer Prices in Germany and Italy relative to USA, 1960–2003**
Source: IMF. See Data Appendix. 1973 = 1.

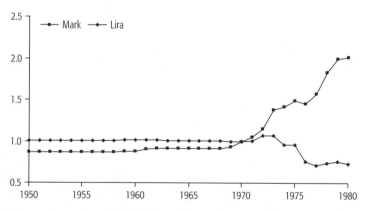

Fig. 1.6. **Deutschemark and Lira Exchange Rates versus Dollar, 1950–1980**
Source: IMF. See Data Appendix. 1970 = 1.

1960s.[17] In the 1970s fluctuations in nominal exchange rates were daily occurrences rather than the rare events of the 1960s, but they did not simply iron out the effect of inflation differentials. Such large year to year changes in the competitiveness of a country's traded goods sectors were probably important in discouraging longer-term investments in manufacturing.

Productivity Slowdown

The slowdown in productivity growth which occurred in the early 1970s was not widely recognized at the time. For example the McCracken Report, an expert review of recent developments for the OECD, concluded that 'We see nothing on the supply side to prevent potential output in the OECD from growing almost as fast in the next five to ten years as it did in the 1960s' (OECD 1977: 16). Given the slack generated by the recession of 1974/5 they believed that output could grow by some 5.5% per year over the period 1975–80. However the slowdown proved to be lasting and made a significant contribution to the turmoil of the 1970s and the form of the stabilization which followed.

The most basic indicator of productivity is output per hour worked (see Fig. 1.7). In the USA labour productivity growth halved after 1973 and stayed very low until the 1990s, when the new economy boom sparked a productivity revival—discussed further in Chapter 6. In Europe and Japan labour productivity growth, which had been much faster than in the USA during the 1960s, nearly halved after 1973 and fell again in the 1980s.

One contributory factor to the productivity slowdown was the lower level of investment. Between 1973 and 1990 the rate of growth of the capital stock in both Europe and Japan fell by more than one-third compared to the period 1960–73 and from the later 1960s business capital accumulation has been on a downward trend in the USA (see Fig. 6.3). The decline in accumulation reflected business anxieties about the decline in profitability, the rise in inflation and the other indicators of instability. The precise effects of slower growth of capital on labour productivity are hard to determine. A very detailed study for the USA estimated that about a half of the slowdown in labour productivity growth could be explained by slower growth of the capital stock.[18] However other factors were certainly involved as well.

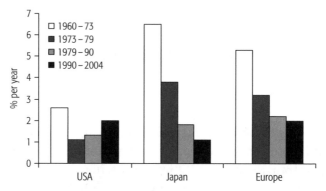

Fig. 1.7. **Growth in Labour Productivity, Whole Economy, 1960–2004**
Source: Groningen Growth and Development Centre. See Appendix.

An obvious influence making for weaker productivity growth in Europe and Japan was that the scope for their catching up with US productivity levels had declined. The boom of the 1950s and 1960s had narrowed the productivity lead of the USA over Japan and Germany as the technologies developed earlier in the USA were rapidly introduced by European and Japanese firms. This could explain a gradual convergence of growth rates in the follower countries on that of the leader (USA). But it could not explain the sharpness of the productivity slowdown after 1973. Moreover catch-up cannot explain the sharp decline in labour productivity growth in the USA, still the productivity leader in most sectors.

The broadest explanation of productivity slowdown, which should apply particularly to the USA as leader country, was that the mass production system known as 'Fordism'—assembly line production with workers performing repeated tasks—was reaching its limits. This would imply that additional investment yielded smaller productivity gains which in turn tended to discourage investment.

One aspect of these limits could be the erosion of factory discipline as the stronger bargaining position of workers allowed them to limit the speed of work. The rather widespread productivity slowdown in the motor industry could be taken as symptomatic of these problems.[19] Again, however, such effects would tend to explain a more gradual deceleration rather than the sharp fall-off in productivity growth which occurred, that also extended beyond the classic assembly line industries.

What particularly distinguished the years after 1973 was the slow growth in demand which resulted from the macroeconomic uncertainties discussed above. Consumers and business were hesitant, real incomes were reduced as oil and other commodities cost more and, even if interest rates failed to keep up with inflation, in nominal percentage terms they were forbiddingly high. With unions still relatively strong after the long period of high employment it was difficult for firms to rationalize production and make workers redundant on the scale needed to keep productivity growing rapidly. In the USA two thirds of the slowdown in productivity in all those sectors where it can be reliably measured took place in pipelines, oil extraction, utilities, motor vehicles and air transport—sectors that were hardest hit by the energy price shocks of the 1970s. The industries with the largest decline in productivity growth suffered declines in output growth of around 5 % per year during the two decades after 1973, four times the average decline. 'This suggests that at least part of the productivity slowdown stemmed from slower output growth in industries characterised by economies of scale' (Nordhaus 2004: 14).

An Alternative System?

Tight labour markets, industrial militancy, commodity price hikes, inflation, profit squeeze, and even productivity slowdown and instability in the international financial system could just be seen as symptoms of a particularly buoyant burst of capital accumulation. Surely things would calm down after a period of financial discipline and demand restraint. But were these problems also symptomatic of, and even encouraging to, a more fundamental challenge to the capitalist system itself?

First of all, as noted earlier, the existence of the Soviet Union and the planned economies of East Europe and China, together with their influence over newly decolonized countries, represented an alternative economic system to one dominated by market forces and private ownership. Although the communist system was bitterly attacked by much of the New Left in the OECD countries for its undemocratic nature, it still appeared to demonstrate that public ownership and centralized planning could work. Growth per head of the population was respectable in the Soviet Union over the period 1960–73—3.4% per year as compared to 4.4% per year in Europe and only 3.0% growth in the USA.[20] Indeed with democratic setting of priorities, and active worker involvement in enterprise operation, why should a planned economy not work better than in 'actually existing socialism' (not to mention actually existing capitalism)?

More than a decade after the collapse of the Soviet system this may seem rather fanciful. However experts on the Soviet economy in the 1970s and into the 1980s were indeed comparing it to Western capitalism by no means wholly unfavourably. Thus Alec Nove, the leading British authority on the Soviet economy, wrote in 1977:

[However] in the last few years the Western industrialised economies have been shaken by inflation and recession. The Soviet-type economies have appeared to be relatively stable in an increasingly unstable world. If their centralized economy, with the help of computers, can continue to grow, even at a modest rate, whilst our own economies decline or are threatened with disintegration, this seems an important advantage, to set against the many micro-irrationalities of Soviet planning. (Nove 1977: 8)

Nearly ten years later, a prominent US textbook called *Soviet Economic Performance and Structure* argued that:

Soviet performance leaves much to be desired, but the bottom line is the extent to which Soviet consumers can be satisfied with *some* increases in the standard of living. Soviet consumers, just like their counterparts everywhere, complain, but why will this form the basis of meaningful pressure when there *is* improvement and the vast bulk of the population has a strong, basic admiration for the system? (Gregory and Stuart 1986: 430)

The final paragraph of their book pointed out that a 'bright spot' for the Soviet leadership amongst rather gloomy economic forecasts was that 'the Western world enters the 1980s with significant troubles of its own. Productivity growth is a problem, high rates of inflation coexist with high rates of unemployment, and real wages are actually declining in some countries.' (ibid. 432).

There was one trend within the rich countries themselves which already seemed to be nudging them away from free market capitalism— the rise in the share of the state in GDP. Total state spending as a share of GDP had not changed much in the 1950s as declining military spending offset some increase in civil expenditure (see Fig. 1.8). In the 1960s the share rose by about 4 percentage points to reach 31% of GDP in 1970 and had exceeded one third in 1974. During the turbulent period which followed the share of state spending lurched up and reached 40% in 1980, as ambitious spending programs collided with a slowdown in GDP growth. In Europe the share was considerably higher (more than 45%), with social democratic Sweden leading the way at 59.8% and the Netherlands close behind.

The total of state spending includes a very large element of government redistribution of spending power (taxes raised to pay pensions,

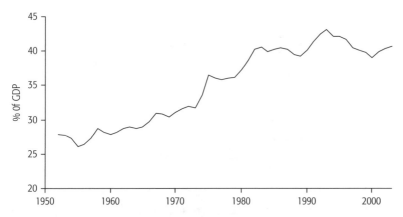

Fig. 1.8. **OECD Government Expenditure, 1952–2003**
Source: OECD. See Data Appendix.

unemployment benefits and so forth); this category of state spending left production (of the goods and services bought by pensioners for example) in the hands of the private sector. Even so there was also rapid growth of welfare state programs that *did* involve the state in producing the services by employing teachers, doctors, social workers etc. These people working for the government were not producing to make a profit for their employer and comprised around one-fifth of total employees in many countries. Thus growing state employment represented a shrinkage of the profit-oriented sector of the economy. In addition most of the taxation to finance state spending had to be paid by taxation on profits and wages in the private sector and this tended to exacerbate distributional struggle as workers sought wage increases to offset rising tax bills and employers sought higher prices to maintain profit margins in the face of rising wages.[21]

On top of the seemingly inexorable rise in government spending came proposals from the labour movement to restrict the prerogatives of capital within its own sphere—private business. A range of plans emerged in the later 1960s and 1970s going well beyond the customary collective bargaining issues of jobs and working conditions. To give a flavour of what was involved a brief discussion follows of German co-determination, Swedish wage-earner funds, the British Labour Party's ideas for planning agreements and finally the French Socialist government's plans for extensive nationalizations in the early 1980s.

In Germany workers had achieved a system of co-determination in the early 1950s with equal representation of employees and shareholders on boards of iron and steel companies. They secured lesser representation within other companies but had the right to appoint the labour director responsible for personnel affairs. In the 1970s there was strong pressure to increase co-determination rights, which resulted in an extension to cover employment contracts and training, and in 1976 the proportion of worker representatives was increased from one-third to a half for larger companies (though with a shareholder-appointed chair having a casting vote). These extensions were strongly resisted by employers, politically and in the courts. German co-determination may have had fairly modest effects on managerial freedom,[22] but a comment in 1984 by a prominent

American economist, Armen Alchian, shows how it was viewed by advocates of shareholder sovereignty: 'The campaign for . . . codetermination on boards of directors appears to be attempts to control the wealth of shareholders' specialised assets . . . a wealth confiscation scheme' (quoted by Gorton and Schmid 2000: 1).

Co-determination was feared for its potential to limit management prerogatives and thus transfer value added to workers, in the form of security or better conditions. The Swedish scheme for wage-earner funds proposed by the trades unions in 1976 had potentially more radical implications:

Firms above a certain size (fifty or a hundred employees) should be required to issue new stocks corresponding to 20 per cent of annual profits and . . . these stocks should be owned by funds representing wage earners as a collective group . . . . Such a reform . . . would also counteract the tendency towards increased concentration of wealth and complement industrial democracy legislation . . . . Under this scheme the higher the rate of profit, the more quickly collectivisation would occur. The committee calculated that it would take thirty-five years for the wage-earner collective to acquire forty-nine per cent of stocks in a firm operating at a ten per cent profit rate. (Pontusson 1987: 13)

Rudolph Meidner, the chair of the committee which drew up the proposals, said in an interview, 'we want to deprive the capitalists of the power that they exercise by virtue of ownership' (Pontusson 1987: 14). The committee also envisaged that wage-earner ownership could chivvy firms into following government industrial policies. Dividends would be used in part to finance 'adult education, wage-earner consultants and various other programs to help wage-earners, and union activists in particular, take advantage of the new labor laws and exercise their ownership role. The gradual transfer of ownership would thus be accompanied by a new competence within the ranks of the union movement.' (Pontusson 1992: 192).

It is important to appreciate just how seriously these proposals were taken at the time. In a lengthy dissection of the 'Rise and Fall of the Swedish Model' in the *Journal of Economic Literature*, a very prominent Swedish economist Erik Lundberg argued in 1985 that the wage-earner funds represented a decisive move away from the

Social Democrats' tradition of pragmatism, which had previously seen radical proposals for socialization or central planning abandoned rather quickly. 'At the present time the socialist goals are more serious and against the background of a crisis in the functioning of the Swedish economy, the plans are more appealing, at least to a strong minority of Social Democrats' (Lundberg 1985: 31). He noted also that 'the bourgeois parties have refused emphatically, to accept the proposal for collective funds in any form. The Opposition includes the entrepreneurial organizations of private corporations, as well as those of small firms. Their antagonism is complete' (ibid. 31). The opposition was largely successful and only a highly diluted form of the plan was implemented, but the point to underline here is that the project was viewed by business with great alarm.

In the early 1970s the British Labour Party formulated an interventionist strategy aimed at industrial modernization. The 1973 Party Conference approved a plan for the next Labour government to compulsorily nationalize 20–25 of the largest manufacturing companies, around one third of manufacturing output. The idea was to take over a leading and profitable firm in each sector and use it to introduce new products or processes forcing, through competitive pressure, the other firms in the industry to follow suit. The other firms would be obliged to sign planning agreements with the government detailing their plans for output, investment and employment which were to be consistent with the government's overall economic objectives. In the event the programme was watered down before Labour came to power and no major firms were nationalized and no serious planning agreement signed.

Labour's plan was neither well worked in terms of how the leverage acquired over the private sector would be used, nor did it have the political support and resolve required to push it through. However it was still seen as a serious threat by the employers. The Confederation of British Industry told the Labour Prime Minister that 'there was absolutely no room for compromise or negotiation about further state intervention in industry and further nationalisation' (*Financial Times*, 16 Sept. 1974).

During the Labour government's 1976 negotiations over a loan from the IMF, the left wing of the Labour Party, led by Tony Benn, pushed unsuccessfully in the cabinet for import controls and other measures as an alternative to spending cuts and deflation. They hoped to maintain economic expansion and help secure the election manifesto objective of a 'fundamental and irreversible shift in the balance of power and wealth in favour of working people and their families'.

Two years after the fall of the Labour government in the UK the French Socialist government of François Mitterrand came to power in 1981 with the plan to double, from 11% to 22%, the share of nationalized industries in industrial employment by taking over five major groups in electronics and chemicals, the largest two steel groups, 39 banks (bringing the share of public ownership of banks to 90%) and a major firm in a number of other sectors. As in the UK, the plans called for these nationalized groups to spearhead industrial modernization, within the context of five-year 'plan contracts' between the management and government.

The extent to which the nationalizations threatened private capital should not be exaggerated. Shareholders in the big five industrial groups received compensation described by the *Financial Times* as 'far too generous' (24 May 1982), and Mitterrand reassured business that he wanted the economy merely 'a little more mixed' (*Financial Times*, 3 Oct. 1981). The Minister for Planning was credited with the view that the market is 'all embracing and irreplaceable' (*Financial Times*, 22 July 1981). Nevertheless the nationalization plans did reflect the belief that private industry was incapable of adequately modernizing the French economy and that this process needed to be strongly state-led. In the event the nationalized firms, many of which were loss making, were given large amounts of capital by the government and they carried out major programmes of rationalization of their activities, which paved the way for their return to the private sector (see Chapter 2).

Challenges Repulsed?

If nothing else, the level of stock market prices is a good indicator of the degree of optimism amongst industrialists, financiers and

investment managers. Equity prices reflect prospects for profit making and in extreme cases even prospects for the survival of capitalism
itself. A sharp way, therefore, of comparing the fortunes of capital
and labour is to examine how equity prices move in relation to a
worker's wage. Figure 1.9 tells a remarkable story. By the mid-1970s
share prices had fallen by about three-quarters relative to average
wages from the peak in the early 1960s as the Golden Age was getting
into full swing. The fall was sharpest in Europe, where in the late
1970s share prices had declined in relative terms by about five-
sixths. However even in Japan and the USA the falls were by around
one-half. This collapse in confidence in financial markets reflected
all the developments discussed above—uncertainties raised by
industrial conflict, rising inflation, profits squeeze, productivity
slowdown, international disorganization, industrial conflict and
threats of deeper state involvement in industry.

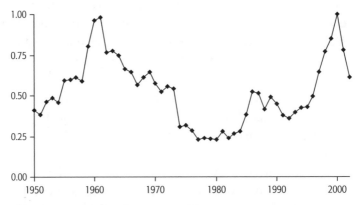

Fig. 1.9. **Share Prices compared to Average Wages, 1950–2002**
Source: IMF. See Data Appendix. 2000 = 1.

By 2000, however, share prices had regained all their previous
losses (Fig. 1.9), strikes had declined towards insignificance (Fig. 1.1),
the inflationary surge had been suppressed and real wages were
creeping up at a quite unthreatening rate (Fig. 1.2), profits had made
a substantial recovery (Fig. 1.3), commodity and oil prices had fallen
back to real levels not significantly higher than in the 1960s
(Fig. 1.4), the dollar appeared to be riding high and a zone of exchange

rate stability was about to be created by the formation of the Eurozone, the rise in government spending had been halted (Fig. 1.8), the Soviet Union, together with its economic system based on state ownership and central planning, had collapsed and radical moves to threaten the dominance of private capital had been abandoned. Whilst new threats were to emerge, as recounted in later chapters, the challenges of the 1970s seemed to have been decisively repulsed.

The four chapters which follow analyse the key components of this decisive recovery in capitalism's strength and stability. The next chapter recounts the dramatic shifts in government policy, followed by an analysis of the growth of the power of the finance sector and the dominance of shareholder profit in the operation of firms. The retreat from government intervention and return to reliance on market forces can be seen as the reassertion of the 'fundamental workings of the capitalist economy'. In Makoto Itoh's vivid formulation 'capitalism seems to be running the film of history backwards by "melting down" the sustained trend of a century, and returning to an older stage of liberalism' (Itoh 1990: 14).

2
Austerity, Privatization and Deregulation

The Federal Reserve had to show that when faced with the painful choice between maintaining a tight monetary policy to fight inflation and easing monetary policy to combat recession, it would choose to fight inflation. In other words to establish its credibility, the Federal Reserve had to demonstrate its willingness to spill blood, lots of blood, other people's blood

(Michael Mussa, Director of the Department of Research at the IMF, reflecting on the tightening of US monetary policy in 1979 (Mussa 1994: 112))

Throughout the 1960s and 1970s the governments of the highly developed economies were reacting to the pressures described in the previous chapter. Budget discipline was breaking down as demands for rising public spending ran well ahead of political capacity to levy high taxes and the inflation resulting from conflict between workers and employers was accommodated with lavish doses of money and credit. Employers were under pressure to accede to more stringent limits on their ability to hire and fire whilst the growth of the welfare state tempered the impact on workers of market forces; further incursions into management prerogatives to allocate capital where and when they liked were threatened. This chapter will outline the counter-revolution in macroeconomic policy which saw tight monetary policy and fiscal austerity imposed in the name of defeating inflation. This was followed rapidly by the unwinding of much of the detailed government intervention into particular sectors and markets which had characterized the previous decades. Privatization, and the deregulation of the industries concerned, the substitution of private sector sources of supply for public sector in-house service provision and the deregulation of labour markets are all aspects of this process.

Monetary Policy and Unemployment

The rise in unemployment in almost all of the OECD in the mid-1970s can readily be accounted for by the jolt both to aggregate demand and to business expectations caused by the rising inflation, oil price increases, profit squeeze and industrial unrest discussed in the previous chapter. Governments were caught in the 'stagflation' dilemma—running an expansionary monetary policy (low interest rates) and fiscal policy (rising deficits) risked 'accommodating' the inflation. Their fear was not just that higher inflation would persist but that it would increase and increase, as argued by Milton Friedman in his famous address to the American Economic Association in 1967.[1] On the other hand, a squeeze on the economy would push unemployment up further, which was felt to be politically unsustainable. Incomes policies, attempting to persuade union bargainers to accept wage increases below the going rate of inflation, were widely introduced. These took varied forms depending on the institutional history of the country and with varying degrees of success. Japan, Sweden and briefly the UK were among the countries where wages increases were sharply ratcheted down in the mid-1970s through agreements of various forms with trades unions.[2]

Figure 2.1 shows the considerable rise in unemployment in Europe and the USA in the mid-1970s. However this was not generally sufficient to squeeze out inflation. The decisive policy shift came in late 1979 when, with US inflation again rising into double digits, Paul Volker at the US Federal Reserve pushed up interest rates to unprecedented levels (see Fig. 2.2). The real interest rate, with inflation subtracted from the nominal cost of borrowing, rose suddenly from being negative (the real value of repayments falling short of the real value borrowed) to more than plus 5%. This precipitated a sharp recession and unemployment rose from around 5% in 1979 to nearly 10% in 1982 (see Fig. 2.1). Inflation fell from 13% in 1980 to 3% in 1983.

The Volker 'coup' against loose monetary policy was aimed at protecting the value of the dollar, internally but also on the foreign

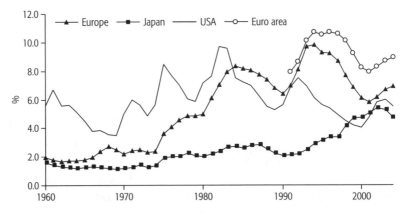

Fig. 2.1. **Unemployment Rates, 1960–2004**
Source: OECD. Data Appendix.

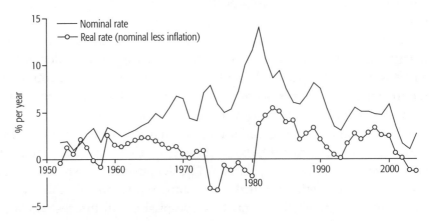

Fig. 2.2. **US Short-Term Interest Rates, 1950–2004**
Source: IMF. See Data Appendix.

exchanges where it had been under heavy pressure, by squeezing out inflation at whatever it cost in terms of unemployment. The minutes of the Fed's Open Market Committee noted that despite a likely rise in unemployment in 1980 the intention was to slow monetary growth further 'in line with the continuing objective of curbing inflation' (quoted Romer and Romer 2002: 44). This was only months after the Council of Economic Advisers' Economic Report to the President had stated that 'We will *not* try to wring inflation out of our economic system by pursuing policies designed to bring about a recession' (quoted ibid. 42). The Fed reiterated its 'willingness to accept high unemployment to bring inflation down' (ibid. 43) several times during the early 1980s. The President of Chase Manhattan bank noted that the policy would 'tend to deepen what has been seen as a relatively shallow recession but is a price worth paying. Inflation is a terrible cancerous disease that takes radical action' (quoted Epstein 1981: 169).

Volker himself, looking back some years later, underlined the links between deflationary monetary policy and the broader issue of the weakening of labour: 'the most important single action of the administration in helping the anti-inflation fight was defeating the air traffic controllers' strike. He thought that this action had rather a profound, and from his standpoint, constructive effect on the climate of labour–management relations, even though it had not been a wage issue at the time' (quoted by Brenner 1998: 191).

Because of the importance of the US economy, and its influence on worldwide interest rates, the turn in policy there is always accorded particular significance. However in reality the USA was following the lead of Germany, which had maintained high real interest rates throughout the inflationary 1970s. The rising mark which resulted had helped to moderate inflation by pressing down on the export sector and established the Bundesbank's credentials as anti-inflationary zealot (in 1979 inflation was 4.1% in Germany as compared to 11.3% in the USA). Mrs Thatcher's government had also begun to squeeze before Volker, and long-term real interest rates in the UK shifted from minus 3% to plus 4% between 1979 and 1982. This not only increased borrowing costs but helped to push up the exchange rate, launching a ferocious squeeze on manufacturing. In the UK case fiscal policy was also aggressively shifted towards restriction, with the budget deficit reduced in 1981 despite the recession which was pushing down tax revenues. Unemployment rose from less than 5% in 1979 to more than 11% by 1983. It was regarded as vital that the presentation of the policy should be phrased in terms of targets for the money supply. Letting the cat out of the bag as to what was implied for jobs would have been a 'very hazardous exercise' according to an adviser to the Governor of the Bank of England because 'the objectives would either have been unacceptable to public opinion or inadequate to ensure a substantial reduction in the rate of inflation, or both' (Fforde 1983: 207).[3] Of course inflation, especially at rates recorded in the 1970s, was itself unpopular as real incomes fell month on month between the dates that nominal incomes (wages, pensions and so forth) were adjusted. In the 1980s the majority of UK workers who kept their jobs saw real wages rising steadily.

Of great symbolic importance was the abandonment in 1983 by Mitterrand's Socialist government in France of their expansionary plans and the launching of the 'Franc fort' policy. 'The Socialist attempt to revive the economy sank on the shoals of rising inflation and a foreign exchange crisis by early 1983, so that the government of the left has in the end introduced a tougher, more market oriented programme than anything considered by the previous centre-right administration' (Sachs and Wyplosz 1986: 262). This policy was labelled 'competitiveness through disinflation', aimed at keeping French goods competitive on world markets by pushing the inflation rate down to, and then keeping it below, that of competitors. This contrasted with the traditional policy of restoring competitiveness through devaluation.[4] By the end of the decade the inflation differential with Germany (6–8% per year higher in France in the early 1980s) had been all but eliminated. However unemployment reached 10% by the mid-1980s and remained stubbornly stuck.

Our final example of the decisive turn to policies aimed at reducing inflation came in 1991 from the Swedish Social Democrats. They had traditionally relied on occasional devaluations to restore export competitiveness whenever their centralized bargaining system had not been able to contain money wage increases at a competitive level.

Ruling out further devaluations, which were becoming unmanageable given financial liberalization and the huge speculative flows (see Chapter 3), the 1991 Budget Statement proclaimed:

in the longer run it is not possible to safeguard employment in an economy which has a higher inflation rate than the surrounding world. In order to protect employment and prosperity economic policies in the next few years...will have to aim at a permanent reduction in inflation. This task must take priority over all other aims and ambitions. (quoted Notermans 1993)

The recession which followed, involving the collapse of a consumer boom (see Chapter 3), pushed unemployment above 9%, a previously unimaginable level for Sweden.

The turn towards restrictive policies was no temporary aberration. Real interest rates throughout the OECD stayed much higher through the 1980s and first half of the 1990s than during the Golden Age, when low real interest rates helped to maintain high investment levels. Even when they fell back towards the end of the 1990s they stuck at around the very long-term historical average (see Fig. 2.3). The spectacular effect of the high real interest rates in helping to push down inflation is clear from Figure 1.2 and applied right across the OECD. In 1980 Japan's inflation rate was 4% and Germany together

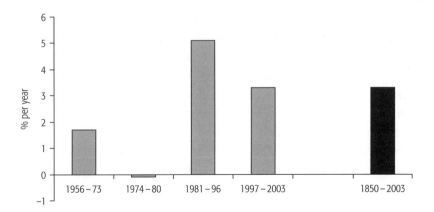

Fig. 2.3. **Long-Term Real Interest Rates, 1850–2003**
Source: Rowthorn (1995). See Data Appendix.

with half a dozen of its close neighbours who were following similarly orthodox policies had inflation rates in the range 5–7%. However, in the same year inflation was running at about 14% in Sweden, France and the USA while UK inflation was 18% and Italy's 21%. By 1997 the range of inflation rates was drastically reduced. Low inflation countries had no inflation at all whilst an inflation rate of only 3% (as in the UK) put a country in the top inflation bracket.

How fundamental was the reversion to tight monetary policy and the hike in real interest rates in generating the higher unemployment over the 1980s and 1990s? Such a case has been strongly argued by Keynesians, who point to the correlation between the tightness of monetary policy in a country and its rise in unemployment in the 1980s.[5] This is no surprise since the immediate factor behind most rises in unemployment is a fall in aggregate demand and tight monetary policy does act in that direction. However when interest rates are the triggering factors the monetary authorities will usually be responding to some perceived problem in the economy, as is clear from the discussion above. For example if they believe that higher unemployment is required to bring down inflation then it is the factors explaining the inflationary pressure which really lie behind the rise in unemployment. The tight monetary policy is the vehicle through which the lower level of aggregate demand and higher unemployment is reached. Governments squeezed harder (via higher interest rates for example) in countries where the 'Non-Accelerating Inflation Rate of Unemployment' (NAIRU) increased by a greater amount.

Of course it is quite possible that monetary authorities may be excessively cautious and depress demand and employment more deeply and for longer than could be objectively justified by inflationary tendencies (as is widely believed was the case in the early 2000s at the European Central Bank, which sets interest rates for the Eurozone). There may also be alternative routes to lower inflation other than increasing unemployment, through social pacts between labour and capital to lever down wage claims. Some countries like Sweden and Austria avoided big increases in unemployment in the 1980s in this way and wage restraint in Japan reflected an implicit agreement with a similar effect.

Explaining the shift in monetary policy discussed in this section is fundamental to understanding why unemployment rose so much in OECD countries in the 1980s. In very broad terms tight monetary policy was the reaction to the turmoil of the 1970s—rising inflation, industrial conflict, profit squeeze and the other developments discussed in Chapter 1. As the Polish economist Kalecki had brilliantly forecast in 1943 at the height of enthusiasm for Keynesian full employment policies:

Indeed under a regime of permanent full employment, the 'sack' would cease to play its role as a disciplinary measure. The social position of the boss would be undermined, and the self-assurance and class consciousness of the working class would grow. Strikes for wage increases and improvements in conditions of work would create political tensions ... 'discipline in the factories' and 'political stability' are more appreciated than profits by business leaders. Their class instinct tells them that lasting full employment is unsound from their point of view and that unemployment is an integral part of a 'normal' capitalist system. (Kalecki 1990 1943: 351)

The concept of the NAIRU is often criticized for suggesting that high unemployment is inevitable or even 'natural' to use Milton Friedman's term. However following Kalecki it is really Marx's 'reserve army of labour' in disguise—the unemployment whose function in capitalism is to keep wages in check.[6] Unemployment could then be seen as a response to industrial conflict, and its various destabilizing economic manifestations like inflation and profit squeeze, as business investment would decline with the fall in confidence and governments would turn to restrictive policies to restore discipline. Such an interpretation is quite consistent with the pattern of unemployment shown in Figure 2.4. Unemployment in the years 1990–9 is plotted against the level of strikes in the country over the years 1968–79 (covering both the wage explosions and workers' subsequent attempts to maintain living standards as inflation rose). Despite all the intervening events (such as German unification) and all the other differences between countries (for example massive agricultural decline in Spain), a country's unemployment is significantly related to the degree of industrial conflict a quarter of a century earlier.[7]

Much was made later in the 1980s of the importance of the Central Bank being independent of political manipulation if it was to implement suitably restrictive anti-inflationary monetary policies. That this was far from necessary was shown by the case of the UK where Thatcherite monetary policy remained firmly under the control of the government, although there could be circumstances where it would be politically convenient to put the blame for unpopular policies on 'independent' experts. Making the Bank of England responsible for setting interest rates was one of the first actions of Gordon Brown as Chancellor of the Exchequer in the Blair government, in a successful bid to convince the financial markets that Labour had fully adjusted to the non-inflationary epoch.

Fig. 2.4. **Unemployment 1990–1999 and Strikes 1968–1979**
Source: Office of National Statistics. See Data Appendix.

Government Deficits

The use of expansionary fiscal policy to maintain demand and employment was repudiated by the deliberate tightening of fiscal policy by the Thatcher government during the early 1980s recession, by the commitment of the Clinton administration to deficit reduction in 1992 and by the adoption by the EU of progressively tougher constraints culminating in the Stability and Growth Pact commitment to balancing budgets on average over the economic cycle.

Keynesian orthodoxy had argued that in a recession the deficit should be allowed to rise through the 'automatic stabilizers' (as tax receipts fell), supplemented where necessary by deliberate fiscal expansion (for example increases in government spending) to help maintain demand. This was not supposed to involve governments running substantial deficits in the longer run. Keynes envisaged that the spending boost would 'prime the pump' of private investment which would take over the running from a government-induced boost to demand. Indeed private investment was sufficiently dynamic in the 1950s and 1960s that sustained government deficits were not needed in the OECD countries to bolster growth (Table 2.1). The Keynesian prescription to run temporary deficits where there was a deficiency of aggregate demand was never intended as a long-term solution to welfare state financing. Indeed in the Scandinavian version, which developed the welfare state most extensively, governments typically ran substantial budget surpluses from which loans were made to the private sector.[8]

Government deficits became substantial and sustained only during the period after the 1974 OPEC oil shock when there was pressure to continue expanding the welfare state and supporting aggregate

Table 2.1 **Budget Deficits, 1952–2004**

General government balance, % of GDP	1952–73	1974–9	1980–90	1991–5	1996–2000	2001–04
USA	−0.8	−1.5	−3.5	−4.5	0.0	−3.2
Europe (Eurozone > 90)	0.2	−3.3	−4.3	−2.2	−2.1	−2.3
Japan	1.0	−3.4	−1.1	−1.7	−5.8	−7.3
OECD	−0.2	−2.5	−3.3	−4.3	−1.3	−2.8

Sources: OECD. See Data Appendix.

demand despite stagnating tax revenue. Deficits were larger still in the early 1990s (considerably larger if adjusted for the smaller effect of inflation in reducing the real value of outstanding debt). It was not until the second half of the 1990s that major reductions in government deficits in Europe and the USA (though not Japan) marked a seemingly decisive restoration of financial orthodoxy in public sector financing.

Why are financial markets so opposed to government deficits, when after all a tidy proportion of their business derives from government borrowing? Alan Greenspan, Chairman of the Federal Reserve, was reported as having spelt out the argument very clearly in his pre-inauguration meeting with President-elect Clinton in December 1992:

Bondholders and traders were sophisticated and anticipated that the federal budget deficit would continue to explode for many years. The anticipated cumulative growth of the deficit over those years was so large that it was perceived to be unstable. History showed, Greenspan said, that with such vast federal expenditures, inflation would inevitably soar at some point. The double-digit inflation of the 1970s had been induced by budget deficits from the Vietnam War. Investors were now wary and demanding a higher long-term return [long-term interest rate on Treasury bonds—AG] because of the expectations on the federal deficit. (Woodward 1994: 69)

Clinton accepted Greenspan's argument.[9] His deficit reduction programme saw the budget in surplus at the end of the decade and was regarded as 'key and indispensable' in generating the 1990s boom in the USA according to Robert Rubin, later to be the Treasury Secretary.

I remember the economic malaise of the early 1990s very well and one of the central features was a loss of confidence . . . in part because our fiscal position was taken to symbolize a larger inability on the part of our country to manage its economic life effectively and with discipline. The consequence of the deficit reduction program of 1993, once the market actually believed that it was real, was not only lower interest rates, but also—in my judgment much more importantly—a great increase in confidence . . . [which] affected business decisions about investment, expansion and hiring, as well as consumer decisions, and produced a greater flow of foreign capital into our savings deficient nation to finance investment here . . . without the boost to confidence provided by the deficit reduction package the investment boom would not have occurred (Rubin 2001: 131, 138)

Rubin's argument turns pump-priming on its head; the adverse effects on bond market and business confidence of a rise in the deficit could make Keynesian fiscal expansion contractionary as real investment fell. The validity of this argument, long proposed by conservative economists in Germany, clearly depends on the economic and political circumstances. Where the government's debt is growing faster than GDP, and threatening to spiral upwards in an unsustainable way, adverse reactions to even larger budget deficits are quite plausible. However this does not mean that increased deficits can never sustain demand. The very expansionary effect of the Keynesian boost to the Germany economy after unification in 1990 or the impact of the George W. Bush tax cuts are just two examples of strong positive effects on demand of expansionary fiscal policy.

Financial markets are far from neutral about how deficit reductions should be achieved; the Business Roundtable in Washington 'believed that deficit reduction should come largely or exclusively from spending cuts, with very little, if any, increase in taxes' (Rubin 2003: 128). Such a focus on spending cuts was given additional credibility by a widely cited study of episodes of deficit reduction in OECD countries.

Fiscal adjustments that relied primarily on tax increases, especially tax increases on households, typically fail to stop permanently the growth of public debt. On the contrary, successful adjustments are those that aggressively tackle the expenditure side, particularly the components of it which are always thought of as untouchable: social security and government wages and employment. (Alesina and Perotti 1995: 239)

The validity of this finding is hotly contested, especially its interpretation of the Irish growth 'miracle' which followed fiscal stabilization in the mid-1980s. If tax increases would be met by higher wage claims, cuts in government employment and welfare benefits could be more effective by weakening labour's bargaining power. In other circumstances organized labour might agree to tax increases in return for preserving welfare spending. Despite these complexities, welfare spending cuts rather than tax increases were promoted in an unqualified way by the European Commission in its quest for deficit reductions ahead of the introduction of the Euro.[10] In the event, budgetary consolidation in the Eurozone came mostly from reduced spending but the biggest part of the decline was in interest payments (as rates fell) rather than spending on programmes. Budget targets for the EU's Growth and Stability Pact—deficits limited to 3% of GDP with the aim of budget balance over the cycle—foundered in 2004 on German and French deficits, which remained stubbornly high as growth in the Eurozone stagnated.

The turn to fiscal orthodoxy was much more successful in the USA than in Europe but was even more short-lived. The recession after the collapse of the stock market/new economy boom in 2000 was met by the Bush administration with tax cuts and spending increases (especially military), pushing the US deficit up to around 5% of GDP in 2004. The US bond market proved remarkably indulgent as evidenced by low long-term interest rates. Few in the Bush administration probably still believed in the 'voodoo economics' of President Reagan that tax cuts to the rich would have major effects on incentives to work and save and thus boost economic growth. But as the *Financial Times* pointed out, if the hoped-for expansion did not materialize, and the deficit proved unsustainably high, the Republicans would be handed a convenient scenario for forcing through cuts in social programmes.[11] Indeed the campaign against government deficits had already provided useful ammunition in the successful battle to limit the upward march of government spending after 1979 (see Fig. 1.8).

By 2005 the aim of 'budgetary consolidation' was in disarray. Japan had had a huge deficit for years, there was a ballooning deficit in the USA and bickering in Europe with France and Germany failing to reach the EU's 3% deficit target. Persistent budget deficits are telltale signs of lack of business confidence in the prospects for profitable investment. For high investment pushes up output and incomes and thus tax revenue and reduces the deficit, as happened in the US boom of the late 1990s. Investment was relatively sluggish throughout the OECD countries after 2000, despite the low and stable inflation, the profits recovery and the absence of industrial conflict. We will return to this puzzle in Chapter 6.

Privatization of Nationalized Industries

The priority given to financial discipline and defeating inflation was complemented by attempts to reduce government intervention in industry. The most spectacular example of this was the privatization of state-owned enterprises.

Nationalized industries have always occupied an uncomfortable position in capitalist economies. Mainly located in utilities and other basic industries they hovered uncomfortably between operating as a socialistic beachhead on the one hand and supplying cheap inputs which boosted the profits of the private sector on the other. In the former conception nationalized firms could influence the structure of the economy, avoid exploitation of monopoly positions and allow experiments in worker involvement in decision-making. Alternatively, as purveyors of inputs to the private sector, they would be criticized for not being efficient enough and for absorbing government subsidies.

Although individual companies had periodically shifted into the public sector as 'lame ducks' and out again when restored to health, privatization as a programme only took off in the mid-1980s, building up to a world-wide peak in the later 1990s before slipping back as the best prospects had been privatized in many countries. The share of state-owned enterprises in global GDP is estimated as falling from more than 10% in 1979 to less than 6% in 2004. More than $1.25 trillion has been raised from privatization worldwide; total receipts up to the end of 2000 raised the equivalent of 3% of one year's GDP in Japan, France and Germany and 10% in the UK. Privatized firms represent around 30% of the total market capitalization of stock markets outside the USA. Privatized oil or telecoms companies were the most valuable companies listed on the stock exchanges of the UK, France, Germany and Italy and the second most valuable firms in Australia and Japan.[12] The discussion below will focus on the UK, the trailblazer in this process. The UK is now held up as a paragon in terms of deregulation and lack of state control, moving from fifteenth to first place out of 22 OECD countries in the Fraser Institute's overall ranking of 'Economic Freedom'.[13]

There are a host of issues surrounding the introduction of competitive pressure into privatized industries, by breaking up existing monopolies, by liberalization of market entry and by public regulation of pricing.[14] Our concern here is with the broad effects on productivity and how resulting gains were distributed between shareholders, consumers and workers.

Privatization reduced the contribution of government-owned companies from 12% of UK GDP in 1979 to less than 2% now. The first major privatization was British Telecom and the motivation at that stage was mainly financial. BT had a major backlog of investment to catch up with new technology and, whilst it remained in the public sector, the finance required would add to the government deficit. Reducing the deficit was a key component of the government's macroeconomic strategy to impose financial discipline on the economy by restricting monetary growth. The resulting sale of over 50% of BT's shares in 1984 was hugely successful with the shares so priced that subscribers secured an instant gain of 33%. British Gas, British Airways, British Steel, the water authorities and the electricity industry followed in quick succession. British Rail and British Coal were privatized after the 1992 election.

The financial motivation for privatization always seemed weak. Although paying off some national debt with the proceeds of privatization would economize on the government's interest payments, it would lose the government an equivalent stream of profits from the corporation. The difference between the government raising money to fund BT's investment by selling bonds and a privatized BT selling its own bonds to the public was rather cosmetic. Nevertheless government deficits were large (4% of UK GDP in 1984) and even 'selling off the family silver', as ex-Prime Minister Harold Macmillan termed it, could be temporarily reassuring for financial markets.

Over and above the immediate financial advantage to the government, the fundamental motivation for privatization was the theory that the firms would be more efficient when subject to competitive private sector disciplines and that this would bring real benefits to the economy in the form of lower prices and higher living standards. These benefits were supposed to swamp the negative effects of a private company being able to exploit its monopoly positions. Opening up markets to competition where feasible, or regulation of prices where it was not, together with pressure from institutional investors to increase profits, were the routes through which new private sector managements would be forced to cut costs in previously sluggish enterprises.

It is hard to find robust evidence of the effects on productivity of a switch in ownership to the private sector.[15] A detailed OECD study of telecoms found lower prices, higher productivity and improved service levels after privatization. However the evidence was consistent with this being the effect of introducing competition into the industry, which can be done without privatizing the dominant state provider. The OECD found no clear evidence of the impact of privatization itself, additional to the effect of competition.[16] The most recent analysis of UK privatizations concluded: 'it is probably fair to characterize our results as showing that firms tended to improve their productivity significantly in the run-up to privatization (with some exceptions) but giving little evidence that the faster growth rate was sustained after privatization. In other words, there is catch-up rather than a permanent change of pace...Whether the commitment to privatize is essential to getting the gains from pre-privatization restructuring, remains an open question...' (Green and Haskel 2004: 91). The government had a great incentive to rationalize the industries before privatization in order to boost profits and thus the prospective sale price;[17] the fact that such rationalizations occurred before privatization showed that private ownership per se was not directly responsible.

The most frequently privatized sectors were utilities and the UK gas, electricity and water sectors provide an interesting example of who gains and who loses from privatization, being privatized at varying dates between 1986 (British Gas) and the early 1990s (electricity). Table 2.2 below shows what happened to capital and labour inputs into the sector, to productivity growth and to wages and profits. The first period shown covers 1970–9, including the turbulent years of the Labour government. The period 1979–90 includes Thatcher's restructuring of industry generally, including serious attempts to rationalize the sector prior to privatization via government imposition of financial targets. Finally 1990–2002 covers a lengthy run of years when the three industries were all privatized and the regulation regimes were settling down.

Capital stock growth only accelerated to a rather minor degree, which must be disappointing for those who anticipated faster introduction of new technology. The trend in jobs was more dramatic however: employment had been declining over the longer term in this sector but the fall speeded up in the 1980s prior to privatization and by even more in the 1990s. A 4% per year loss of jobs over 12 years represents a near halving of the workforce since 1990. The effect of this rationalization was a sharp increase in labour productivity.[18]

Table 2.2 **Production and Incomes in UK Utilities, 1970–2002**

Average annual percentage changes	Real output	Employ- ment	Capital stock	Labour Productivity	Real wage bill	Real profits
1970–79	3.7	−1.1	1.1	4.9	5.5	2.7
1979–90	2.0	−2.0	0.6	4.1	1.6	0.7
1990–2002	2.5	−4.1	1.4	6.9	−2.8	1.6

Source: Office of National Statistics. See Data Appendix.

How were the benefits of this rationalization distributed? After 1979 prices of energy and water grew less fast than the consumer price index overall.[19] This differential doubled to 2.7% per year after 1990. This suggests that competitive and regulatory pressure was distributing some of the benefits from higher productivity to consumers.

After 1990, real profits rose as the wage bill fell. However the growth of profits was not spectacular and this is consistent with the finding that long-term shareholders did no better from the privatized industries than from shares as a whole in the private sector.[20]

The big gainers from privatization were those that 'stagged' the issues of shares (selling them for a quick profit), the firms in the City which earned large fees from arranging the privatizations and management, whose pay was ratcheted up.[21] The main losers were those workers who lost relatively well-paid, unionized jobs. Although privatization of the coal industry was termed the 'ultimate privatization' because of its effect on the power of the mineworkers, studies suggest little evidence that in the UK the act of privatization per se was associated with a decline in union membership or bargaining rights. In contrast, in Japan the privatization of railways, telecoms and the tobacco and salt monopoly had a major impact in weakening the militant wing of the Japanese union movement.[22]

Even the OECD's very positive assessment of restructuring and privatization admits that they 'tend to be accompanied by some degree of dislocation and job loss, at least in the short term. Furthermore ... in many instances employment reductions have continued after privatization.' They also noted that while employees in privatized companies receive generous salaries, they are 'reported to often have longer hours, decreased job security and union power' (OECD 2003a: 43). An industrial disputes arbitrator noted that privatized and deregulated bus operators in London had little scope to compete by means 'other than worsening employees' terms and condition' and that this brought 'a declining sense of employee commitment to public transport as a service' (quoted by Sachdev 2004:16).

Privatization in OECD countries shifted within a decade or so from being a radical policy of hard-line right-wing governments (notably Mrs Thatcher's) to being the conventional wisdom even amongst governments of the left. The experience of France exemplifies this. In 1981 Mitterrand was elected to the presidency with a strong programme to extend state ownership by taking over major industrial groups in electronics and chemicals, 39 banks (raising the state's share of banking from 60% to 90%) together with major firms in other industries (see Chapter 1). These nationalizations doubled the state's share of industrial employment to 22%.[23] The programme was first put on hold after the 1983 macroeconomic crisis and policy shift (see above), and successive right-wing governments privatized selected companies whilst preserving interlocking cross-holdings of companies in conglomerate groups. Finally, in the second half of the 1990s the Socialist government of Lionel Jospin privatized more than the previous six governments put together, including almost all government holdings in the banking and insurance sectors. *Le Monde* noted that 'never had the sales of public companies generated so little controversy' (quoted by Gordon and Meunier 2001: 22). Overseas financial firms took large stakes in many of the privatized firms.

Privatization is just one, highly visible, aspect of government's withdrawal from intervention in the market sector of the economy. The OECD has produced an index of the degree of regulation in seven industries covering energy, post and telecoms and transport (rail, air and road freight). The index, covering not only public ownership, but ease of entry into the industry and aspects of its market structure, charts the course of deregulation over the 1980s and 1990s. In 1978 the USA had least regulation out of 21 OECD countries.[24] By 1998 only three countries (Greece, Italy and Portugal) had a greater degree of regulation than the USA had in 1980. In 15 countries the index was at least one-third lower in 1998 than 20 years earlier and the UK had become the least regulated country of all, with a level of regulation one-quarter of the US level in 1978.

This process of product market deregulation took off in the 1980s really only in the USA, becoming widespread in the 1990s. A more extensive analysis by OECD covering the years since 1998 showed deregulation continuing apace in all three areas considered—state controls on industry, barriers to entrepreneurship (administrative and legal difficulties in starting a business) and barriers to international trade and investment (ownership barriers, tariffs and so forth). Taken as a whole the OECD's assessment[25] is that regulation was reduced by about one-quarter in that five-year period alone, with a strong tendency for the most regulated countries to be cutting regulation by most (Italy and France being good examples).

Government Services and Private Procurement

Government spending has always involved services provided within the public sector and purchases of goods and services from the private sector. Along with privatization of nationalized industries which produce goods and services for sale, there has been a trend towards government procurement moving from in-house provision of services to purchases from the private sector. Shifting to private provision *may* result in savings if the private provision is cheaper (contracting out hospital cleaning services) and the threat of such a switch can also be used to put pressure on workers in the public sector. Between 1987 and 2003 the proportion of UK government current expenditure on goods and services which represented purchases from the private sector rose from 37% to 48%. The trends to outsourcing, and to putting contracts out to competitive tendering, are common to most countries.[26]

A review of the effect of contracting out services previously provided in the UK public sector concluded that cost savings have frequently been in the range 10–30%.[27] Some, though not all, studies suggest that the savings are similar if the contract is retained in-house after being opened up to competitive tender. As with privatization the issue is whether cost savings come from the shift to private ownership of the enterprise supplying the service or from tighter financial controls and competition, which may not require privatization. The UK results noted above are broadly similar to those reported in a review covering other countries. Fears that cost savings were funded by quality reduction were not borne out by studies of school cleaning. However it seems very plausible that the biggest element of cost-cutting costs often comes from 'raising effort...lower wages and less favourable work conditions' (Lundsgaard 2002: 84–5). The *Guardian* reported that a government review of outsourcing, set up after trade union pressure but abandoned for undisclosed reasons, had found that 'efficiency' savings came from cuts in staffing and lowering of pay rates mainly for manual workers (8 Mar. 2002 quoted by Pollock 2004:193).

The UK government has also pioneered the use of private finance to fund investment projects for use within the public sector (PFIs). Begun under the Conservative government, this form of funding has contributed 10–15% of public services investment since 1997 and by the middle of 2003 had delivered 600 new public facilities including 34 hospitals, 119 other health facilities and 239 new and refurbished schools.[28] Just as with privatization a decade earlier, an important attraction for the government was the fact that some investment spending was removed from the public spending total. This was particularly absurd given that the Chancellor's own Fiscal Rules explicitly permit budget deficits in order to finance public investment. Indeed the main effect has been to push spending into the future as building costs are paid in an annual rental rather than as lump-sum construction costs. Moreover more is paid out over the life of the project than would be the case with ordinary contracts. This is because of the considerably higher rates of return allowed to the private sector contractors than the government would pay on its own borrowing. A recent review of the costs of this kind of finance concluded:

In certain situations where contracts are easy to define, risks are well understood, transaction costs are low, and competition to provide finance is active, then the costs of public and private finance are likely to be very similar. Unfortunately for many public services such conditions simply do not hold, and insisting on private financing will impose significant costs on taxpayers in general, and/or the users of the services. (Jenkinson 2003: 333).

Over and above temporary accounting advantages from PFI, the contractor constructs and often then manages the whole project. Over-runs with construction projects in terms of cost and completion date have been found to apply to 20–25% of PFI projects as compared to 70–75% of public projects.[29] When the private contractor has a contract to maintain the building and provide services such as cleaning, PFI in effect involves the contracting out of some of the ancillary services (with the potential for cost savings noted earlier).

Mainly as a result of privatization, but assisted by the developing trend to purchase for the public sector inputs made in the private sector, the share of UK employment which was in the public sector fell from 27.4% to 18.1% between 1981 and 2003.[30]

A feature of the increasing involvement of the private sector in the British NHS, depressingly familiar from the defence sector, has been the interchange of personnel between those responsible for making policy for the NHS and the private sector companies hoping to profit from outsourcing.[31] If the provision of public services was no different in kind from the provision of goods and services for private consumption then the logic of importing private sector methods into the public services would be clear. But many public services, like health and education, have been publicly provided because they have been produced 'for the benefit of the public'. This reflects the egalitarian idea that everybody, regardless of income or foresight, should have access to a decent standard of these services, and that all in society benefit from a healthy and well-educated population. These features give additional motivation to those who work in public services, recently summarized as follows: 'not-for-profit activity and public-sector bureaucracies are organisations that try to cohere around a *mission*. The notion of a mission replaces the conventional focus on profit. We argue that people work harder when they buy into the mission of the organisation and this raises productivity' (Besley and Ghatak 2003: 237). The danger is that work to high standards out of commitment to the public services will be undermined by the profit-oriented goals of private sector management. An influential adviser suggested that the UK government has made exactly this mistake in its attempts to 'reform' public services with its stress on rewarding individual performance 'rather than providing proper pay for each grade and stressing the importance of the job and of the professional norms and professional competence' (Layard 2005: 160).

Labour Market Deregulation and Unemployment

The rise in unemployment in the 1980s brought a concerted drive by international organizations to champion the case for labour market deregulation. The OECD took the lead on publishing a massive *Jobs Study* in 1994. Some of the recommendations of the resulting Jobs Strategy were uncontroversial, such as setting macroeconomic policies to encourage sustainable growth and improving labour force skills and competences. But they included the following more contentious proposals:

Make wage and labour costs more flexible by removing restrictions that prevent wages from reflecting local conditions and individual skill levels, in particular of younger workers.

Reform employment security provisions that inhibit the expansion of employment in the private sector.

Reform unemployment and related benefit systems—and their interaction with the tax system—such that societies' fundamental equity goals are achieved in ways that impinge far less on the efficient functioning of labour markets.

Examples of the policies advocated were

If it is judged desirable to maintain a legal minimum wage as part of an anti-poverty strategy, consider minimising its employment effects, including
• Indexing it to prices, rather than average earnings
• Ensure sufficient differentiation by age and region . . . .

loosen mandatory restrictions on dismissals where the current provisions appear to seriously hinder economic restructuring and the hiring chances of new labour force entrants

Restrict UI [unemployment insurance] benefit entitlements in countries where they are especially long to the period where job search is intense and rapid job-finding remains likely.

Reduce after tax replacement ratios where these are high and review eligibility requirements where these require little employment history before withdrawing benefits (OECD 1994a: 43–8)

The OECD went beyond general injunctions for reform and made specific recommendations to each country as part of its programme *Implementing the Jobs Study*.[32] These came under 30 sub-headings. Fourteen of the headings covered benefits and taxation, such as lowering replacement rates or tightening eligibility conditions. Six related headings referred to wage formation, including widening the wage distribution. Ten covered employment protection, such as easing severance regulations and regulations covering temporary workers. At one extreme, Australia and the USA received four recommendations whilst Finland received 21 and Germany 23. The OECD also published measures of the degree to which their recommendations had been followed. New Zealand and the UK led the field with over 80% compliance; France languished near the bottom.

More recently the IMF joined the clamour with a chapter in their flagship *World Economic Outlook* entitled confidently: 'Unemployment and Labor Market Institutions: Why Reforms Pay Off.' As the IMF noted, international organizations have long argued that 'the causes of unemployment can be found in labor market institutions.

Accordingly, countries with high unemployment have been repeatedly urged to undertake comprehensive structural reforms to reduce "labor market rigidities" ' (IMF 2003: 129). Indeed they claimed that 'high and persistent unemployment can only be solved through structural reforms' (ibid. 133 n. 8). They described reducing unemployment benefits, labour taxation and employment protection legislation from Euro-area levels to US levels as 'popular measures' and claimed (their table 4.1) that this would reduce unemployment by nearly 3 percentage points.

How strong is the evidence that these policy recommendations would have the desired effect? It is far less conclusive than is suggested by the confidence with which labour market reforms are advocated. As a simple example take the case of unemployment benefits, which are widely thought to cause unemployment. Replacement ratios did rise, especially in Europe from the late 1960s to the early 1980s. But if we look at the cross-country position at the turn of the century, we can use the considerable degree of variation in both replacement ratios and unemployment rates across Europe to try and pin down the relationship with unemployment (see Fig. 2.5). According to the OECD data, six European countries had a lower NAIRU than the USA, and three more (including Germany) were not very much higher. The relation between unemployment and benefits is, if anything, in the 'wrong' direction (higher benefits go along with lower unemployment). Of course there are a host of other influences on unemployment but if benefits were very important we might expect *some* degree of correlation in the 'right' (positive) direction. Baker *et al.* (2005) show that such a lack of a simple relation with unemployment applies to the other likely suspects such as employment protection and union membership.

Such simple cross-country comparisons, whilst very seductive when they seem to support the point at issue, are *very* simple and ignore a host of factors which should be controlled for. These include differences across countries in the 'shocks' their economies have had to contend with, changes in labour market institutions over time, interactions between them and so forth. There is a huge literature on all this, which is far too vast to even briefly summarize. However a comparison of such studies, which use a variety of data sets and methodologies, concludes that the statistical results are quite 'unrobust' in the sense that the magnitudes of the effects found vary widely between the studies.[33] This does not mean that there may not be some effects in the supposed direction but that their quantitative importance is not well measured and may very well be small.

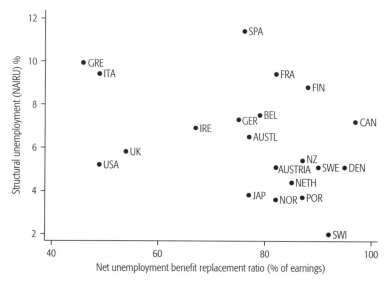

Fig. 2.5. **Structural Unemployment and Unemployment Benefits, 1999**
Source: OECD. See Data Appendix.

Further consideration will be given to the impact of labour market deregulation in Chapter 5 below. However the point to stress here is that it has been strenuously promoted despite weak evidence for the magnitude of its benefits and in almost total neglect of its costs. There are immediate and obvious costs,[34] namely the cut in the incomes of a badly off section of the community (the unemployed) or the extra precariousness of the jobs of large numbers of workers (including the low one paid). If the pay-off in terms of higher employment was clear and substantial then the costs and benefits could be compared. But employers would unambiguously benefit from greater latitude in hiring and firing and so forth. Thus there is plenty of support for such deregulation from business even without strong evidence that unemployment would be reduced.

Conclusions

This chapter has documented the turn towards tight monetary policies, with priority accorded to maintaining low inflation and the efforts at limiting budget deficits. These measures were quite successful in economies which were growing rapidly but foundered successively in Japan, Europe and the USA as stagnation or the fear of recession took over. Complementing the turn to financial austerity, the degree of government intervention in the dominant market sector of the economy has been drastically cut through privatization and latterly reductions in a wide range of product market regulations. Finally there has been a forceful campaign from the international organizations in favour of freeing up market forces in the labour market by cutting unemployment benefits, minimum wages and employment protection, the hard-won gains of the 1960s and 1970s. The broad impact of these developments on growth, stability and inequality will be reviewed in later chapters. First, however, the reassertion of the power of capital ownership over the functioning of private sector firms, and the associated rise in the importance of the financial sector, must be examined.

3
Finance and Ownership

It was deliciously intense and exciting to have been a part of creating LTCM [Long-Term Capital Management]. For making it possible, I will never be able to adequately express my thanks to my extraordinarily talented LTCM colleagues.

The distinctive LTCM experience from the beginning to the present characterizes the theme of the productive interaction of finance theory and finance practice. Indeed, in a twist on the more familiar version of that theme, the major investment magazine, *Institutional Investor* characterized the remarkable collection of people at LTCM as 'The best finance faculty in the world.'

From Merton Miller's autobiographical notes on receiving the 1997 Nobel Prize in Economics. On LTCM see below.

Adam Smith described money as the 'great wheel of circulation' and traditionally the finance sector has been seen as playing a rather passive role in economic development, channelling credit more or less effectively towards profitable firms. However financial liberalization and advances in communications encouraged financial innovation and brought finance into much greater prominence—with effects both on the economy as a whole (aggregate demand) as well as on the behaviour of individual firms.

A number of aspects of the heightened role of the financial sector are considered in the chapter which follows. The development of consumer and mortgage credit seems to free mass consumption from the age-old budget constraint encapsulated in the epigram 'workers spend what they get'. Financial markets claimed spectacular success in generating the 1990s 'new economy' boom in the USA and have increased their control of corporate managements, pressing them to cut costs and maximize short-term profits. International financial flows hold out the promise of liberating a country's rate of investment from the limitation imposed by its savings. Increasingly elaborate financial instruments allow hedge funds and others to parcel out yield and risk in ever more complicated ways, promising to detach returns for the sharpest investors from the profitability of the under-lying assets.

In what ways is the rise of finance linked to the shifts in government policy discussed in the previous chapter? The financial sector was always in the forefront of demanding orthodox financial policies and the defeat of inflation. High inflation, and particularly unpredictable inflation which tends to be associated with it, cause sudden shifts in the real value of financial assets such as bank deposits or bonds. Whilst the most agile or well-informed investors like such 'volatil-ity' as it opens up anomalies in financial markets which they can exploit, the financial sector overall is much more comfortable with macroeconomic stability. In this respect, however, there is no major difference of interest between finance and the big industrial firms, which also stood to gain from wages being brought under control and profits being restored. Industry also stood to gain from financial lib-eralization if it opened up cheaper sources of funds. The possibility of replacing the instability of the 1960s and 1970s, which derived in good part from conflict between bosses and workers, with instability deriving from bubbles and crashes in unfettered financial markets was not one that was contemplated in advance.

The Rise of the Financial Sector

Numerous indicators testify to the increasing role for finance in the rich countries—burgeoning ratios to GDP of stock market cap-italization, of consumer borrowing, of derivatives turnover and of cross-border financial flows. All this activity has been reflected in the profits of the financial sector, viewed (like Wall Street or the City of London) as comprising a distinct set of interests. The expansion of finance has been at its most dramatic in the USA, where aggregate profits of financial corporations rose from being one-fifth as big as non-financial profits in the 1970s and 1980s to a half after 2000 (see Fig. 3.1). The stock market valuation of US financial companies (a reflection of expected long-term profits) was 29% of the value of non-financials in 2004, a fourfold increase over the previous 25 years; in the UK there was a slower increase in this 'capitalization ratio' from a higher starting point to some 40% now. However the ascent of finance has not been without setbacks. In the 1990s both the German growth slowdown and the Japanese banking crisis saw the relative capitalization of the financial sector halved since heady peaks in the 1980s.

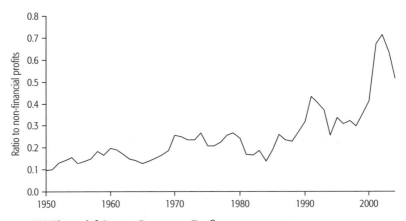

Fig. 3.1. **US Financial Sector Corporate Profits, 1950–2004**
Source: Bureau of Economic Analysis. See Data Appendix.

Finance and Household Consumption

From Marx to Keynes at least, consumption was viewed as an essentially passive component of the growth process. Capital accumulation, investment spending on machinery and buildings, was the essential driving force on the demand as well as on the supply side. It was the capitalists' access to finance which allowed capital spending to exceed the previous period's savings and fuelled the expansion of demand; future profits ensured that such borrowing was repaid with a real return. Deficit spending by the government could, in wartime for example, impart a similar impulse to demand, at least till capital markets took fright at the growing debt interest burden and worries about inflation. However household consumption, some two-thirds of aggregate demand, was seen as playing the role of sustaining the current output level rather than driving it up.

Savings ratios often fell during recessions, as consumers attempted to maintain spending in the face of falling incomes. Indeed, Milton Friedman criticized the Keynesians for exaggerating the dependence of consumption on current income and ignoring the extent to which savings could be used to 'smooth' out the path of consumption. More recently, rather than acting as a stabilizing influence, sharp *falls* in the savings ratio have occurred during expansions. By boosting consumption proportionately more than the rise in incomes this has intensified upswings, with the danger of sharp falls in demand if savings rebound sharply when the expansion slackens and pessimism builds up.

Buoyant household consumption has been most notable in the USA where household savings have slumped. From the 1950s to the 1980s the household savings ratio averaged 8–9.5% each decade. In the 1990s the ratio fell to 5.2% and then averaged 1.9% over the period 2000–3. Without this fall in savings consumption would have grown 1% per year slower during the long expansion from 1992 to 2000. Household spending on consumption and residential investment contributed nearly 80% of the total increase in US demand during the new economy boom of 1995– 2000 as compared to 65–70% during the comparable periods at the end of the 1960s and 1980s booms.[1] There were similarly powerful boosts to consumption from falling savings ratios in the UK, Netherlands, Sweden, Italy, Finland, Canada and Australia at various periods in the 1990s.[2] Whilst this list extends beyond the most market-oriented group of economies, France and Germany are notable absentees with consumption remaining more closely confined to the growth of real incomes.

The expansion of household borrowing, from banks, credit card companies, mortgage companies, has been very rapid in the 1990s. The ratio of this borrowing to disposable income rose by 20–40% between 1991 and 2003 in the USA, Germany and the UK to exceed previous peaks. Mortgage borrowing, which is more comparable across countries, exceeded 100% of GDP in the UK and was 60–85% of GDP in the USA, Germany and Japan.[3]

Before the 1980s financial institutions had been constrained in many countries as to the interest rates they could offer and charge, what sort of loans they could make, what type of financial assets they could purchase and whether they could gain access to overseas markets. People who wanted to borrow for house purchase had to make substantial deposits up front, and could only borrow relatively small multiples of their income. Removal of such restrictions (financial deregulation) generated aggressive competition for customers and much easier access to credit. The result was greater access to borrowing and periodic boosts to household spending, particularly in the USA and UK. Another factor probably contributing to increased consumer borrowing was that the slower growth of household incomes in the 1980s and 1990s lagged behind consumption aspirations which could therefore only be realized by increased borrowing. Moreover, as it became easier to borrow against increases in wealth, capital gains on assets held by consumers were more likely to be translated into higher consumption. With housing supply expanding slowly, credit expansion itself increased house prices in many countries. These capital gains then provided the backing for further borrowing, which consumers could use to finance purchases of cars or holidays. For a time at least consumption took over as the motor of economic expansion.

Shareholder Value and the Stock Market Boom

The US financial system has been widely taken to be the model for flexibility and dynamism. The pricing of companies' securities by active financial markets is supposed to provide a rational allocation of capital as companies' prospects are assessed by people with every interest in exploiting all available information. So finance chases after those investment prospects which are likely to realize the greatest return. Managements with the greatest entrepreneurial skills in seeking out profitable opportunities from new technology or products will find it easy to raise funds to make those investments. The same financial markets keep the pressure on incumbent managements to minimize costs and rationalize wherever this is profitable. Poor profit results leave the firm vulnerable to takeover with control passing to more effective or aggressive management.

In economics textbooks firms maximize profits by their marginal pricing and output decisions. Cost minimization, a necessary condition for profit maximization, is presumed to be unproblematic. These assumptions were challenged by Berle and Means in the 1930s who pointed out that many companies had large numbers of owners with relatively small shareholdings and thus little ability to assess whether management was really up to scratch. This gave managements, especially in industries where product market competition was not so fierce, considerable latitude to pursue their own objectives (for example growth even at the expense of profits or a quiet life in preference to cost minimization). The rise in the power of organized labour, discussed in Chapter 1, acted as a constraint over what management could achieve. This was manifested in conflicts on the shop floor on manning levels and production line speeds, collective bargaining over job security and in some countries like Germany it was institutionalized in co-determination legislation. The crisis in profitability of the 1960s and 1970s, outlined in Chapter 1, showed the extent to which the prerogatives of the owners of capital had been undermined. The period since has seen a strong counter-attack under the slogan 'shareholder value', with the financial markets playing a crucial role in transmitting the pressure for improved profitability.

An important factor behind the drive for shareholder value in the Anglophone countries was the rise in the proportion of corporate equity owned by financial institutions. Pension funds have swelled; traditionally they were tightly controlled by governments as to what assets they could hold, in order to protect savers from risk. However, partly in response to the low or negative real returns on safe financial assets in the 1960s and 1970s, the financial sector lobbied successfully to have these restrictions relaxed, allowing these funds to invest in corporate equities and in risky ('junk') bonds rather than safe government assets.[4] Big institutional shareholders have the resources and incentives to closely monitor company performance and bring pressure on laggards. In the UK and USA (largest 500 companies) around 40% of equity is held by financial institutions. Proportions are much lower elsewhere—15–18% in France and Germany and 6% in Japan—with dominant blocks of shares often held by families or by other (non-financial) companies.[5] They may be less concerned with maximizing short-run profits than with the long-run fortunes of the company better served by increasing market share or maintaining good relations with customers, suppliers, banks and even the workforce.

Widespread benefits have been claimed for the US trend towards institutional investment.

'As institutional investors with larger stakes took over from individual investors... the power of investors vis-à-vis management has grown....' the paramount duty of management and the board is to the shareholder and not... to other stakeholders' (Business Roundtable)... Because governance has been improved, firms have been paying more attention to the utilisation of the funds they generate.... The consequence of this newfound awareness has been a substantial increase in the rate of return... As governance improves, and managers begin to work in their investors' interests, *everyone benefits*. (Rajan and Zingales 2003: 74–5; emphasis added).

Such claims assume that financial markets do indeed make rational appraisal of the prospects of the firms whose shares they are holding.

Stock markets are viewed as being high if equity prices are high relative to the profits of the companies concerned. Since owning a stock entitles you to a share in the future growth of profits, high equity prices are justified if there is good reason to expect rapid growth of the profits and thus the dividends of the companies concerned. The US stock market boom of the later 1990s brought it, by this measure, to the highest peak it had ever achieved. In 2000 US

equities were valued at about 45 times underlying corporate earnings, as compared to around 30 times earnings before the Great
Crash in 1929.[6] Enthusiasm for new economy stocks, particularly
connected with the internet, reached incredible levels. In February
2000 the market valuation of internet-involved companies (including portal companies like Google and e-commerce companies like
Amazon) was estimated at $943 billon despite the fact that these
companies were together reporting *losses* totalling $6 billion per
year. After surveying a mass of evidence Ofek and Richardson (2002)
conclude that it is very difficult to explain the internet boom as
being consistent with financial market rationality. One of their
examples of absurd valuations was Zapata, founded in the 1950s by
former US President George Bush as an oil and gas company, but by
1998 specializing in meat-casings and fish oil. After an earlier
abortive foray into an internet venture it announced that it was
forming an internet business subsidiary called Zap.com. This
brought an immediate rise in its share price of 98%!

A recent survey by a leading finance specialist concluded that 'the
recent worldwide stock market boom, and then crash after 2000, had
its origin in human foibles and arbitrary feedback relations [rising
prices promoting expectations of further price rises, increasing
investor demand—AG] and must have generated a substantial real
misallocation of resources' (Shiller 2003: 102). Another assessment
was even more damning:

In part the massive overvaluation of equity that occurred in the late 1990s
and early 2000s was an understandable market mistake. Society often
seems to overvalue what is new—in this case high-tech telecommunications, and Internet ventures. But this catastrophic overvaluation was also
the result of misleading data from managers, large numbers of naïve
investors, and breakdowns in the agency relationships within companies, in
investment banks, and in audit and law firms many of whom knowingly
contributed to the misinformation and manipulation that fed the overvaluation. (Jensen 2003: 14)

The circumstances which led to this bitter reproach to US business,
from one of the leading prophets of shareholder value, deserve some
explanation, and this is the subject of the next section.

Shareholder Value and Corporate Governance

In the 1980s extra pressure on management which was exerted by US financial markets came via hostile takeovers. The consequent restructuring often involved major increases in borrowing by the companies taken over, the idea being that the obligation to pay interest on the debt would force management into cost-cutting. The 'leveraged buy out' firms, such as Kohlberg, Kravis Roberts, gave management teams 'high-powered' incentives in the form of stock options which allowed managers to buy shares in the company at a later date at what would be an extremely favourable price if the company was successful. This gave managers a very strong incentive to do whatever would help to boost profits and thus the share price. This trend was then taken up by institutional investors: 'With the implicit assent of institutional shareholders [e.g. pension funds—AG], boards substantially increased the use of stock option plans that allowed managers to share in the value created by restructuring their own companies. Shareholder value thus became an ally [of management—AG] rather than a threat' (Holmstrom and Kaplan 2003: 8).

This is a very mild way of describing the frenzied increase in management pay, mainly by the issuing of stock options. In 2001 the ten most highly rewarded CEOs in the top 500 companies were granted option packages with an estimated average value of $170 million, an amazing amount, especially since several of them already held large amounts of stock. 'It is hard to argue that these people needed stronger shareholder incentives. An obvious explanation is that they have been able to use their positions of power to command excessive rewards' (Holmstrom and Kaplan 2003: 13). For the largest 500 US companies the ratio of CEO pay to production worker earnings rose from 30 in 1970 to 570 in 2000, with most of the increase taking the form of stock options. This contrasts with ratios in the 10–25 range in Japan and Europe. CEO compensation (that is for *one person* per company) averaged 7.9% of corporate profits in a large US sample of companies. Stock options (on shares which management still held) reached 15% of equity currently outstanding. It is hardly surprising that all this potential for personal enrichment caused 'management to obsess over their firm's day-to-day share price' (Coffee 2003: 32).[7]

There was a close link between this change in executive compensation and the wave of corporate scandals (Enron, World Com etc.) that engulfed the USA after the stock market boom subsided in 2000: 'a system that lavishly rewards executives for success tempts those executives, who control much of the information available to outsiders, to fabricate the appearance of success. Aggressive accounting, fictitious transactions that inflate sales, whatever it takes.' (Krugman 2004: 111). An example helps to clarify the potential benefits to top management of inflating current profits, for example by somehow bringing hoped for future revenues into this year's accounts: 'assume a CEO holds options on 2 m[illion] shares of his company stock and that the company is trading at a price to earnings ratio of 30 to 1 (both reasonable assumptions for this era). On this basis, if a CEO can cause the "premature" recognition of revenues that result in an increase in annual earnings by simply $1 per share, the CEO has caused a $30 price increase that should make him $60 m richer. Not a small incentive!' (Coffee 2005: 202).

WorldCom admitted in July 2002 that it had hidden some $7 billion of operating expenses over the previous two years as capital expenditure, thereby inflating earnings by the same amount.[8] A study by the *Financial Times* of 25 major corporate bankruptcies calculated that 'between 1999 and 2001 the senior executives at these doomed firms pocketed some $3.3 billion in salary, bonuses, and the proceeds from sales of stock and stock options' (Cassidy 2002: 336).

Doing business with these companies was extremely important to the auditors, lawyers and bankers involved, discouraging probing questioning of deals and accounts. 'Put as bluntly as possible, the audit partner of a major client (such as Enron) is always conflicted by the fact that such a partner has virtually a "one-client" practice. Should the partner lose that client for any reason, the partner will need to find employment elsewhere' (Coffee 2003: 37). Fees from Enron represented one-quarter of Arthur Andersen's auditing revenue in Houston, thus making that branch of Andersen highly dependent on business from Enron. Moreover these auditing companies frequently also provided lucrative consulting services to the firms they were auditing; for example, Andersen earned a further $27 million in consulting fees from Enron. Buying consulting services from the auditor gave firms like Enron an effective but discreet additional source of leverage. Whilst sacking an auditing firm which was proving uncooperative in reporting rapid profit growth would lead to plenty of unwelcome comment, threatening to shift consulting contracts away from the auditor was a 'low visibility' method of keeping up the pressure. Rather chillingly, in view of Andersen's collapse in the wake of the Enron meltdown, Coffee (2003: 35) concludes 'The available evidence in fact suggests that Andersen was no different from its peers (except possibly less lucky).'

Investment banks earned $125 million in underwriting fees from arranging share or bond issues for Enron over the period 1998–2000. Analysts working for investment banks, supposed to be advising investors but eager to curry favour with Enron in the hope of future business, forecast increases in Enron's share price that were twice as big as the increases forecast by analysts not working for investment banks.[9] More broadly, as the Initial Public Offering (IPO) market grew, analysts' objectivity became increasingly compromised as they became 'the principal means by which investment banks competed for IPO clients, as the underwriter with the "star" analyst could produce the biggest first-day stock price spike' (Coffee 2003: 39).

Finally the financial press signally failed to act as an effective counterweight to analysts' hype and auditors' timidity. A review of the treatment of Enron in the business press reported 'a parallel universe of cheer-leading and obsequiousness, a universe where applause obliterated scepticism'. According to a *Wall Street Journal* writer, financial journalists 'outsourced their critical thinking to Wall St analysts, who are not independent, and by definition were employed to do nothing but spin positive company news in order to sell stock' (quoted Dyck and Zingales 2003: 88, 89).

But surely the increasingly important investment managers of pension and other funds would invest in line with long-term 'fundamentals', and would thus act as a counterweight to the 'momentum' trading of investors who just pile in after the prevailing trend. Unfortunately the highly competitive nature of the fund management industry prevailed over what might have been their better judgement:

> Whilst investment management firms were selected on the basis of long-term records kept by pension fund consultants, consultants naturally began to help corporate [pension—AG] plan sponsors monitor the performance of investment managers by collecting quarterly performance results. As competitive pressures built in the very profitable investment management business, this quickly evolved into a quarterly performance derby . . . investment time horizons collapsed, investment performance became defined relative to a benchmark or index portfolio, asset allocation and market timing skills were made obsolete by a monomaniacal focus on stock selection and risk became defined solely in relation to departures made from benchmark weightings. Each of these consultant-inspired moves had the unintended consequence of enhancing herding dynamics among institutional investors. (Parenteau 2005, p. 123, 126)

Equity bubbles become much more likely.

The discussion in this section has concentrated on the weaknesses in the US system based on 'outsider' ownership by pension funds and other financial institutions focussed on shareholder value. Just before the system was engulfed by Enron and other scandals at the end of the boom, the superiority of its shareholder-oriented corporate governance structure was pronounced as representing the ultimate system—the 'end of history'—for corporate law by a pair of Yale and Harvard law professors.[10] Their justification was the superior performance of the US economy compared to Germany, Japan or France. How rapidly fashions had changed is shown by a 1992 *Harvard Business Review* article called 'America's Failing Capital Investment System' by Michael Porter, one of the most influential management writers. This argued that US ownership structures and corporate governance optimized short-term private returns whilst '[b]y focusing on long-term corporate position and creating an ownership structure and governance process that incorporates the interests of employees, suppliers, customers and the local community, the Japanese and German systems better capture the social benefits that private investment brings' (Porter 1992: 74).

Of course scandals are by no means unique to the US financial system. Europe produced a worthy competitor to WorldCom in the

Italian company Parmalat where more than $17 billion mysteriously vanished from the balance sheet, with huge sums apparently being siphoned off by controlling shareholders. Although auditors should presumably have detected fraudulent transactions, which apparently stretched over a decade, a comparison of US and European scandals notes that 'one suspects they would have likely been dismissed at the point at which they began to monitor earnestly' (Coffee 2005: 208). Nevertheless what was so striking about recent US experience was that there was such a comprehensive and systematic set of incentives for all the many professional groups involved in the financial markets to acquiesce in such widespread abuse.

Despite all its evident problems, are the systems of other countries being forced by competition towards the US model? Indications that this is the case include the spectacular takeover of the giant German company Mannesman by Vodafone reflecting the sudden emergence of a wave of hostile takeovers in Europe, the growing number of European companies listing on the US stock exchange bringing with it disclosure requirements and pressures for shareholder value and the effects on French and German corporations of large ownership stakes built up by US financial institutions.[11] This latter development has provoked a sharp reaction in Germany, with a senior official of the ruling SPD denouncing the US financial institutions involved as 'locusts'. The Chairman of Toyota explained to a finance industry conference in 2001 that it would be irresponsible to run Japanese companies primarily in the interests of shareholders as this would result in the pursuit of short-term profits at the expense of employment and research and development (R&D) spending. This approach, however frustrating to investment managers, may be much more successful in the longer term, at least in some sectors. With its long-term perspective Toyota has recently been valued more highly by the stock market than Ford, General Motors and Chrysler combined.[12] This is hardly consistent with the proclaimed universal superiority of the UK/US system—the battle of competing models for industrial organization and corporate governance is far from over.

In the wake of all the scandals in the USA there was a flurry of proposals about how the law on corporate governance should be tightened. The Sarbanes–Oxley Act which passed in 2002 required

CEOs to disgorge any profits from bonuses or stock sales during the 12 months after a financial report which was subsequently 'restated' because of 'misconduct'. More detailed disclosure is required of off-balance sheet items and 'special purpose entities' (much used by Enron), the power and independence of the company's audit committee was increased and criminal penalties for misreporting were raised. The authorities, having sat on their hands whilst the boom and the scandals were boiling up, acted to head off further excesses. One assessment concluded that Sabanes–Oxley dealt with 'some of deficiencies of US corporate governance' and probably helped to restore confidence (Holmstrom and Kaplan 2003: 21).

Who Bears the Costs?

The costs and benefits of the great drive for shareholder value and the US stock market boom can be examined at two levels. First, there is the impact of the frauds and scandals. Secondly, there is the boom itself—what was its role in launching a major wave of new innovations?

The cases of fraud and deliberate malpractice have often brought financial disaster for tens of thousands of the employees involved (lost jobs and frequently pensions). Moreover the companies concerned invested in assets which turned out to be useless. Enron spent nearly $1 billion on information technology during its last three years and there was heavy spending on R&D, broadband and IT technologies by other prominent manipulators such as WorldCom, Tyco and Global Crossing. Such companies also acquired companies with their inflated shares and often ran them into the ground. An analysis of earnings manipulation suggested 'waste, probably running into hundreds of billions of dollars, is a direct result of accounting manipulations' (Lev 2003: 43).

There was, of course, more to the great US stock market boom, and the new economy it was supposed to reflect, than accounting scandals. Venture capital partnerships grew spectacularly from committing around $5 billion of new funds to start-up companies in the mid-1990s to more than $60 billion in 2000, 60% of which went to companies in the IT sector. The bloated stock market valuations of such companies brought the prospect of mouth-watering returns for the venture capitalists if the companies they financed could be floated on the stock market. By 2000 venture capital portfolios represented twice as much capital in the USA than in Europe and 20 times more than in Japan.[13]

Venture capitalists could boast of having supported many companies which proved very successful (like Apple, Cisco, Microsoft or Sun) but the collapse of the internet boom revealed a vast over-commitment of resources. The momentum of rising investment was so strong that capacity in the US telecommunications equipment sector doubled between the beginning of 1999 and the end of 2002. However the utilization of this capacity fell from the exceptional level of 94% in mid-2000 to a bit less than 50% in the second half of 2002. The whole high-tech sector (including computer and semi-conductor manufacture) exhibits the same pattern in milder form with capacity utilization subsiding by 20% as the boom collapsed.[14]

This contradictory picture—extraordinary successes in introducing new technologies combined with extremes of waste and overinvestment—encapsulates the dynamic side of capitalism. The finance theorist, Andrei Shleifer, recalls Keynes's verdict on the boom of the second half of the 1920s: 'Whilst some part of the investment which was going on . . . was doubtless ill-judged and unfruitful, there can, I think, be no doubt that the world was enormously enriched by the constructions . . .' (Shleifer 2000: 189). Shleifer argues in a similar vein that the internet stock price bubble meant that 'a large number of creative entrepreneurs have moved into this line of activity . . . , which may well be efficient in light of the possibly significant external benefits from innovation in this area' (Shleifer 2000: 189).

Even leaving aside the extreme effects of boom and slumps shareholder value is immediately increased by actions which cut costs and raise profits. Cutting jobs is often the easiest route to 'taking out costs', to use the slightly sinister management jargon. Job destruction was higher in US manufacturing in the 1980s and 1990s than in the 1970s, with both more employment falls within continuing plants and more job losses due to plant closures. The pattern of involuntary job loss in the USA over the past 20 years is consistent with there having been increasing pressure on management to cut costs through rationalization of production. At the end of the upswing (1997–9) the rate of job loss was higher than a decade earlier, despite a tighter labour market. If anything plant closures were more important in the 1980s, which may reflect the strength of the takeover boom of that decade, whereas in the 1990s focus was on 'positions abolished' in continuing plants, which is consistent with greater pressure on all managements to take out production costs. Hostile takeovers, a prime means of pursuing shareholder value in the USA, often boosted profits at the expense of workers who lost out in terms of jobs, wages or pension levels.[15]

International Finance

The growth of international financial flows has been one of the more notorious aspects of the expansion of finance, stimulated by progressive abandonment throughout the OECD of the capital controls. These had more or less severely constrained the extent to which a country's firms and residents could invest overseas through purchasing shares, putting funds in a bank abroad or even financing the setting up of factories overseas. There were often corresponding restraints on overseas funds entering a country. This is an aspect of financial liberalization which has been well documented and it has broader significance as opening the borders up to financial flows makes it much more difficult to maintain tight controls on the domestic financial system. Amongst OECD countries, five out of 19 were classified by the IMF as having open capital markets in 1976, including the USA and Germany. The UK and Japan followed suit by 1980. By 1988 only one OECD country was classified as having controls in one of the five strongest categories, compared to half the countries in 1973. In the late 1980s and early 1990s the rest of the OECD liberalized with Norway the last of the social democratic strongholds to succumb in 1995.[16]

World foreign exchange trading reached \$1,900 billion per day in 2004, more than three times the level of 1989. Massive two-way flows of funds have built up as banks and other institutions simultaneously borrow and lend abroad. Estimates show the total value of stock of foreign assets of a large sample of countries doubled from the equivalent of 36% of GDP to 71% of GDP between 1980 and 1995, having already more than doubled over the previous two decades. By the early 2000s the ratio probably reached 100%, getting on for double its peak in 1900. Transactions in overseas securities by US residents increased 60 times in relation to GDP between 1977 and 2003.[17]

The theory is that all of this activity parcels out risks and returns between holders of financial assets in an efficient way. Of particular importance is the impact on payments balances. Has greater capital mobility allowed countries to run balance of payments deficits on current account and has this helped or hindered stability and growth? Have capital flows facilitated rapid movement of exchange rates towards appropriate levels or tended to exaggerate overvaluations and undervaluations which have serious consequences for the real economy?

During the Bretton Woods period exchange rates were pegged with devaluations only allowed in situations of 'fundamental disequilibrium'. The current account of the balance of payments was generally regarded as a constraint to which domestic policy had to respond and current account deficits were small. This constrained countries' investment to their own level of savings.[18] Since the early 1980s, and especially in the 1990s, however, there has been a substantial increase in the average size of balance of payments surpluses or deficits (in relation to GDP).[19] Is this a good thing? If larger deficits reflected borrowing to invest productively by poorer OECD countries like Portugal, or those particularly well endowed with natural resources like Australia, then the effects would be beneficial. However deficits have often been associated with the consumer booms discussed above. In Portugal for example most of the increased deficit reflected reduced savings rather than increased investment. The rising US deficit at the end of the 1990s expansion could be regarded as facilitating the great IT investment boom. However by 2004, with the current account deficit at 5% of GDP, the deficit was funding high levels of consumption and military spending.

Free mobility of capital is supposed to ensure that exchange rates smoothly offset trends affecting the competitiveness of a country's exports (rate of wage increases out of line with competitors' for example). This would mean that the real exchange rate—the nominal rate adjusted for price or wage cost inflation—would be maintained, or only adjust smoothly in response to long-run changes in underlying competitiveness. Here the record must have been very disappointing to free-marketers. On average the real exchange rate of OECD countries changed by about 3% a year in the 1960s, and then 6% per year in the 1970s as the Bretton Woods system collapsed.[20] Real exchange rate fluctuations subsided somewhat after the 1970s, but in the 1990s these year to year movements were still half as large again as in the 1960s. If these were merely random fluctuations around satisfactory trends then they could hopefully be absorbed by the real economy without undue costs, especially as the greater sophistication of financial markets and its participants made it easier to hedge (insure against) fluctuations in nominal exchange rates. However, these year to year movements have also coincided with longer-term swings in real exchange rates (and thus the cost competitiveness of the traded goods sectors) of individual economies which can have a lasting, distorting effect on the structure of the economy.

Confining attention to the three major currencies (dollar, yen and the Euro superseding the German mark), Figure 3.2 shows the real revaluation of the dollar of around 70% in the first half of the 1980s followed by a sharp fall and then another substantial increase after 1995 (US policy towards the dollar is discussed in Chapter 4 below). The Euro and the yen have also delivered large changes in real competitiveness, generally mirroring the dollar. Such sustained movements in the real exchange rate can be extremely damaging to the capacity of the economy. Investment is discouraged by the extra risk and adjustments are made which are not readily reversed if the real exchange reverts to a more appropriate level.[21] For example sustained real appreciation causes companies to withdraw from export markets and make workers redundant. A detailed study of

US manufacturing found that dollar appreciation substantially increased job destruction (the rate of job loss in manufacturing plants) and that was *not* compensated by correspondingly lower job destruction or increased job creation (manufacturing plants increasing employment) when the dollar depreciated again. The authors also noted the damaging effects of bursts of job destruction: 'Workers are likely to have an easier time finding suitable reemployment when job destruction is gradual and diffuse than when an external shock [e.g. dollar appreciation—AG] causes job destruction to spike and, consequently, a glut of displaced workers are searching for new jobs simultaneously' (Klein *et al* 2000: 29).

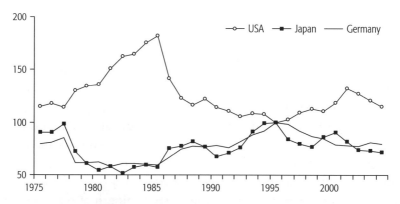

Fig. 3.2. **Real Exchange Rates, 1975–2004**
Source: IMF. See Data Appendix. 1995 = 100.

The pathological case of exchange rate fluctuation is a full-blown currency crisis. This is conventionally defined in the academic literature as a month when a combination of exchange rate and foreign currency reserve changes exceeds a threshold level. One study found that each of the OECD countries in the sample (four Scandinavian countries and Spain) had experienced four or more crisis episodes since 1970. As well as instances involving big budget deficits, current account deficits or 'financial excesses', there were also crises caused by sudden shocks in international capital markets and self-fulfilling speculative attacks—'crises also happen in economies with immaculate fundamentals' (Kaminsky 2003: 2). The incidence of crises with a currency element rose in the period of floating rates since 1973, with the period up to 1987 being worse than the following decade.[22] In an admittedly rough and ready calculation Eichengreen (2004) suggests that reimposing capital controls, with the presumed effect of suppressing currency crises, could add as much as $100 billion dollars per year to the *growth* of world GDP. However he did not favour such a move since he estimated the costs, in terms of reduced depth of financial intermediation, as 50% more than the benefits. It seems unlikely that controls focused on short-term financial flows would have such dire effects on the financial system and thus economic growth. More fundamentally, the issue of who bears the costs or receives the benefits from financial liberalization should be brought into the calculation. The World Bank estimated that the Asian crisis of 1997, discussed briefly below, increased the incidence of poverty in the region by 22 million.

Financial Instability

Exchange rate crises were discussed in the previous section, but financial crises customarily include banking crises as well—episodes where there is severe 'financial distress' in the banking system. The most comprehensive historical study of financial crises found that crises involving banking crises, which had almost died out in the Golden Age, reappeared in strength from 1973 onwards and became practically as frequent after 1987 as during the interwar period. These banking crises, in Scandinavia for example, caused very large output losses estimated as adding up to 7% of the GDP of the country over the period affected and, where they were combined with a currency crisis, the output loss was some 16% of GDP.[23]

The Bank for International Settlements in Basle is the international institution charged with maintaining stability in the financial system through formulating rules on how banks and other financial institutions should meet standards on capital adequacy and so forth. Its Annual Report for 2005 (BIS 2005: 5) noted that 'The global financial system seems to have become prone to financial turbulence of various sorts'. A recent paper from the Head of the Monetary and Economics Department of the BIS argued that there seems to be a 'common structural thread' linking the increasing number of financial crises: 'Increased risk taking on the part of private sector participants in financial markets has been facilitated by financial market deregulation and technical change. Liberalized financial systems seem inherently more prone to ... intermittent financial crises than do repressed financial systems ... Increased competition could bring a "sharpening dilemma". Financial institutions find it harder to maintain rates of return even as shareholders demand that returns rise.' The author notes the tendency for the finance sector to take greater risks: 'Consider how the loan losses to emerging market economies (EMEs) in the 1970s seemed to spark a series of risky initiatives to reconstitute profits. In turn banks went into leveraged buyouts, property lending, proprietary trading and then lending to EMEs all over again.' He gloomily concludes that 'the modern financial system seems to be subject to a wide range of problems: operational disruptions, institutional insolvencies, short-term market volatility, medium-term misalignments and contagion across countries and markets' (White 2004: 1, 2 n. 4, 24).

Amongst the many financial crises which have plagued the markets two may be selected as exemplifying the problems. The crisis over Long-Term Capital Management in 1998 emphasized that the increasing sophistication of financial markets has widened the scope for drastic miscalculation rather than simply parcelling out risk in smaller and more manageable bundles. In this case prompt coordinating action by the financial authorities saved the day. Finally the Asian crisis of 1997–8 underlined the contagion in contemporary financial markets and the destructive role of the policies of the 'Washington Consensus' pushed by the IMF.[24]

(a) Long-Term Capital Management

The collapse of Long-Term Capital Management (LTCM) in 1998 involved a mixture of 'institutional insolvencies, short-term market volatility ... contagion across countries and markets', to quote from the menacing BIS list. Moreover it featured the most threatening new breed of financial institutions—hedge funds[25]—and the most alarming new class of financial instruments—derivatives.[26] LTCM was a US hedge fund which in July 1998 held assets of $125 billion, financed by $4.1 billion of its own capital and the rest by borrowing. It had been extremely profitable and held more than 50,000 derivatives contracts with a notional sum involved in excess of $1 trillion. LTCM was betting heavily that the yields on certain bonds were out of line with short-term interest rates and this 'should' have brought it a tidy return when relative values returned to a more normal relationship. Unfortunately for LTCM the Russian government's debt default intervened to prevent the shifts in yields anticipated by LTCM, which then started racking up losses.

'As it made losses, it sold some assets, which put pressure on prices, but more importantly the market perceived that liquidation of its positions became more likely. Traders who knew about LTCM's portfolio could position themselves so that they would not get hurt by a liquidation, and might even benefit from it. Their actions put pressure on prices, reducing further the value of LTCM's portfolio, which made liquidation more likely... investors and banks which under normal times would have bid for assets in the event of an LTCM liquidation were facing problems of their own, as they had also made losses on their positions. Some were forced to sell assets that LTCM also held, putting further pressure on prices' (Stultz 2004: 31–2). A compounding factor was that other financial institutions had set out to copy the particular deals which had been proving very lucrative for LTCM. This was a worrying example of the broader problem of 'herding' behaviour in financial markets. 'Hedge fund investors are notorious for copying each other's strategies, so it is not unusual for similar momentum based bets to race through the hedge fund community at the same time. On top of this... copycat trades are initiated by the proprietary trading desks of investment banks and sometimes leaked to the trading desks of institutional investment managers as well' (Parenteau 2005: 122).[27]

In the event LTCM was rescued from bankruptcy by a $3.6 billion injection of funds from creditor banks. They were cajoled by the New York Federal Reserve Bank into contributing to a rescue whilst individually they would have opted to free-ride on other people's efforts. The President of the New York Fed later explained:

Had Long-Term Capital been suddenly put into default, its counterparties would have immediately "closed out" their positions . . . [I]f many firms had rushed to close out hundreds of billions of dollars in transactions simultaneously . . . there was a likelihood that a number of credit and interest rate markets would experience extreme price moves and possibly cease to function for a period of one or more days or even longer (quoted MacKenzie 2003: 366–7).

Alan Greenspan testified to Congress that if LTCM had failed this could have triggered the seizing up of markets, threatening the economy of the USA and many other countries.

Although the bailout of LTCM prevented serious longer-term repercussions the crisis brought into sharp focus the potential fragility of the financial system at its most sophisticated end. This is a continuing worry for the financial authorities charged with regulating the sector and minimizing the likelihood of major crises. A recent, very sophisticated and elaborate analysis found that a conclusive assessment of the systemic risks posed by hedge funds required data that was unavailable and likely to remain so. However the results of their modelling suggested that 'we may be entering a challenging period' and that 'systemic risk is increasing' (Chan *et al.* 2005: 97). Moreover the banks are heavily involved with the hedge funds. 'With margins in traditional business squeezed, big banks are falling over themselves to provide prime brokerage services to hedge funds, which include extending credit, securities dealing and settlement and so forth. Competition has led to an erosion of credit standards . . . One respondent [to a recent survey] even refers to prime brokerage as "the crack cocaine of the financial system"' (Plender 2005: 17).

Problems like those at LTCM seem endemic given the search for ever more exotic ways of beating the market. In May 2005 there was a 'near systemic meltdown' in the 'Over the Counter' derivatives market, according to a senior figure in the securities industry. This followed the reduced credit rating of GM and Ford bonds, which affected several popular hedge fund trading ploys. Some funds had arranged complicated deals based on these corporation' bonds and stock tending to move in the same direction. However, a takeover bid for GM pushed its stock price up whilst its lower credit rating pushed its bond price down. This left hedge funds that were holding the bonds and committed to sell the stocks, which they did not yet own, at a low price 'doubly exposed and with leverged positions [having borrowed a lot]' (Dodd 2005: 4). A number of major hedge funds subsequently closed, including the one designated Hedge Fund of the Year for 2004. Unfortunately very rich owners of, or investors in, these funds are not the only people whose finances are put at risk by such instability. As the OECD noted: 'Public pension schemes are being scaled down to reduce fiscal pressure and to increase space for contributions to occupational and personal pension arrangements' (OECD 2001: 13). If financial markets are made volatile then growing numbers of workers will face increasingly risky retirement incomes.

(b) The Asian Crisis

The Asian crisis which developed in the second half of 1997 illustrated above all how inextricably intertwined the world's financial system had become. Speculative pressure against a previously obscure currency, the Thai baht, spread from currency to currency and threatened disaster for the world economy. Orthodox financial policies, dogmatically applied by the IMF, became widely recognized as destructive in the circumstances and seriously undermined the credibility of that institution.

The underlying cause of speculative pressure was the serious overvaluation of these currencies, which were pegged to the dollar. When the dollar appreciated in the second half of the 1990s their manufacturing sectors became uncompetitive. This coincided with the coming on stream of manufacturing capacity resulting from the earlier high rates of investment. This investment, which extended into speculative office building, was strongly encouraged by plentiful supplies of overseas finance. Firms and banks in these countries took on huge levels of debts, denominated in dollars. The real value of these debts, in terms of domestic production and exports, would rise in proportion to any decline in their currency's value against the US dollar.

A brief chronology compiled from the Bank for International Settlements, Annual Report for 1998 and 1999, illustrates the contagious nature of financial market behaviour.

July 1997	Thai baht forced to float after exchange controls failed to stem speculative pressure; wider fluctuations for other Asian currencies.
August	Floating of Indonesian ruppiah. IMF-led support package of $20.1 billion for Thailand.
October	Sharp falls in equity prices in Asia, Latin America and Russia. Strong exchange rate pressure in Brazil, Hong-Kong, Korea and Taiwan.
November	$40 billion IMF-led support package for Indonesia.
December	$57 billion IMF-led support package for Korea. Korean won floated.
January 1998	Rouble pegged to dollar with +/- 15% band. Indonesian corporate debt 'pause'.
May	Russian interest rates reach 150%.
June	Indonesian corporate debt restructured. South African rand depreciates sharply.
July	$23 billion IMF-led support package for Russia.
August	Russia suspends payments on short-term government debt and moratorium on commercial debt payments to non-residents.
September	Rouble floated. Malaysia pegs exchange rate and imposes stringent capital controls. Latin American equity markets fall sharply; interest rates double in Brazil to 50%. Chile widens bands for exchange rate, increases interest rates and tightens exchange controls.
December	$41.5 billion IMF-led support package for Brazil after budget balancing programme.
January 1999	Brazilian real floated.

The charge against the IMF (and the American Treasury whose views they tended to follow to the letter) is that it had pushed countries into capital market liberalization which, combined with fixed exchange rates, encouraged firms and banks to borrow abroad recklessly. As Joe Stiglitz, ex-chief economist at the World Bank and scourge of the IMF, pointed out, the Managing Director of the IMF was still repeating the call in September 1999 'after the global financial crisis had so vividly demonstrated the risks of capital market liberalization' (Stiglitz 2004: 58). In a remarkable volte-face the IMF as good as admitted this when the Chief Economist of the IMF concluded that 'those countries that made the effort to become financially integrated . . . faced more instability' (quoted by Stiglitz 2004: 57).

All the countries concerned suffered serious output declines as they raised interest rates and cut budgets as instructed by the IMF: 'the initial demands for fiscal cuts on the part of the crisis countries were excessive; by further compressing demand in an already depressed environment, they made post crisis recessions worse' (DeLong and Eichengreen 2002: 227).

The increase in interest rates which the IMF claimed was necessary to limit falls in currency values also had the perverse effect of further weakening domestic economies at the very time that overseas investors' confidence had to be maintained. Companies with debts owing to local banks faced higher interest costs which compounded their having to pay more on their overseas loans as their currencies depreciated. Instead of trying to sustain production and investment in countries whose currencies were under pressure, the IMF's focus was on 'structural reforms'. The very features of Asian economies, particularly the close relation between banks and firms, that had previously been heralded as contributing to rapid growth, were now retitled 'crony capitalism' and blamed for the crisis.

The Asian economies suffered big falls in output in the wake of the crisis, but mostly recovered quite rapidly. Even so in Korea the lost growth was never made up and unemployment has remained 1 percentage point above the pre-crisis level. In Indonesia the consequences were much graver still as the financial crisis developed into a full-blown political and social crisis.

Conclusions

This chapter has traced the remarkable shifts in the financial landscape over the past 25 years. The importance of financial activities has grown spectacularly along almost every dimension of financial activity. Consumer credit has boomed allowing consumption to acquire temporary independence from the constraint of current incomes. Particularly in the USA shareholdings have become more concentrated in the hands of financial institutions, which pile on remorseless pressure for the maximization of share prices. Corporate management whose pay was extravagantly boosted by share options, auditors, lawyers and analysts, were entangled in a mutually beneficial game of talking up profit prospects. Together with some genuine investment opportunities in sectors in high-tech sectors, such manipulation brought stock markets to record highs. International capital flows brought extended periods of exchange rate misalignments. Financial crises have increased in frequency, both in the most sophisticated financial markets of the rich countries and in 'emerging market' economies induced to liberalize regardless of domestic circumstances. The most significant winners have been chief executives and successful speculators on the domestic and international financial markets. The losers were workers whose jobs, working conditions and pensions were put at risk and investors not in the know.

More volatile consumption, violent stock market and foreign exchange swings in valuations, and periodic financial crises might be expected to bring 'boom and bust'—greater fluctuations of output and employment. Whether the economies of the rich countries have indeed become more unstable will be discussed in Chapter 6. First, however, we need to examine developments in international economic relations which have added further elements of instability, much debated under the broad heading of 'globalization'.

4
Globalization and International Economic Relations

Is that to say we are against Free Trade? No, we are for Free Trade, because by Free Trade all economical laws, with their most astounding contradictions, will act upon a larger scale, upon the territory of the whole earth . . . .

(Karl Marx; text of a speech on Protection, Free Trade and the Working Classes in 1847, reproduced in Engels (1847: 290)).

The economy is *shot*, Ma, we can't hack it, we don't have the discipline the Germans and Jap[anese] do.

(Harry Angstrom in John Updike's *Rabbit is Rich* (1981)).

So far economic relations between countries have played little part in this account of the response of the most developed economies to the challenges of the 1970s. Subsequently globalization, which we will take to mean international economic integration, has claimed a leading place in economic discussion. This chapter will examine first the changing economic fortunes of the USA, now restored to its position of pre-eminence amongst the rich countries. Then the challenge posed to the economies of the most developed economies by the spectacular rise of China will be discussed. Finally the broader issues of international economic integration will be analysed, as a backdrop to the discussion of the pressures on the labour movement, which is the subject of the next chapter.

The USA and its Rivals

As discussed in Chapter 1, Europe and Japan made considerable headway during the Golden Age in catching up with US levels of productivity and this continued through the 1970s and 1980s. This generated widespread concern in the USA, reflected in the setting up of an MIT Commission on Industrial Productivity. The introduction to its report, published in 1989, began:

To live well a nation must produce well. In recent years many observers have charged that American industry is not producing as well as it ought to produce, or as well as it used to produce, or as well as some of the industries of some other nations have learned to produce. If the charges are true and the trend cannot be reversed, then sooner or later the American standard of living must pay the penalty.

. . . Products made in the United States are said to be inferior. . . . American factories are accused of inefficiency; the work force is said to be indifferent and ill-trained; and managers are criticized for seeking quick profits rather than pursuing more appropriate long-term goals. (Dertouzos *et al* 1989: 1)

In each of the eight industry case studies carried out by the Commission, including cars, computers and consumer electronics, the seriousness of the competition posed by European, or more often

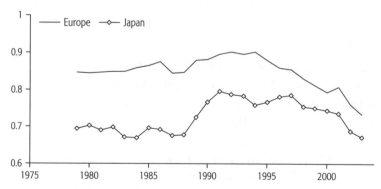

Fig. 4.1. **Manufacturing Productivity relative to USA, 1979–2003**

Note: The series are for output per hour worked. USA = 1

Source: Groningen Growth and Development Centre, Bureau of Labour Statistics. See Data Appendix.

Japanese, companies was stressed. In the light of the excitement surrounding nimble US high-tech companies in the new economy boom of the 1990s the Commission's comment on US semiconductors is striking: 'The contest was between small, single-product, inexperienced under-financed American start-ups and the heavyweights of Japanese industry. David did not defeat Goliath' (Dertouzos *et al* 1989: 10).

The period after 1995 saw a striking turn-round. US productivity growth accelerated and both Europe and Japan fell further behind again as Fig. 4.1 brings out very starkly. These comparisons of productivity levels, which can only be very approximate, suggest that manufacturing industry in Europe and Japan having got within striking distance (80–90%) of US productivity by the mid-1990s, then sank back to around 65–75% of the US level. The factors behind this change in fortunes are considered in Chapter 6 below; for the present the important point is that the stronger productivity growth helped bolster confidence in the US economy.

The Dollar and the US Balance of Payments

The improvement in US economic performance encouraged massive inflows of capital into US financial assets. This drove up the value of the dollar, which appreciated against the currencies of its main trading partners by 29% between 1995 and 2001. The dollar plays a pivotal role in the world monetary system as other countries hold their foreign exchange reserves in dollars and it is used for many international transactions between non-US firms and banks. Its fluctuations, including the slide in 2004–5, need to be set in longer-term context.

Figure 4.2 shows the shifts in both the nominal value of the dollar against other currencies and the real exchange rate measuring the cost competitiveness of US manufacturers. It is clear from the chart that the overwhelming influence on the real exchange rate has been the fluctuations in the nominal exchange rate of the dollar against other currencies. The real dollar exchange rate appreciated by some 40% in the first half of the 1980s, fell rather more than that in the later 1980s and early 1990s, before appreciating by around one-third during the subsequent boom. The real depreciation in the early 1990s was a bit more than the nominal depreciation, as US costs also rose relatively slowly. However for each of these big swings, including the most recent dollar depreciation, shifts in the nominal exchange rate have dominated.

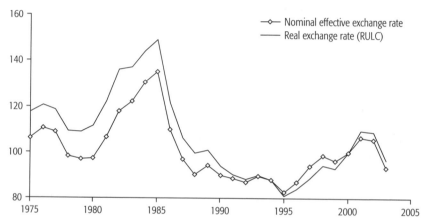

Fig. 4.2. **US$ Exchange Rate: Nominal and Real, 1975–2003**
Source: IMF. See Data Appendix. 2000 = 100

The rise in the dollar in the early 1980s can be explained by the attraction of the rise in US interest rates implemented by Volker at the Fed (see Chapter 2), and then reinforced by a rising US budget deficit. The US government maintained a policy of 'benign neglect' towards the exchange rate until in 1984 it pressurized the Japanese government to open up their capital markets. This was supposed to lead to a capital flow towards Japan (thus reducing the dollar's value) but it probably had a greater effect in making it easier for Japanese investors to chase the rising dollar. The perverse effect on the dollar was of little concern to Wall Street, which had wanted access to Japanese markets. Indeed it appears that many US banks were 'unsympathetic to industry's problems in the early 1980s...some bank CEOs hoped, with the Federal Reserve, that the appreciation of the dollar would force rationalization and cost-saving upon what they perceived to be a spendthrift and undisciplined manufacturing sector' (quoted by Frankel 1994: 325). However, by the beginning of 1985, the strength of the complaints from manufacturing about the neglect of the dollar 'had multiplied greatly' and was 'certainly a major influence' on the shift of the administration to a more activist policy (Frankel 1994: 322). The (gross) profit share of US manufacturing value added was 24.8% in 1985, very close to the 24.3% level of 1979 before the recession and recovery. Given the extraordinary decrease in US competitiveness implied by the rise in the dollar, a sharp decline in profitability might have been anticipated. That it did not materialize suggests that US manufacturers were rationalizing effectively.

The speculative nature of the dollar's rise became hard to dispute as it carried on into 1985 after US interest rates had begun to fall relatively to those on competing investments. In February the bubble deflated and the dollar fell back. In September 1985, and with a less dogmatic team at the US Treasury, finance ministers of the G5 meeting at the Plaza Hotel agreed that 'some further orderly appreciation of the non-dollar currencies is desirable' and that they 'stand ready to cooperate more closely to encourage this when it would be helpful'. Background papers mentioned a 10–12% dollar depreciation. The dollar fell by 4% immediately and then resumed its downward slide, encouraged by sales of $10 billion dollars by central banks including the Fed. By the end of 1986 Japanese exporters were feeling the pinch and at the Louvre Accord in February 1987 the G7 finance ministers announced that the previous dollar decline had brought currencies within the range 'consistent with underlying economic fundamentals' and that further changes could be damaging. Though it was not made public, there were apparent understandings that exchange rate fluctuations should be kept inside a 'reference band' by central bank intervention in the foreign exchange markets and, if necessary, by coordinated macro policies. Heavy central bank intervention (including $100 billion purchases of dollar securities by the Japanese government) restrained and then halted the dollar's fall. The fall in the dollar after 1985 helped push up the manufacturing profit share by 5% points to reach 30% in 1988–9.

The first two years of the Clinton administration saw a further decline in the dollar and in 1995 policy switched with Clinton announcing that he wanted a 'strong dollar'. The G7 finance ministers were persuaded to declare that a reversal of its decline against the yen was now desirable and there was heavy foreign exchange intervention to support the dollar. Larry Summers, later Secretary of the Treasury, justified the policy by arguing that pushing the dollar down leads to a lack of confidence in financial markets and 'undermines the discipline needed to increase productivity' (Summers 2002: 261). As Figure 4.2 shows the dollar rose again, though to nowhere near the level, in real terms, of the early 1980s.[1] The 'strong dollar' policy may have initially helped the dollar up but the more important influence was the excitement surrounding the new economy boom. Overseas purchases of US assets such as equities and bonds were four times as high in 2000 as they were at the end of the 1980s boom. As one observer put it: 'The capital inflow is the way foreigners share in the higher profits and future profits that new technology is expected to bring' (Meltzer 2002: 266). With both the stock market and the dollar rising, returns on such investments in the USA were very high and this in turn attracted more speculative inflows.

The gyrations in exchange rates noted above do more than simply redistribute wealth between speculators. The real economy of exports and jobs are involved, as noted in Chapter 3, and we next turn to the

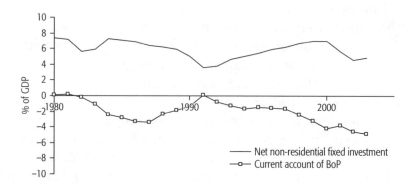

Fig. 4.3. **US Current Account and Domestic Investment, 1980–2003**

Source: Bureau of Economic Analysis. See Data Appendix.

story of the US balance of payments. The US current account has been in deficit every year since 1982 (Fig. 4.3). Whilst there was an obvious improvement in the current account when the dollar fell in the second half of the 1980s (compare Figs. 4.2 and 4.3), the deterioration through the 1990s looks quite inexorable. So the deficit in 2003 was considerably larger as a percentage of GDP than it had been in the mid-1980s when the real exchange rate was vastly more appreciated and thus manufacturing less competitive.

The consumer boom of the late 1990s sucked in huge quantities of consumer goods, from China in particular, and so the volume of imports into the USA rose by 75% between 1995 and 2000. Imports took 26% of the US market for manufactures in 2000, including 80% for leather and shoes, 57% for apparel, 51% for computers and electronic equipment and 33% for cars and a wide swathe of machinery.[2]

The overvaluation of the dollar and the collapse of the high-tech boom, which had boosted exports of ITC equipment, took their toll on US exports which lost one-fifth of their world market share between 2000 and 2003. The growing current account deficit reflected a growing deficit in goods and even the services account declined a little to near balance in the early 2000s. By 2004 the debts of the US government and firms overseas exceeded US-owned foreign assets by the equivalent of some 30% of its GDP. Even so it was still making a small net surplus on the returns from its investments overseas, much of which had constituted high return 'direct' investments by US companies with subsidiaries overseas. Though there was a big inflow of direct investment into the USA in the 1980s and especially during the new economy boom, a good deal of this was invested in taking over existing US assets, yielding a lower return than US multinationals earned on their direct investments abroad in new production facilities. Nevertheless if the current account decline persists and the overseas debts continue to pile up the investment income account will inevitably go into the red pulling the current account further into deficit. A persistent current account deficit of 5% of GDP implies an overseas debt ratio rising towards 100% of GDP if the underlying growth rate of the economy is 5% in nominal terms (say 3.5% growth and 1.5% inflation).

So the prospect is of increasing indebtedness until the pattern of growth can be twisted away from consumption and imports and towards exports. Despite some decline in the dollar from its peak value, detailed analysis in 2005 suggested that a further real depreciation of one-third was necessary to bring the USA into reasonable balance; the nominal fall in the dollar would have to be considerably greater than the 'necessary' real change since some of the competitive advantage would inevitably be eroded by faster US inflation as the dollar price of imports rose.[3]

Figure 4.3 also plots the amount of net fixed investment in buildings and machinery by US business that is investment in excess of depreciation. The current account deficit of the balance of payments represents the amount that the economy as a whole is borrowing from overseas. By 2002 the amount borrowed from overseas matched net business investment. It was as though the whole of the meagre US savings was absorbed by the government's budget deficit and by housebuilding, leaving *all* net business investment in the USA to be financed by US corporations borrowing the savings of other countries.[4] This was an astounding position for the richest country in the world.

If the USA was borrowing so much, who was doing the lending? The first row of Table 4.1 shows the average size of the current account deficit, building up to more than 5% of GDP from 2003. One possible source of finance is from overseas firms investing more in new factories in the USA or in purchasing US companies than US firms were investing abroad. However this category of 'direct investment' (inflows minus outflows), having been small throughout the 1980s and 1990s, became a net outflow from 2003 on as US firms were investing more overseas than their counterparts were doing in the USA (Table 4.1 row 2). A second source of finance is if individuals and financial institutions overseas buy US government or other bonds, shares in US companies, or simply deposit money in US banks. Again the issue is the balance between finance coming into the USA like this and corresponding outflows by US residents and financial institutions. In fact the private sector overseas provided modest finance for the modest average US current account deficits in the 1980s and 1990s, and provided almost all the extra finance

required when the deficit blew out over the years 2000–2 (row 3).
It seems surprising that the collapse of the US stock market and
of exaggerated expectations about the new economy boom did not
undermine the supply of private sector finance earlier. The third source
of finance is when foreign governments pile up foreign exchange
reserves in the form of US Treasury bills and bonds. Extra official
holdings were quite small until 2003–4 when Asian governments
in particular began to acquire huge amounts of dollars when they
intervened in foreign exchange markets to sell their own currencies
which were in heavy demand (row 4) They did this to prevent their
currencies from rising in value relative to the dollar, which would
have made their exports less competitive. In 2003–4 the dollar was
only prevented from free-fall by governments in the Far East being
prepared to accumulate seemingly endless piles of dollar assets as a
counterpart to export surpluses. By the end of 2003 overseas governments held 1.474 trillion dollar assets equivalent to 13% of US GDP.

The Bank for International Settlements underlined the precariousness
of the position of the dollar in 2005:

Table 4.1 **Financing the US Balance of Payments Deficit, 1980–2004**

Percentage of GDP	1980–9	1990–9	2000–2	2003–4
Current account	−1.7	−1.5	−4.3	−5.6
financed by				
Direct investment (net)	0.3	−0.1	0.4	−1.0
Other private capital	0.5	1.0	3.3	4.2
Overseas governments' holdings of US assets	0.4	0.7	0.6	3.2

Note: − means deficit or capital outflow; sources of finance are positive. Some smaller sources of finance are excluded so rows 2–4 do not precisely offset the deficits in row 1.

Source: Bureau of Economic Analysis. See Data Appendix.

the widening current account deficit of the United States is a serious longer-
term problem. That is, it could eventually lead to a disorderly decline of the
dollar, associated turmoil in other financial markets, and even recession.
Equally of concern, and perhaps closer at hand, it could lead to a resurgence

of protectionist pressure. The unprecedented size of the deficit, the speed with which external debts are growing, the increasing reliance on the official sector for deficit financing, and the fact that US borrowing has primarily financed consumption (rather than investment) all suggest an eventual problem. Moreover, given the interdependency of modern financial markets, it is likely that problems would not be confined to the dollar alone. (BIS 2005: 144)

Capital Accumulation on a World Scale

Capital accumulation is the fundamental driving force of the economy. Increases in investment are usually the most dynamic element in aggregate demand expansions, particularly on a world scale where one country's exports are another's imports. On the supply side the growth of the capital stock is necessary to expand capacity. Investment has a symbiotic relation with new technology, being made more profitable by it and at the same time being the route through which it enters the production system.[5] Table 4.2 shows how the rate of accumulation on a world scale slid back after the 1970s and how the industrial countries are now accumulating at a slower rate than the world as a whole, implying that the developing countries are accumulating distinctly faster. It should be emphasized that the calculations are based on partial information and many assumptions so small differences in growth rates should not be taken literally.

Table 4.2 **Capital Accumulation: Growth Rates of Fixed Capital Stock, 1960–2004**

Average annual percentage changes	World	Industrial countries	USA	Europe	Japan	Korea	China	India	Brazil
1960s	5.0	5.0	4.0	4.6	12.5	8.9	1.9	4.5	5.8
1970s	5.1	4.2	3.8	3.8	8.5	14.6	7.2	4.1	9.6
1980s	4.0	3.1	2.8	2.9	6.1	11.2	8.4	4.9	4.1
1990s	4.0	3.3	3.0	2.8	4.0	9.6	10.9	6.2	2.2
2000–4			2.0	2.6	2.1				

Source: Bosworth and Collins (2003). See Data Appendix.

The numbers in bold are for substantial countries whose accumulation rate is estimated to be more than 1 percentage point above the world growth rate for capital at the time. The fall in the capital stock growth is clear across the OECD, and especially in Japan. The baton of 'super-accumulator' was passed from Japan in the 1960s to Korea (and Taiwan) in the 1970s and 1980s and then to China in the 1990s. In the early 2000s the growth of capital stock in China could easily be 12% or more.

In the early stages of China's high growth period there was an expansion of state employment, including in the dynamic and crucial manufacturing sector. However from the mid-1990s onwards state employment began a sharp decline. 'Through a combination of management and worker buy-outs that converted firms from public to private, some bankruptcies and a substantial workforce downsizing in firms that remain state owned, manufacturing jobs in the state sector have declined by almost three quarters from their peak' (Lardy 2003: 12).[6] Thus, in its most recent phase, private capital accumulation dominates the growth process in China, although the state still strongly influences the pattern of investment through its control of the credit system and its policy of creating 'national champions' in sectors such as cars and steel.

A fast growth of the capital stock requires high ratios of investment to GDP. Maddison (1998) adjusted official figures give a Chinese investment share of about one-third for 1978–94, which is very close to that reached in Japan and Korea.[7] Indeed machinery and equipment investment, often seen as the main driver of growth, has been running at around 20% of GDP—about 6% points less than in Korea and Japan during their maximum growth periods and only 3–4% points more than France and Germany in their Golden Age.[8] So, even with a further sharp rise in the investment share in 2003 and 2004, China's productive investment effort is not wholly unprecedented. However it is playing out on a massive canvas and with vastly larger supplies of surplus labour than its Asian predecessors in the catch-up process.

After some decline in profitability in the later 1990s, industrial profits in money terms rose by a factor of five between 1999 and 2004 and profits in the distribution sector rose at an even faster pace.

Conventional calculations for the rate of return to equity holders suggest a higher return on capital in 2004 than in the mid-1990s. Domestically funded companies have considerably lower reported profits than foreign owned, with those owned in Hong Kong, Macau and Taiwan most profitable of all despite a tendency to under-report profits for tax reasons. Foreign-owned companies export around one-third of their sales, three times the share for domestic companies.[9]

Total employment in China is estimated at around 750 million, or about one and a half times that of the whole of the OECD and nearly ten times the combined employment of Japan and Korea. About a half of China's employment is still in agriculture. This constitutes an enormous labour reserve available to flood in from the less developed interior of the country as labour markets tighten in the coastal industrial areas. Estimates of the numbers who may be pulled out of agriculture, where their incomes are very low, into industrial and service jobs in the towns range as high as 150–300 million depending on the time scale.[10] There are already very large numbers of workers making some kind of living in the informal sector of the urban economy, including both new recruits from the countryside and those made redundant from state enterprises. They constitute an additional part of China's huge reserve army of labour, to use Marx's very appropriate term.

Very rapid capital accumulation has brought a spectacular rise in China's share of world GDP, nearly tripling from 5% to 14% in a quarter century. China on its own made up for all the collapsed output share of the ex-Soviet Union and Eastern Europe and much of the downward drift in the share of Europe and Japan.[11] It is easy to see from Fig. 4.4 that, if current trends continued for another decade or so, then China would be challenging the US's title as the world's largest economy.

Whilst becoming the world's largest economy will be a notable development, China's vast population means that this would occur at less than one-quarter of the US level of GDP per head. Figure 4.5 sets the growth of China in the longer-term perspective of Asian catch-up. Despite the doubling of the ratio of per capita GDP compared to the USA over the past 20 years, China is still as far behind the USA as Korea and Taiwan were before their three decades of

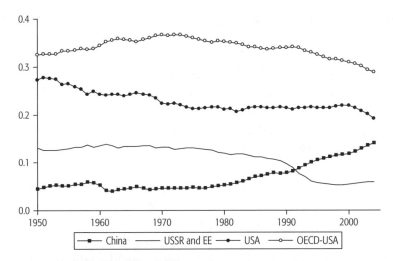

Fig. 4.4. **Shares of World Output, 1950–2004**
Source: Maddison (2001). See Data Appendix.

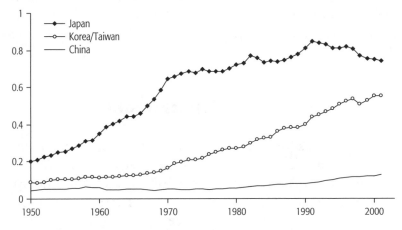

Fig. 4.5. **Catch-Up to USA in Asia—per capita GDP, 1950–2001**
Source: Maddison (2001). See Data Appendix. USA = 1

rapid catch-up beginning in the late 1960s; it is still well below the position from which Japan started its spectacular growth climb in the mid-1950s.[12]

China is obviously far larger, in terms of population, than the earlier examples of Asian catch-up. However it is also, after two decades of spectacular growth, still far behind, in relative terms, the positions from which their growth spurts were launched. Both aspects contribute to China's gigantic growth potential. Of course there is nothing inevitable about China continuing along its present trajectory. If it does, the problems of adapting to this major shift in the structure of world trade and output will be correspondingly severe.

The current and prospective development of China dwarfs all other current trends in the world economy. For example it more than accounts for all the reduction in the inequality of the distribution of income on a world scale.[13] Large numbers of poor Chinese people have received increases in their real incomes which has pushed up an important part of the bottom of the world income distribution. Despite major increases in inequality *within* China, the improved living standards of millions of poor Chinese have been more important in reducing income differences on a world scale. However the latter issue, and the broader questions of China's development process, lie outside the scope of this book.[14] Even world inequality is an abstraction for people in the advanced countries. Where China has a very real impact is in the shops and perhaps on the dole queue.

China's Export Boom

Table 4.3 records the tenfold growth in Chinese manufactured exports as a share of world exports over the past 25 years. Since 1990 the growth of Chinese exports has exceeded in absolute amount that of the next largest nine low-wage manufacture exporters put together.[15] Ominously for them, since 2000 their combined export share has fallen whilst China's rose rapidly. An analysis of the impact of Chinese exports on its Asian competitors found that countries producing consumer goods based on low wages were suffering whilst capital goods producers, like Korea, were gaining from the expanding market in China. Between 1980 and 2000 a half or more of the increase in China's export share in labour-intensive sectors like clothing, travel goods, footwear and toys was at the expense of Korea, Taiwan and Singapore, with the pressure now rising on India and Indonesia. Up to one-third of Chinese manufactures are produced from foreign owned plants, mostly Japanese, and this generates a flow of machinery and component imports into China from Japan to sustain export production. In 2003 China (including Hong Kong) ran a trade surplus of nearly $100 billion with the USA, whilst it was in substantial deficit with Japan, Korea and Taiwan. Although foreign owned plants account for around one-half of Chinese exports, more of their production is sold to the rapidly expanding home market than is exported.[16]

Table 4.3 **China's Exports, 1980–2003**

Percentages	1980		1990		2000		2003
Shares of world exports of manufactures							
China	0.8		1.9		4.7		7.3
Nine other major low wage exporters	6.8		10.5		16.1		15.0
Chinese share of imports into:	North America		Europe		Japan		
	1995	2003	1995	2003	1995	2003	
All manufactures	7.6	15.9	2.2	4.7	15.1	29.3	
Toys and games	52.3	76.9	26.0	39.8	26.4	56.7	
Clothing	14.9	16.9	7.9	12.2	56.6	80.0	
Office etc equipment	5.4	23.7	2.5	10.0	5.8	28.0	

Source: World Trade Organization. See Data Appendix.

China now makes nearly one-third of the comparatively limited amount of manufactured imports into Japan (Table 4.3). It accounts for a larger fraction of imports into both Europe and North America than does Japan. In each case China's market share has more or less doubled in less than a decade. China dominates imports of toys and games and has 40% of imports of clothing from low-wage countries and is set to gain more market share for clothing now that quotas have been phased out under the end of the Multi Fibre Agreement. Its share in office equipment, several rungs up the technological ladder, is already rising rapidly. In 2002 China displaced the EU and Mexico as the biggest exporter to the USA of computers, consumer electronics and other IT products,[17] though a high proportion of these exports involved assembly of high-tech components sourced abroad. China's is rapidly developing the capacity to produce more sophisticated goods. By 2010 it is likely to be turning out more Science and Engineering PhDs than the USA. Already China is ranked fourth in the world, after USA, Japan and Germany, in research publications in four emerging technologies and multinational companies are locating research facilities there. Such activity is 'moving to china because China is graduating huge numbers of scientists and engineers' (Freeman 2005b: 27)

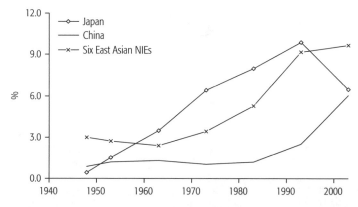

Fig. 4.6. **Shares of World Commodity Exports, 1948–2003**
Source: World Trade Organization.

The growth of China's involvement in world trade is spectacular but, thus far, not without precedent. Just as the take-off of accumulation in China followed the pattern set by Japan and then Korea, so has the trajectory of its exports. Figure 4.6 shows that China's exports have not yet reached the shares of world trade achieved by Japan in the 1980s and 1990s, and then by the Asian NIEs (the Newly Industrializing Economies including South Korea and Taiwan etc.). Even though the rising share of Japanese exports was a more measured and protracted process than China's, the latter's steep climb was matched by the NIEs in the 1980s. Sharply rising competition from the East has been a persistent trend over the past 40 years and China's export growth is its latest manifestation, rather than a qualitatively new phenomenon.

However, as noted earlier, China's size and current backwardness means that it has the potential to carry this process a great deal further.

Another couple of decades of Chinese growth at something like current rates *must* involve an enormous expansion of Chinese exports to pay for the rising bill for imports of food, materials, fuel, semi-finished manufactures, capital goods and even luxury brands of consumer goods. Fast compound growth in China's exports has a greater and greater absolute impact on its low-wage competitors and on domestic producers in the rich countries as its share of world trade grows. Thus China's share roughly doubled in the 1980s, increasing by around 1.5 percentage points; it doubled again in the 1990s, pushing it up by 3%. If per capita GDP growth rates of around 6% per year in China persist, a further doubling of the export share in the next decade would probably be necessary to pay for the rising import bill. This would raise China's export share by another 6 percentage points or so, more than the impact of the 'Asian tigers' in the 1980s (see Fig. 4.6). Moreover, even after another decade of rapid growth, China's per capita GDP would not nearly have exhausted the possibilities of further rapid growth as China's productivity would still be far below that of the rich countries. Of course economic crises can stifle growth of countries at any level of development, as the stagnation in both Japan, after the collapse of its bubble, and Indonesia in the wake of the Asian crisis illustrate all too well (see Chapter 3). But barring a collapse into longer-term stagnation

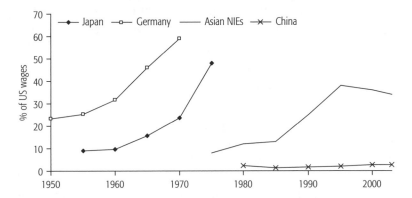

Fig. 4.7. **Manufacturing Wages during Catch-Up, 1950–2003**

Source: Bureau of Labor Statistics, China Statistical Yearbook. See Data Appendix.

China will continue to have a massive effect on the evolution of the world trade structure.

A further huge expansion of Chinese exports will certainly increase competition for markets in the OECD countries, causing serious problems for the other Southern industries in competition with them. China will at some stage move up the 'value chain' in the same way as did Japan and the Asian NIEs; when wage levels grow industries can no longer compete so effectively in 'low value' markets where low wages for unskilled workers are the main source of competitive advantage. The historical experience is that at a certain stage in the 'catch-up' process wages do start rising substantially. At present, however, wages are still much lower in China than they were during the boom periods in Japan and the Asian NIEs and are not yet threatening China's position as low-wage producer par excellence (see Fig. 4.7).

Real incomes have been rising in urban areas at over 5% per year on average during the 1990s, though this exaggerates improvements since residents faced much higher charges for education and health. Moreover these estimates do not include rural migrants, who make up much of the workforce for the exporting factories. In Guandong province, where many export factories are situated, base wages are reported at about $80 per month and working hours can be up to 80 per week. Wages are reported to have hardly risen in nominal terms in a decade and inflation has eroded their real value by up to 30% despite the rapidly growing employment, suggesting that this group of workers has not shared in the general urban prosperity.[18] The migrants have to go through elaborate and expensive bureaucratic procedures to obtain permission to work in the cities and it is frequently made very difficult for them to change jobs. Labour discipline is very harsh, especially in Korean and Taiwanese owned factories, where apparently in some cases: 'workers are even marched to and from meals and to and from dormitories in tight military style squads' (Chan 2003: 46).

Independent unions are banned, workers are often jailed for organizing strikes and the official All-China Federation of Trade Unions 'for decades has aligned itself more with management than with workers' (Gough 2005). A senior provincial ACFTU official explained the union's attitude to poor conditions. 'It's better than nothing', he said.'Labor protections, working conditions and wages are related to a country's level of economic development. Of course we want better labor protections but we can't afford it. We need the jobs. We need to guarantee people can eat' (Goodman and Pan 2004). Foreign firms locating in the Industrial Parks find 'There is no union representation in the plant....There is no interference by unions in operations management. The Labor union also seemed not to exert influence in the area of wages' (Jürgens and Rehbehn 2004: 17). Despite all these obstacles, websites.[19] regularly report on quite major strikes and other actions, including disputes over unpaid wages and compensation for redundancy.

There have been successive relaxations of the restrictions on migration to the towns, but labour shortages are reported in the coastal areas giving 'button-sewers and shoe stitchers a bit of bargaining power for the first time. Factory owners cannot replace disgruntled employees as easily as they once could; wildcat strikes can cripple output for days or weeks. Almost imperceptibly workers are starting to win concessions' (Gough 2005).

Provided the boom keeps going and the labour reserves are whittled away, then at some stage market forces will overwhelm the repressive measures and wages will start growing for the exporting factories just as they did in Japan and the Asian NIEs. Moreover, continued export success will bring currency appreciation of the yuan which will further increase wages valued in terms of dollars, which determines competitiveness. Rising wage costs will force Chinese firms to switch to production and export of products requiring more skilled labour. This will relieve the pressure on the other very low-wage exporters now suffering from Chinese competition. In their stead it will be the producers of the more sophisticated goods into which China moves, in the North and in the Asian NIEs, who will feel increasing pressure.

China's imports have been growing very rapidly and now comprise around 5% of world imports of both agricultural products (food and materials) and mining products (metals and fuel), including 12% of world imports of iron and steel.[20] Such imports of the basic inputs into manufacturing have received much attention, with press stories of shortages of steel capacity and China's voracious demand for oil and other inputs. However imports of manufactures into China are currently worth about four times as much as its imports of agricultural and mining products. Imports of high-tech components, of computers for example, for re-export play a very substantial role. However imports of capital goods for domestic investment and consumer goods for domestic consumption are becoming increasingly important. The fundamental point is that China is important for the OECD countries not only as a source of cheap, and potentially disruptive imports, but also as an increasingly important market for exports. Although OECD countries have no monopoly on supplying China, if Persian Gulf oil producers or Brazilian soy bean farmers receive higher incomes through exporting to China they in turn will tend to buy more imports. Thus, both directly and indirectly, China is becoming an increasingly important influence on the economies of the rich countries.

International Economic Integration

The arrival of wave after wave of Chinese exports in the shops of the rich countries is the most dramatic manifestation of their increasing integration into the world economy. This section examines the extent to which their economies are affected by international competition as a prelude to the discussion in the final chapter of whether such competition is undermining regulation and egalitarian policies. The flows of financial capital were discussed in the last chapter so the focus here is on international trade, flows of foreign direct investment (FDI) and international migration.[21]

Trade

Exports are the most visible form of production geared to the world market. World exports have grown faster than world production and this comparison is often used to measure rising globalization.

In fact the ratio of world exports to GDP has doubled since 1960 to around 25% of world GDP,[22] with the rate of increase being slower in the second half of the period (having lost the boost from higher oil prices). Much of the increase reflects rising export shares in Europe and the USA (see Fig. 4.8); in both cases however, the ratio of exports to GDP in 1913 was only exceeded at the end of the 1960s.[23] Japan however shows an extraordinary stability of trade shares since 1950 (with oil-price induced humps)—in striking contrast to China.

The impact of international competition within domestic economies is most clearly displayed in the degree of import penetration of the domestic market for manufactures (see Table 4.4)

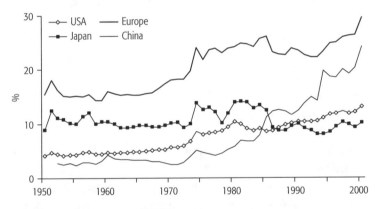

Fig. 4.8. **Trade as a Percentage of GDP, 1950–2000**
Source: Penn Tables. See Data Appendix.

Table 4.4 **Import Penetration of Domestic Markets for Manufactures, 1913–2001**					
Percentage	1913	1950	1974	1991	2001 All	From 'South'
USA	3	2	6	14	21	10
Japan	34	3	5	7	12	7
Europe	13	6	17	28	39	8

Source: OECD. See Data Appendix.

Increasing import competition was noticeable during the Golden Age and, with the partial exception of Japan, it has continued unabated with import market shares doubling in Europe after 1974 and rising more than threefold in the USA. Most of this competition has traditionally come from other OECD countries. However imports from the 'South' have grown rapidly and now take nearly one-tenth of domestic markets in USA and not far short of that in the rest of the rich countries, with China playing a major role as discussed earlier.

The impression of dramatically increasing international integration through trade surely derives from this growing penetration by imports of domestic manufacturing markets. But manufacturing only constituted 18% of OECD employment by the end of the millennium (ranging from 15% in USA to 24% in Germany); for the OECD this represents a decline of one-third as compared to 1974. Does trade integration amount, therefore, to increasingly fierce competition for a diminishing and relatively small, but highly visible, share of the economy?

The significance of manufacturing is in fact underplayed by its share of employment since other sectors make a contribution as suppliers of inputs to manufactured commodities. So part of the output of agriculture, mining, energy, construction, transport and finance and business services is, at one remove, subject to the international competition within manufacturing. Thus it is dependent on the success of the country's manufacturing sector in maintaining its share of the domestic and world markets. If we extended the calculation to include service inputs into manufacturing, and the value of agricultural and mining output which is heavily traded internationally, it would seem that around 30% of the UK economy is directly or indirectly contributing to the production of internationally traded goods.

Of course some services are traded directly as well. In the late 1990s exports of commercial services were about 20% of total exports for the world as a whole and for high income countries.[24] But these are concentrated in a narrow range of specialized business services (international transport, international finance, consulting, call centres and so forth) and imports are practically irrelevant for the mass of domestic service producers (distribution, education and health care for example).

There is no obvious way of quantifying what part of services is seriously internationalized in this sense; but any plausible estimate would leave a majority of employment in OECD countries, possibly a substantial and even a growing majority, largely untouched by international trade competition.[25] Outside agriculture, mining and manufacturing only a small proportion of workers are subject to international competition directly or indirectly through services provided to traded goods sectors. Wholesale and retail trade, community, personal and social services, utilities and construction together comprise some 60% of employment in the OECD as a whole, rather more in the USA. These sectors are largely insulated from international trade competition. Recently there has been much publicity about 'outsourcing' some service activities, call centres or clerical work for the financial sector being relocated in India for example. Available estimates suggest that this activity is fairly limited in terms of its employment effects—one estimate puts such new outsourcing at only 1% of jobs destroyed and created annually in the USA. Outsourcing of computing and business services in the USA had doubled in each of the last two decades but is still only 0.4% of US GDP. Both the USA and the UK, where there is more outsourcing, have substantial overseas payments surpluses in these services and Japan and Germany only have small deficits.[26]

The impact of internationalization through trade, therefore, is quite complicated. For one section of the economy, comprising manufacturing production and its suppliers together with some specialized enclaves in the services sector, international integration through trade has grown considerably and this will continue if rapid growth continues in China. Meanwhile large sections of the economy, including growing ones like social and community services and retail, are highly insulated from international trade.

The impact of this rapid growth of trade on Northern workers is mixed. Living standards have been boosted by low wage imports. On the other hand there has been a substantial effect in terms of job loss as discussed in the next chapter.

Foreign Direct Investment

Foreign direct investment (FDI), in factories and purchase of companies overseas, rose rapidly over the last three decades, especially in the second half of the 1990s. Corporations in the rich countries were both investing overseas (outward investment) and meeting competition from overseas companies investing in their domestic markets (inward). The quantitative importance of FDI may be assessed by comparing the annual flow with the total amount of domestic investment going on in the recipient country in that year. If the inflow of FDI were to continue at a particular percentage of investment, eventually it would constitute that percentage of the accumulated capital stock. Table 4.5 suggests that should recent trends continue, around 13% of the capital stock in both the developed and developing countries would be owned abroad. This would bring the share of FDI above its previous historical peak before 1914, though not by a large margin.[27] Within the developed economies FDI is exceptionally high in the EU, with much of the investment being within the EU (and thus showing up as both inward and outward). It is also exceptionally low in Japan, with the stagnant Japanese economy attracting little inward FDI, and more surprisingly Japanese firms investing abroad very modestly. The US economy attracted more FDI than US multinationals invested abroad.

Although the Chinese figure for inward investment does not look exceptional, the enormous share of gross investment in Chinese GDP, approaching 50% by 2004, means that the FDI inflow was

Table 4.5 **Foreign Direct Investment Flows, 1992–2003**

Percentage of gross investment	World		Developed countries	USA	EU	Japan	Developing countries	China
	1992–7				1998–2003			
Inward	5.2	12.7	12.6	9.1	23.5	0.7	12.5	11.6
Outward	5.5	12.0	14.8	7.7	30.1	2.7	3.7	0.7

Source: UNCTAD. See Data Appendix.

very large in relation to GDP—some 5%. Much FDI into China comes from other overseas Chinese capitalists in other Asian developing countries. Newspaper reports suggest that substantial inflows of FDI into China actually originate within China itself, masquerading as FDI in order to obtain tax breaks. In addition, however, Western multinationals were carrying out substantial investments in industries like electronics and cars. Chinese companies have also begun to make investments abroad, in search of supplies of energy and other inputs or of brand names and manufacturing expertise. Even though this is in effect reinvesting back the equivalent of a small part of the inflow of FDI, it created a furore, especially when a Chinese bid went in during 2005 for a modestly sized US oil company.

The sectoral composition of FDI is less biased towards manufacturing than is foreign trade. In the 1990s around one-half of outward FDI was in the services sector. Obviously FDI can reach into parts of the service sector like retailing or restaurants immune from direct competition from imports, as when McDonald's or Walmart invests in a new country. Well over half of FDI inflows into OECD countries represent cross-border mergers and acquisitions rather than companies setting up factories or offices from scratch. However this may still represent a heightening of competition for the other domestic firms. FDI represents an important qualification to the remarks above about the insulation of large parts of the services sector in the rich countries from international competition. Countries, like the USA and UK, with strong service sector companies have been pushing hard for the liberalization of service provision, and the FDI required to support it, in international economic negotiations at the World Trade Organisation.[28] Whilst the numbers presented above are useful to gain an impression of the magnitudes involved, it may be that the most important aspect of FDI is the enhanced potential for mobility of location for companies in the rich countries. Even if the threat is only exercised periodically it can still serve to weaken workers at the bargaining table when it comes to wage or employment negotiations, as discussed further in the next chapter.

Migration

The labour market is surely the least integrated of global markets. For the USA, despite a strong rise in the 1980s, inward migration in the 1990s was still only at one-third of the rate seen during 1900–10 as a proportion of the population.[29] The proportion of the world's population resident in countries where they were not born is estimated to have risen from a little over 2% to a little under 3% during the last 30 years and is around 10% in both Europe and the USA. Rising supply of migrants has been met in most developed countries with a tightening of controls against most unskilled migrants. In countries where unemployment is now relatively low, inward migration of both skilled and unskilled workers is an attractive option for employers worried about keeping down wages. As we shall see in the final chapter, migration is being used as an argument for cutting back generous welfare states for fear that they will attract migrants. It is simultaneously being promoted as a solution to the 'pensions crisis' looming because of stagnating or declining populations in many rich countries. Policy on migration will be of central importance in coming decades and is likely to continue to be highly conflictual.

Conclusions

This chapter has reviewed the contradictory position of the USA, which has been the most strongly growing amongst the rich countries, yet maintains its consumption by a huge amount of overseas borrowing. The extraordinary rise of the Chinese economy has also been outlined and its growing impact on world trade patterns was described. The degree of international integration of the rich economies varies from industry to industry along a continuum, with extremely competitive electronics production at one end to hairdressing at the other. Although exports of services, and FDI in services, have been growing rapidly there is probably still a majority of the workforce in the rich countries in sectors where international competition plays a relatively small role. Migration is likely to be an increasingly important influence on employment, work and pay patterns, which are the focus of the next chapter.

5
Labour's Retreats

'I wish it was the sixties.'
(From 'The Bends',
Radiohead (1995))

The rise in unemployment after 1973, evident in Figure 2.1, is a powerful symbol of labour's weakening position since very low unemployment was the most fundamental gain that labour secured during the Golden Age. Rising unemployment undermined labour's bargaining power, formally in collective bargaining, and informally on the shop floor, with fear of the sack becoming much more potent. The three previous chapters have discussed the succession of pressures to which labour has been subjected—the turn to restrictive macroeconomic policies, the renewed emphasis on market forces and profit maximization bringing privatization, deregulation and the drive for shareholder value and finally the intensifying international competition in important sectors of the economy. Unions were forced onto the defensive, if not into retreat, and this chapter reviews the patterns of employment, wages and working conditions which developed across the OECD countries.

Employment and Structural Change

As is clear from Figure 2.1, Europe presents the gloomiest employment picture with the unemployment rate rising by a factor of nearly five times between the 1960s and early 1990s, before a significant fall in the second half of the 1990s. However it was only in the early 1990s that most European countries had much higher unemployment than the USA. The Eurozone countries, including the unemployment-plagued quartet of France, Germany, Italy and Spain, experienced a higher peak than the rest of Europe in the early 1990s and a smaller decline thereafter. It is Eurozone joblessness which still (in 2005) compares unfavourably with the USA.

It was noted in Chapter 1 that growth during the Golden Age involved the rapid run-down of agriculture and a rising share of employment in services. These trends continued after 1973, with the addition of a rapid fall in the employment share in industry. This deindustrialization was particularly severe in Europe. Figures 5.1 and 5.2 contrast US experience with that of Europe,[1] a comparison used repeatedly from the mid-1990s in policy debates to argue for US-style deregulation. The experience of men and women was rather different. Men in Europe lost more than one-third of their industrial jobs (measured as compared to the population of working age) as male jobs in industry converged down to the US level (Fig. 5.1). Although service jobs for men grew rapidly, this was not fast enough to make up for all the lost jobs in industry (and the continuing drain out of agriculture) or to bring service employment for men up to the US level.

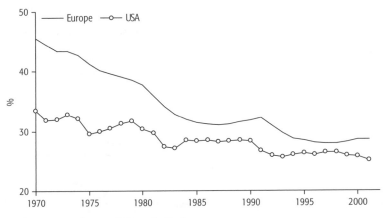

Fig. 5.1. **Men's Employment Rate in Industry, 1970–2001**
Source: OECD. See Data Appendix.

Women lost many fewer jobs in industry than men and employment in services for women grew very rapidly, but not as fast as in the USA until the 1990s (Fig. 5.2).

The net result of these trends was that men's employment declined in Europe and women's failed to rise as fast as in the USA (Fig. 5.3).

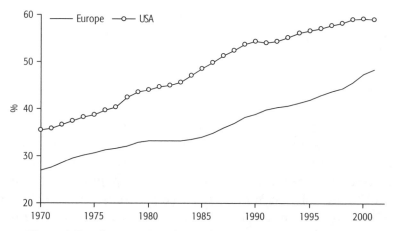

Fig. 5.2. **Women's Employment Rate in Services, 1970–2001**
Source: OECD. See Data Appendix.

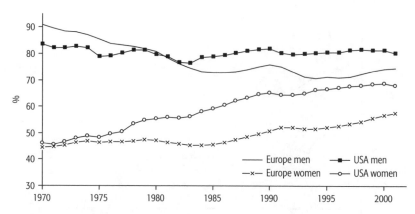

Fig. 5.3. **Employment Rates, Men and Women, 1970–2001**
Source: OECD. See Data Appendix.

The shortfall in jobs was reflected in rising male unemployment, especially in Europe. However more men became 'inactive' in Europe than became unemployed. Some of this was welcome (staying on longer in education or voluntary early retirement) but large numbers of men who would otherwise have worked also dropped out of the legitimate labour market. In some countries, like the UK and the Netherlands, many found their way onto sickness benefit. But the key issue here is that the rise in inactivity was very closely associated with lack of work. Across the UK, for example, there was a strong positive correlation between numbers on sickness benefits and the local unemployment rate.[2] And the areas with the lowest activity rates for men were those where deindustrialization, leading to factory closures and major job loss in local areas, was most severe. Much inactivity therefore flowed from employment decline. In this sense the unemployment rate (for men especially) far underestimated the true extent of joblessness and its increase in the 1980s. Women's labour market inactivity rates fell as they obtained jobs in the expanding services sector. However, in less dynamic regions, inactivity fell less as women did not bother to enter the labour force and look for work where jobs remained scarce.

The Low-Skilled

The declining position of the low-skilled has been an important preoccupation in the OECD countries since 1979. Although the relative supply of low-skilled workers has been declining as educational qualifications have increased, the demand for their work appears to have declined even faster, leading to either falling pay and/or lack of work.

It is extremely difficult to compare skill or educational levels across countries or even to get comparable data over time within a country. One way to get round this problem is to focus on the least educated one-quarter, say, of the workforce. Their skill levels will not be the same across countries or over time, but what happens to the least educated quarter is a good measure of what is going on at the bottom end of the labour market.[3] In the late 1990s in the typical OECD country 84% of the most educated quarter of the population aged 25–64 were working whereas 57% of the least educated quarter had jobs. The differential in employment rates (proportion of working age population who are working) was 30 percentage points for women and 19 percentage points for men. Figure 5.4 summarizes the trends in Europe and the USA over the 1980s and 1990s.

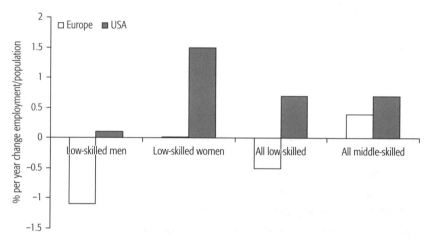

Fig. 5.4. **Employment Rate Changes by Skill Groups, 1980–2000**
Source: Glyn (2001). See Data Appendix.

In Europe the percentage of low-skilled men who had work was declining by around 1% each year, a very sharp decline. The least qualified women just held on to the existing number of jobs. So, overall, the proportion of the less qualified in work fell by about 0.5 percentage points per year—over a 20-year period this represents a 10 percentage point fall. By contrast, employment rates for the middle group (middle two-quarters of the distribution) rose. So the employment position of the least qualified declined in Europe absolutely and by even more relatively to those better qualified. In the USA, however, the least qualified men in work kept jobs and the least qualified women increased employment as fast as did the better qualified.

It looks as though the least skilled did much better in the USA than Europe. In fact the level of the employment rate for low-skilled men was not that much higher in the USA than in many European countries since many low-skilled American jobs had disappeared earlier in the 1970s. At the end of the 1990s the employment rate for the least qualified quarter of men was 77% in the USA, which was less than Switzerland and Japan and compares to 69% in West Germany and over 70% in Netherlands, Austria, Sweden and Norway. Moreover the US figures for employment rates of low-skilled men are exaggerated to the tune of several percentage points by the very large number of predominantly low-skilled men who were in prison and not counted in the (non-institutional) population. The bigger contrast is for low-skilled women where the USA provided many more jobs than the typical European country (though Sweden has the highest employment rate of all for low-skilled women).[4]

Why have the less skilled been falling behind in terms of jobs, especially in Europe? Three important influences are believed to have been technical progress favouring the employment of skilled workers, the displacement of low skilled manufacturing by imports from the low-wage South and the less qualified being 'bumped down' off the jobs ladder as weak demand for labour overall allowed employers to be more choosy and recruit better qualified workers for what had previously been jobs open to the least qualified.

A good deal of evidence has accumulated that technical advance has favoured the employment of more qualified workers. Replacement of the unskilled has taken place within individual industries (manufacturing and services) across a range of OECD economies and it has been strongest in industries producing machinery including computers, electrical machinery and printing and publishing, where there has been significant technological change. Detailed analysis of occupational patterns has traced the link between skills and computerization. Labour has been displaced mainly in tasks which can be routinized. This includes many unskilled assembly line jobs, which are repetitive and can easily be replaced by computerized technology.[5]

However it is important not to conclude that unskilled work is about to disappear. There are still large numbers of unskilled workers which are very hard to replace: cleaning, restaurant work, shelf-filling rely on 'hand-eye co-ordination that virtually all humans find easy but machines find enormously difficult' (Goos and Manning 2003: 2).

In the UK between 1979 and 1999 the fastest growing job category was care assistants (nearly 400% increase and very poorly paid) beating software engineers into second place. Two of the largest lowest paid groups in the UK (shelf-fillers and check-out operators) nearly doubled their share of employment.

Moreover not all skilled work is insulated from the effects of technical change. Some skilled craft and record-keeping jobs require precision and so require skill if done by humans, but they are repetitive and thus can be replaced by technology. However there are rising numbers of professional and managerial jobs which cannot easily be mechanized and there is no question but that on balance the demand for skilled work has risen rapid relative to jobs for unskilled workers.

The most debated issue is the impact of trade with the low-wage economies of the South in hastening the replacement of low-skilled jobs in the North by work requiring higher educational levels. At first sight it seems implausible that imports of manufactures from low-wage countries could have played a very important role. After all they took a bit under 10% of the domestic market for manufacturers in the USA and Europe in 1999 (see Table 4.4).

These imports of manufactures are usually more or less balanced by the expansion of manufactured exports, of machines for example, to Southern producers like China and the countries which supply them with raw materials. However, as Adrian Wood (1994) has argued, many more jobs will be at stake from cheap imports than will be gained from high value exports since the imports are so cheap because labour is paid so much less than in the North. Thus even balanced trade between North and South involves a substantial loss of manufacturing employment. A recent comprehensive study[6] supports this, estimating that for every job in high-skill manufactures created by additional exports to the South there are as many as six jobs displaced by the same money value of low-tech manufactured imports from the South. This disparity is just a reflection of the potential gains from trade. If it took as many workers in the North to produce the machine tools which paid for the shirts as it would have taken to produce the shirts at home, then there is no benefit to the North from the trade.

The qualification 'potential' to the gains from trade is important—the realization of these gains depends on the workers concerned being re-employed. A study of employment change in US manufacturing over the 1980s and 1990s found that the industries most subject to import competition, including toys, clothing and electronic goods, accounted for more than one-third of job losses. Around 40% of those affected were out of work two years later, and of those with jobs one-half suffered a wage cut of 15% or more. Over the decade 1992–2002 trade with the South may have accounted for one-quarter of the loss of manufacturing jobs in the EU and nearly one-half of the loss in the USA. These job losses can have such disruptive and damaging effects because manufacturing employment tends to be geographically concentrated. Where the plants comprise a significant part of local labour markets it is particularly difficult to reabsorb such displaced workers.[7]

This loss of manufacturing jobs through trade is substantial, but it should be remembered that manufacturing accounts for one-quarter or less of total employment. This has left the 'non-traded sector' (including retailing and many personal services) as the main source of demand for unskilled labour. Whilst some of these services are financed by the state (hospitals have to be cleaned and food cooked in them), many are dependent on 'physical proximity to richer high-skill workers as it is the expenditure of these individuals that is the main source of labour demand for low-skill workers' (Manning 2004: 4). Spending in shops and restaurants and on care for the elderly by managers, computer programmers and financial advisers creates jobs for the unskilled, but not fast enough to absorb the loss of other unskilled jobs in traded goods and in repetitive tasks in other sectors.

The above explanations for declining demand for the less qualified depend either on the decline of industries where the less qualified are particularly concentrated (e.g. textiles) or on falling numbers of jobs for the unqualified within individual industries (replacement of assembly line workers by robots). It is possible, however, that part of the problem is that the less qualified are being increasingly bumped out of jobs that they could adequately carry out by an excess supply of better qualified workers. Employers may prefer those with qualifications, believing them to be more adaptable, diligent or reliable. If demand for labour was higher then workers would tend on average to shift up the jobs ladder and more of the least qualified would get back onto the lower rungs.

A detailed study of US occupations and qualifications has claimed that such bumping down has been important:

Although the number of jobs requiring more education has risen considerably faster than the number with lower educational requirements, the number of educated workers has risen even faster. Moreover, women have filled an increasing proportion number of these jobs. These two circumstances have initiated a chain reaction of job displacements. More specifically, university-educated women have replaced men with a similar education, but with lower cognitive abilities than others with the same education. Those displaced have taken jobs previously held by workers with less education who, in turn, have displaced those with even lower cognitive skills. Many of the least educated workers have been knocked completely out of the labour force. (Pryor and Schaffer 1999: 217)

Over the 1990s in the UK, increasing numbers of workers, especially those in less skilled jobs, have reported that the educational qualification required for their job is not necessary to do it.[8]

Where the overall demand for labour does grow strongly, then those at the bottom of the skill distribution tend to do relatively well as employers cannot afford to be so choosy. Thus in the periods of strong employment growth in the Netherlands and USA during the 1990s employment of the least qualified grew faster than employment of those in the middle. However bumping down is certainly not the whole story and may rather be exacerbating the long-run shift away from unskilled work connected with new technology and international trade.

A final influence on employment prospects for the least qualified has been the power of unions. In most OECD countries substantial numbers of less educated industrial workers had been well organized in trades unions and had achieved relatively decent wages. The weakening of these unions in countries like the UK, as discussed later in the chapter, left them less able to protect the jobs of their members in the face of rationalization drives by employers facing recession or heightened international competition. Jobs stacking supermarket shelves do not necessarily provide enough work for redundant industrial workers.

Hours, Work Intensity, Employment Protection, Unemployment Benefits

It was noted in Chapter 1 that average hours of work declined up to the 1970s and this reflected longer holidays and a shorter working week. The trend continued with average hours worked for employees in 12 OECD countries falling from around 1,750 in 1979 to 1,625 in 2003. The picture is complicated by the growth of part-time work, which reduced average working hours, particularly in Netherlands. But French and German workers are now also working under 1,400 hours a year after considerable battles over working time. In France the cut in working time from a 39 to 35 hour week (combined with wage restraint and cuts in social security contributions) is estimated to have increased employment by some 300,000 or 2%.[9] However the shorter working week has been under severe pressure in Germany. *The Economist* (29 July 2004) reported that Siemens had 'persuaded its workers, and their union IG Metall, to accept a week of up to 40 hours, with no extra pay, to avoid the relocation of Siemens' mobile phone production to Hungary. "Blackmail" said a union spokesman'.

Sweden was unusual amongst European economies in not recording falls in working time after 1979 but hours there were already short. The major contrast was between most of Europe where working hours continued to fall steadily and the USA where the decline in working hours virtually stopped. The European trend was often presented by US writers as anomalous, with high taxation discouraging work effort frequently taking most of the blame. In fact the stability of US hours represented the real break with long-established trends. Between 1870 and 1979 average hours worked fell by around 0.5% per year in both Continental Europe and the USA and this was in the context of hourly productivity rising at about 1.5–2.5% per year.

Thus about one-quarter of the rise in living standards was taken in the form of reduced working hours.[10] After 1979 trades unions continued to press for hours reductions in Europe with fear of unemployment bringing additional impetus to the campaign. Hours of work continued to fall at roughly the long-term average rate in Europe but flattened out in the USA as average living standards stagnated.

How hard people work has only recently been at all systematically measured. A very careful and comprehensive survey of the evidence (mainly derived from workers' and managers' answers to questionnaires) summarized the conclusions as follows:

work in Britain was being intensified, especially in manufacturing, in the 1980s... work intensification continued in Britain through the first part of the 1990s... more workers were operating at high speeds and to tight deadlines. By the end of the decade, however, work intensification had apparently reached the point of satiation: there were no further increases in work effort over the 1997 to 2001 period.... Work intensification was also experienced by workers in almost all European Union countries during the 1990s, though to a varying extent and with different timing.... For France, the work intensification that took place in the 1990s was a continuation of change that was already taking place in the 1980s.... Almost certainly intensification also took place in Australia and in the United States... (Green 2006: 64–5)

Work intensity apparently rose in Europe at a slower pace in the second half of the 1990s, when unemployment was generally falling.

The rather widespread rise in employment protection up to the late 1970s was noted in Chapter 1 as a reflection of labour's stronger bargaining position. The most detailed data for the 1980s show reductions in the strength of employment protection in around half the countries analysed. In most countries this involved relaxation of conditions on temporary (fixed-term) working or on the related activities of temporary work agencies. The OECD has examined employment protection since the late 1980s in great detail. They found marked declines in employment protection in eight countries including Germany, Italy, Spain, The Netherlands and Sweden. In every case except Spain the relaxation referred to temporary and not to regular employment. France was the most notable high-unemployment/tight-regulation absentee from this list; temporary employment had been deregulated there to some extent in the 1980s but this was reversed in the 1990s. In the 'liberal', more free market, economies (North America, the UK and Ireland, Australasia), there was little regulation to begin with and little change.[11]

Fear of losing one's job—job insecurity—is widely regarded as having risen in the rich countries. A comprehensive analysis of survey evidence for the UK, Germany and the USA concluded that feelings of insecurity do fluctuate with unemployment. Not surprisingly, this would suggest greater insecurity recently than during the 1960s and 1970s. Insecurity, which has long been a feature of blue-collar occupations, became more prevalent amongst white-collar workers in the US in the 1990s and for finance workers in the UK. In the UK in 2001 workers in foreign-owned enterprises, and in particular workers subject to competition from low-wage country exports, felt more than average levels of insecurity.[12]

For those workers who do lose their jobs the level of unemployment benefits is crucial for their living standards. Figure 5.5 shows a rise in the replacement ratio—benefits divided by average earnings—in the 1960s and 1970s which was particularly rapid in Europe. By 1980 rates easily exceeded those typical of liberal economies. Replacement rates were on average held steady in Europe after 1980,

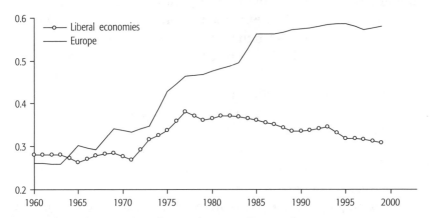

Fig. 5.5. **Unemployment Benefits: Ratio to Earnings, 1960–1999**
Source: OECD. See Data Appendix.

whilst in the liberal economies they fell quite markedly; Mrs Thatcher's indexation of benefits to inflation brought a steady decline in the UK ratio which was not halted by the Blair government. A number of countries have tightened eligibility criteria for unemployment benefit; there was a tighter definition of obligation to accept suitable work in Denmark and the UK, combined in the Netherlands with an increase in the number of benefit sanctions.

Wages

It was already noted in Chapter 1 that real wages have grown very slowly in OECD countries since 1979, an extraordinary turn-round from the 3–5% growth rates of the 1960s (see Fig. 1.2). In the USA the median wage, that is a wage half-way up the pay distribution, was $13.62 in 2003; in 1979 it was $12.36 reckoned at 2003 prices.[13] Indeed average wages actually declined until 1995, after which the 'new economy' boom of the late 1990s pulled them up a little, leaving an average growth rate of less than half of a per cent a year. In Europe and Japan average wages have done only a little better, having grown around 1% per year.

What explains the stagnation of real wages? The most important influence is the rather slow rate of productivity growth, which is further discussed in the next chapter. But real wages do not automatically grow as fast as labour productivity. The general increase in the share of profits discussed in Chapter 1 pulls real wage growth behind productivity growth and this has been a significant influence in many countries. Secondly, these earnings measures do not include employers' contributions to social security or to pension and health-care schemes, which have been tending to rise. Thirdly consumer prices, which determine the real purchasing power of wages, often grow faster than the prices of domestic output as a whole, for example if rents rise especially rapidly.

The fanning out of the pay distribution has been discussed more than the slow growth in average wages. OECD collates changes in the pay inequality for a number of countries for the 1980s and 1990s.

Figure 5.6 compares pay at the top end with the middle (a worker 10% from the top compared to a worker half-way down the distribution) and compares the middle to the bottom end (a worker 10% from the bottom). The evolution of pay differentials is shown for two groups of countries—three liberal economy countries with deregulated labour markets at least by the end of the period (the USA, the UK, Australia) and five countries (Finland, France, Germany, The Netherlands and Sweden) representing continental Europe.

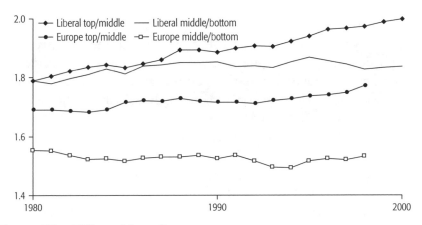

Fig. 5.6. **Wage Differentials, 1980–2000**
OECD. See Data Appendix.

Wage differentials, in both halves of the distribution, are considerably higher in the UK/US group than in Europe. By 1998 the gap between the top and the middle was about one-quarter higher in the US/UK group than in Europe and the gap between middle and bottom was more than half as big again. Differentials between the top and middle have grown generally but faster in the liberal group. Thus in the USA real wages at the top grew by 27.2% between 1979 and 2003 as compared to 10.2% in the middle. The most surprising result is that differentials between the middle and bottom have not grown at all in Europe, implying that real wages grew at the bottom at a similar rate to the average. In the liberal economies, differentials in the bottom half have expanded, but considerably slower than in the top half. Even so their relative decline means that US real wages at the bottom (first decile) did not grow at all between 1979 and 2003.

Since women make up a disproportionate share of the low paid, one factor limiting the rise in pay inequality overall has been that women's pay has tended to grow relative to men's. In the 1990s women were catching up at a moderate rate; on average across OECD countries the radio of womens to men's pay rose from 74% to 80% by the end of the decade. In many countries, especially Northern European ones with comparatively high pay for women, catch-up stopped completely in the second half of the 1990s. Part of the pay gap reflects the lower educational qualifications of women on average. However a study which matched pay differentials across countries against attitudes suggested that discriminatory attitudes, through declining, 'continue to play an important role hindering women's quest for equality in the labour market' (Fortin 2005: 21).

Although measuring the 'top' by somebody 10% down the distribution, as in Figure 5.6, shows a sizeable relative gain for that group, especially in the USA/UK, it misses the more startling rises in some countries for those really at the top. The extraordinary increase in the compensation of top US executives, discussed in Chapter 3, is the extreme case of this. However the phenomenon extends beyond this tiny group. Piketty and Saez (2003) show the top 1% of wage-earner households nearly *doubling* their share of total wage earnings in the USA between 1979 and 1998 (from 6.2% to 10.9%) whilst the top 0.1% of wage earners practically *tripled* their share to 4.1% (where they were earning 41 times the average!). Virtually all of the increase in the share of the top 10% occurred amongst the top 5%, and about two-thirds of it within the top 1%. Comparable data seem only to be available for France, but these show no trend at all in the share of the top 1% in total wage earnings, which stayed at the same 6–7% share found in the USA at the beginning of the 1980s.[14]

One important influence on the pay distribution, and also a telling indicator of attitudes, is a statutory minimum wage. There is a great variation across the OECD over minimum wage policy.[15] In a number of European countries without a statutory minimum wage (Sweden, Germany) minimum rates are set by collective bargaining. These tend to be in the range of 50–60% of average earnings, similar to European statutory minima in countries which have them. With the recent introduction of a minimum wage in the UK and Ireland all the liberal economies now have legal minimum wages. They tend to have somewhat lower statutory minimum wages than in mainland Europe; minimum wages in both groups have tended to drift down compared to average earnings. As well as showing the average minimum wage for nine countries with a long run of data, Figure 5.7 takes two of the most contrasting cases. France has had a high level of minimum wages and has kept them high whilst in the USA there has been a downward slide in what was a low rate to begin with.

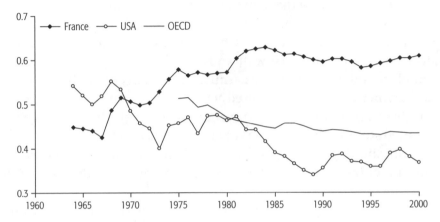

Fig. 5.7. **Minimum Wages—Ratio to Average Pay, 1964–2000**
Source: OECD. See Data Appendix.

Less Pay or Fewer Jobs—The Nasty Trade-off

In the 1990s, as the share of profits rose in many countries (Fig. 1.3) the emphasis in policy discussion shifted away from urging overall wage restraint to a focus on greater wage flexibility for the less skilled to overcome the decline in demand for their labour discussed above. The 'Unified View', that rising unemployment in 'Europe and growing wage dispersion in the USA were two sides of the same trade-off, offered a simple explanation of unemployment patterns and one with obvious policy implications.[16] In the face of technical progress and structural change the less skilled had to accept lower relative pay if they were to keep in work (as in the USA); the alternative was unemployment.

However the evidence for the importance of this trade-off in explaining European unemployment is quite weak. Bertola *et al.* (2001) do report a negative correlation between unemployment and wage dispersion patterns and Iversen (2001, fig. 2) shows a positive relation for the growth of employment in the private services and the level of wage inequality. More direct and thus convincing evidence focuses specifically on less qualified workers. Nickell and Bell (1995: 46) examined decreasing demand for unskilled labour in the 1970s and 1980s and found no evidence that 'unemployment effects are any more severe in countries where wage effects [increases in pay dispersion] are small'. Howell and Huebler (2005, figs. 2.11, 2.12) found no relation between earnings inequality and the level of employment of the less qualified across OECD countries or between changes in these measures. Card *et al.* (1999: 3) conclude from a very detailed study of the USA, France and Canada that 'it is very difficult to maintain the hypothesis that the "wage inflexibility" in Canada and France translated into greater employment losses for less-skilled workers in these countries'.

There can be many partial explanations for the lack of a strong trade-off relationship. One is that the lower wages for skilled labour may have rather little effect on the extent to which employers switch towards employing less skilled people and to which industries dependent on them expand in response to lower costs. Countries also differ widely in just how 'less skilled' the bottom of the education distribution is—in Northern Europe there is a much smaller tail of workers with extremely low numeracy and literacy than in the liberal economies. Whatever the full explanation, the conclusion should be that the impact of declining relative wages at the bottom on generating jobs is quite unclear whilst the adverse effects on those already in unskilled work is obvious.

The way in which reducing benefits, allowing the minimum wage to erode and cutting employment protection, is supposed to generate jobs is by forcing down wages in the part of the labour market where these measures of social protection make a real difference—that is the bottom. Thus the weakness of the evidence for the importance of the low wage/unskilled jobs trade-off should have given the advocates of labour market deregulation cause to tread warily. Far from daunted, however, and armed with the presumption that because economic theory identifies the trade-off, then it *must* be important, OECD, IMF and the EU have been unreservedly pushing for deregulation or labour market reform as noted in Chapter 2. However if the OECD's own compilation of reforms is used to construct an index of 'reform intensity' across countries, there is no evidence that the countries which carried out more reforms secured significant falls in unemployment.[17]

Union Decline

Until the end of the 1970s a rising proportion of employees were joining trade unions (and more and more workers were employees rather than self-employed). Since 1979 the proportion of unionized employees has fallen in many countries. Figure 5.8 shows strikingly similar patterns of decline in the three most important advanced economies, although from rather different starting points.[18] The halving of union membership in the USA is not untypical of the six liberal economies. In Australia and New Zealand membership

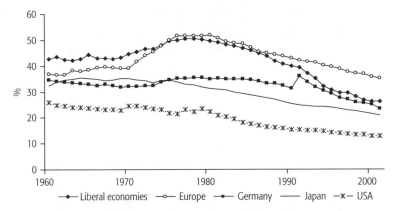

Fig. 5.8. **Trade Union Membership as a Percentage of Employees, 1960–2001**
Source: OECD. See Data Appendix.

also declined by more than a half. In the UK, often derided as exhibiting a particular destructive form of union organization and militancy, union membership fell by 40%. The downward trend has been less drastic in Europe, but still severe, with the unions typically losing more than one-fifth of their membership rate. The trend in Germany is particularly striking—a cut in union membership of one-third of employees even if we discount the spike associated with unification due to initially higher union membership in East Germany. In some of the smaller North European countries unions have an important role in unemployment insurance and in several of these membership rates grew.[19] In Italy and France (the latter with very low membership to begin with) membership fell by one-third and a half respectively. In a number of countries unionization is very much higher in the public sector than in the private sector (more than double in the UK and Germany for example).

In one respect at least, the data for membership may exaggerate the decline of union influence. Whilst the average union membership in the OECD fell from 47% to 36%, the average proportion of employees covered by collective agreements negotiated by unions declined from 67% to 64%. There were drastic declines in coverage in the UK (from around 70% to around 30%), in New Zealand (60% to 25%) and the US (26% to 14%), but in many European countries there was an increase in coverage (France from 80% to the 90%, the Netherlands from 70% to 80%) and there were even increases in some countries (like Australia) where membership fell heavily. In about half the countries the extension of agreements to other firms is by some form of legal or administrative extension; in the other half it is a voluntary extension by employers. How long unions can sustain very high coverage of collective agreements with falling membership seems an open question.

The way in which wage bargaining takes place varies enormously across OECD countries. In the UK wage bargaining is predominantly at the company or plant level, it is fragmented with little or no co-ordination by the TUC or CBI, collective agreements are not legally enforceable and there is no tradition of 'peace obligations' whilst the agreement is in force. In Finland bargaining is centred at the national level between highly coordinated employers and unions and collective agreements are legally enforceable and with automatic peace obligations. The general trend has clearly been towards decentralization of bargaining. In the early 1970s, out of 19 countries, six countries had rather decentralized bargaining (predominantly or importantly at the company level) whereas in seven countries central-level agreements were of overriding or periodic importance (with bargaining otherwise at the industry level). By the late 1990s ten of the 19 countries were in the decentralized groups and three in the centralized ones. Ireland stands out as the only country which made a major move towards greater centralization of bargaining when national wage agreements were reinstated in the late 1980s. However a move towards decentralizing bargaining does not necessarily undermine coordination and in a number of countries including Denmark and Italy, there was more coordination in the bargaining process in the 1990s. In the later 1990s a majority of countries were ranked by OECD as having a high degree of coordination in the bargaining process, with only the UK, USA, Australia and France having distinctly low levels.[20]

Although the general level of strikes has been at a low level (see Fig. 1.1) there have been an average of two general political strikes in Europe per year since the late 1980s, mainly over such issues as public spending cuts or reforms to the pensions, employment protection or unemployment benefit systems.[21] Obviously each country has its own complex history of union influence over the past 25 years and space precludes attempting a survey here. What follows is therefore a brief account of developments in the UK where, in addition to all the pressures from mass unemployment and deindustrialization, the unions were under sustained legislative attack in the 1980s from the Conservative government.

Union membership declined in the UK from 51.6% of employees in 1979 to 30.4% in 2002, with the private sector unionization rate being below 20% by 1999. Although the manual unions have been heavily hit by deindustrialization, this has been offset by rapid expanzion of heavily unionized public services like heath and in the UK at least 'changes in industrial structure are not a principal explanation for the decline in unionism' (Pencavel 2004: 199). Added to the members, some 14% of employees are 'free-riders'—covered by collective agreements but not union members—whilst 7% are union members not covered by a collective agreement (Metcalf 2004: 19). In the private sector the 1990s saw the total abandonment of collective bargaining in one out of every three workplaces that had practised collective bargaining in 1990, indicating that 'it was the exercise of managerial power which led to the removal of bargaining' (Charlwood 2003: 13). Unions have also failed to gain recognition in newly formed workplaces.

This anti-union attitude of increasing numbers of employers was encouraged by legislative changes under Conservative governments. Unions' legal immunities became more qualified, picketing became more circumscribed, notice had to be given before strikes, strike ballots became essential to protect the unions from financial liability. Employers could no longer refuse to hire or dismiss a worker because of their non-membership of a union, leading to the virtual extinction of the closed shop, which had previously covered a quarter of workplaces and nearly 90% in nationalized industries. In 2000 the Labour government changed the law which now gave the unions the right to a ballot on representation which required a majority of those voting and 40% of the workforce to vote yes.

An important milestone in the weakening of unions was the defeat of the epic miners' strike of 1984–5 over the issue of colliery closures. The state used police on an unprecedented scale to combat miners' pickets and to allow the Nottingham coalfields to continue working and power stations to receive coal. The secret services were heavily involved in undermining the strike (see Milne 1994). The wider union movement itself was bitterly divided over the NUM's failure to call a nationwide ballot on the strike. Its defeat after a year spelt the virtual elimination of the industry (described in Chapter 4) and demoralization amongst union activists ('if the miners can't win...').

Unions in the UK have struggled to maintain any premium in the wages they negotiate as compared to those received by comparable non-union workers. Two recent studies conclude 'there are real questions as to whether there is a significant union wage premium for workers at the beginning of the 21st century' (Blanchflower and Bryson 2003: 18) and 'For men it used to pay to be in a union [in the early 1990s] and it used to pay to join a union, but by the end of the 1990s it does not. For women the answer is: it does still pay to be in a union, but not by as much as it used to, and it does not pay to newly join' (Machin quoted by Metcalf 2004: 7).

Unions were widely blamed in the 1970s for the low level of labour productivity in UK manufacturing, and there is some evidence that in 1980 productivity levels were lower in unionized plants. Productivity growth in the 1980s was faster in these same plants, consistent with the notion that the pressure of the recession and weakening unions was greatest where they previously had greatest effect. A study of the most recent data for the end of the 1990s concluded that there was only any productivity shortfall in the very small number of plants where bargaining was still fragmented, with many unions bargaining separately (suggesting demarcation between different trades may have been inhibiting productivity).[22] It will be recalled that work has intensified considerably in the UK since 1979, which again is quite consistent with the weakening of union influence over speed of production lines and so forth. It is a salutary reminder that productivity growth frequently involves harder work for those involved.

The example of the decline of unionism in the UK shows how the norm for industrial relations can be undermined (in this case by legislation and the miners' strike). Whereas previously employers in new workplaces, in industry at least, were expected to bargain collectively, this changed decisively in the 1980s, bringing a steady decline in union membership in the private sector. The remaining union members were left with less bargaining power, less able to use the strike weapon and with declining political influence even when the Labour government was finally elected in 1997.

It might be assumed that these developments in the UK represent the neo-liberal offensive against unions in unvarnished form, and that the only factor holding back employers elsewhere from following suit is some combination of political circumstances and union strength. This is probably an oversimplification, however. In a number of European economies coordination between employers permits a training system where large employers invest heavily in the skills of their workforce and take full advantage of the workers' expertise in the firm's specific system of production. This gives such skilled workers a particularly strong objective interest in the competitive success of their firm, especially if their skills would be of less value to other employers. This can lead to 'enterprise egoism' in the workforce, as it is termed in Germany, which has long been a feature of Japanese industrial relations in the big exporting firms. The need to respond to international competition has apparently seen a trend towards greater cooperation between labour and management within this type of firm in countries such as Germany and Sweden. In this situation unions or works councils could continue to play a more important role at the firm level than more authoritarian employers in more free market economies would ever contemplate. However such a development can in turn heighten the problem of maintaining union solidarity between different groups of workers, such as the employees of large firms and those in small firms less involved in international trade or between industrial and public sector workers.[23]

A Balance Sheet

The period since 1979 provides an extraordinary contrast with the gains made by labour over the previous 30 years which covered jobs, pay, working conditions and worker representation. In the Golden Age unemployment fell to very low levels and workers moved out of agriculture into better paid jobs in industry and services. Pay levels rose steadily, differentials were often narrowed, hours of work fell and legal protection for workers was extended. Unions became stronger and exerted this strength in industrial action. Since 1979 labour markets have slackened and the unskilled men who lost jobs in industry have shifted into poorly paid service jobs, unemployment or even out of the labour force. For women job opportunities have improved but many of these jobs are still low paid. Average pay levels rose in real terms slowly if at all. Those at the top of the pay distribution tended to gain substantially relative to the middle. Work intensity typically increased. Employment protection legislation, particularly affecting temporary workers, was scaled back. Outside Scandinavia the proportion of employees in unions fell substantially.

Superimposed on this generally bleak picture, labour's position tended to be more eroded in the more free market economies like the USA and UK than in European economies where social protection was already stronger. Thus unemployment benefits fell somewhat in the liberal economies but hardly in most European countries. Those at the bottom of the pay distribution lost out in the liberal economies but not generally in Europe where minimum wages tended to decline less in relation to average wages. The extraordinary gains at the very top of the income distribution, such a striking feature of the USA and UK, were not repeated in those European countries for which data are available. Coverage of union agreements generally held up even in those European countries where union membership fell, whilst coverage fell rapidly in most of the liberal economies, and the impact of unions on pay and conditions was measurably lessened there. However even in countries like Germany and Sweden, traditionally seen as bastions of union power, international competition may be making union solidarity more difficult to sustain.

It seems impossible to depict all of this as signalling anything other than a major retreat for labour. As noted in Chapter 1 demands to extend control over the operation of firms were abandoned and replaced by the defensive stance of holding the line over basic terms and conditions of work. Whilst the retreat was headlong in some liberal economies like New Zealand and the UK, in some Scandinavian countries it appears more like a tactical withdrawal. The latter countries are small, however, and with a strong social democratic tradition. How far their experience could be generalized and extended is far from clear. We return to these difficult issues again in Chapter 7 which looks more broadly at equality and welfare across the OECD. First however we need to examine how the rich countries have fared, and are likely to fare, in terms of growth and stability. These macroeconomic conditions constitute the background against which struggles over labour issues, income distribution and the welfare state take place.

6

Growth and Stability

Even if the crises that are looming up are overcome and a new run of prosperity lies ahead, deeper problems will still remain. Modern capitalism has no purpose except to keep the show going.

(Joan Robinson, Professor of Economics, Cambridge University, writing in 1971 (Robinson 1971: 143))

The previous chapters reviewed first the challenges faced by capitalism in developed economies in the 1960s and 1970s and then the responses. Chapter 2 recounted the return of macroeconomic policy to financial orthodoxy, with control of inflation taking over from high employment as the primary objective. It also described the retreat of governments from intervention in industry through privatization and deregulation of product markets. Chapter 3 analysed the increasing role of the financial sector and the reassertion of profit maximization as the overriding objective of corporate management. Chapter 4 covered the increasing international economic integration and enhanced competition in the traded goods sectors. Chapter 5 analysed the weakened position of labour, reflecting its reduced organizational and political strength in the face of the heightened competitive pressures.

The story is not one of universal triumph for free market orthodoxy. For example, earlier chapters have recounted the difficulties in achieving sustained fiscal consolidation, the scandals over corporate governance especially in the USA, the erratic behaviour of exchange rates and stubbornly high coverage of collective bargaining even in some countries where union membership was declining. Even so, the rich countries have followed the orthodox prescriptions with more vigour than could possibly have been anticipated by neo-liberals in the 1970s. How should their economies have responded and have such expectations been borne out?

A supporter of this fundamental shift to the right in economic policy-making would have hoped that

(a) the strengthening of the position of employers and the weakening of organized labour would have brought rationalization of existing activities and a restoration of profitability;

(b) the response to intensification of product market competition domestically and internationally, combined with heightened surveillance by capital markets, would have been increased investment in new products and processes.

In short there should have been renewed dynamism in the economies of the advanced countries, bringing faster growth. Realistic assessments would have conceded that a likely by-product would be greater instability as financial liberalization brought with it busts as well as booms, with governments less ready to intervene to shore up demand. More intense competition in product markets would also bring greater instability in the market shares of established large producers. All this instability would be seen as an aspect of 'creative destruction' in Schumpeter's famous phrase, the destructive but unavoidable side of dynamic capitalism. The task of this chapter is to assess how far the unleashing of market forces over the past quarter century conforms to these patterns.

Dynamism in the Rich Countries?

The growth of output per head of the population is a simple indicator of the dynamism of the economy. The slowdown in growth during the turbulent 1970s comes as no surprise given the oil shocks, profit squeeze and vacillating macroeconomic policies (Fig. 6.1). The fact that there was no general improvement in growth in the 1980s could be explained away by the fact that the deflationary policies, giving priority to inflation, were being pursued quite fiercely and that the policies of privatization and deregulation, initiated under Reagan and Thatcher, were only picking up steam. But the real puzzle is the 15 years since 1990. Why has the combination of macroeconomic stabilization, involving the return to low inflation and the freeing up of market forces, failed to bring an increase in the growth rate?

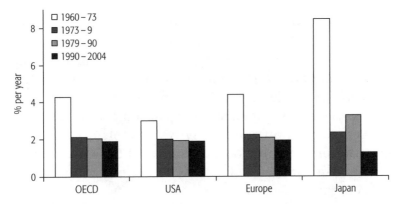

Fig. 6.1. **Growth of Output per Head of the Population, 1960–2004**
Source: Groningen Growth and Development Centre. See Data Appendix.

Before turning to developments in the different parts of the OECD, one looming global issue should be brought into play, namely environmental constraints. As noted in Chapter 1 these have long been forecast as threatening to tighten and drag down growth. Has this begun? In an authoritative estimate Nordhaus (1992) concluded that resource depletion and pollution reduction had shaved some 0.25% per year off productivity growth. If environmental constraints had been biting harder in the 1990s as minerals and energy became scarcer, this should be reflected in their prices. Moreover traders have a strong interest in forecasting scarcities and these become priced into current market values. Strong rises in oil and some other commodity prices did not really emerge until 2004 when the impact of prolonged Chinese industrial growth, absorbing increasing volumes of energy and materials, became widely noticed. These price rises could portend persistent scarcities, rather than temporary supply problems. However it is unlikely that environmental pressures have played a major part in holding back a growth rebound over the past decade or two.

The USA and the New Economy

Of the growth patterns in Figure 6.1 that of the USA is perhaps the most surprising. The 1990s brought the new economy boom and a productivity rebound which apparently re-established the US economy as top of the league. Yet the growth of per capita GDP in the USA taking the whole period since 1990 is not outstanding. It was only from the mid-1990s that US expansion became at all exceptional. Before examining productivity, a simple decomposition of US growth from 1992 to 2000, as compared to two earlier periods with sustained expansion (Fig. 6.2), is quite revealing about the character of that expansion.

Although the growth of consumption was not exceptional it contributed a higher proportion of overall growth in the 1990s (70% as compared to 60% in the 1960s expansion). As noted in

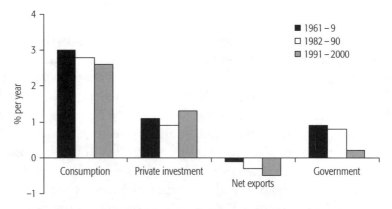

Fig. 6.2. **Contributions to US GDP Growth: Three Long Expansions**
Source: Bureau of Economic Analysis. See Data Appendix.

Chapter 4 the US balance of payments deteriorated drastically, reflected in the figure in declining net exports, and this represented a substantial drag on US growth (but a stimulus to the rest of the world). Private investment (and specifically business investment) made a bigger contribution to growth in the 1990s. This was despite fears that pressures from financial markets were forcing companies to disgorge more and more of their cash flow to shareholders as dividends or buy-backs of shares, thus starving them of investment funds.[1]

Government spending on goods and services grew unusually slowly. Military spending declined as a share of GDP and civil spending grew relatively slowly. Given that the budget balance was also moving into underlying surplus at the rate of more than half a per cent of GDP per year, government spending and taxation overall was contributing nothing to the expansion. Arguably this was the first prolonged expansion in the USA since the 1920s that did not include a major stimulus from public budgets, usually involving greater military spending.[2] This expansion was overwhelmingly generated within the private sector, and as we noted in earlier chapters, it came to a sticky end.

The much-heralded productivity growth in the late 1990s (2.5% per year growth in hourly productivity in the non-farm business sector) represented a decent improvement over the past 25 years' average of 1.7% per year. However the really spectacular productivity growth occurred after the bust in 2000. The average growth rate of hourly labour productivity in the non-farm business sector was 3.8% per year for 2000–4. So the usual productivity slowdown in a recession never happened in the early 2000s and instead there occurred the fastest four-year growth rate since 1951.

Since so much hangs on it, the acceleration of US productivity has been closely examined, though as yet most of the analysis focuses on 1995–2000. Despite spectacular productivity growth in computer production, the glamorous new economy sectors as a whole (computers, machinery, telephone and telegraph and software) only accounted directly for around one-fifth of the productivity acceleration in the second half of the 1990s. A rise in productivity growth in mundane wholesale and retail trade was about twice as important.

Purchases of new economy goods (computers, software) must also have boosted productivity in these 'old economy' sectors. One widely quoted study estimates that the accumulation of ICT capital was responsible for nearly half the acceleration. Such estimates are based on specific assumptions. The impact of ICT investment could really be less than this, since much of it was underused especially after the boom collapsed, as noted in Chapter 3; alternatively it could be greater, if its impact on the technological level and thus productivity was greater than its weight in the capital stock would suggest.[3]

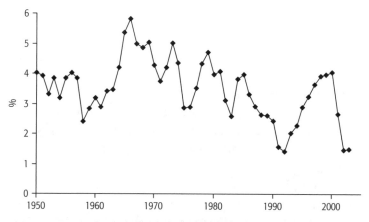

Fig. 6.3. **US Capital Stock Growth: Private Business, 1950–2003**
Source: Bureau of Economic Analysis. See Data Appendix.

As noted above private investment increased very rapidly and thus contributed substantially to the demand increase during the 1990s. Although this meant a very sharp increase in the growth rate of the capital stock, as Figure 6.3 demonstrates, it did not drive the growth rate of the capital stock to unprecedented heights. This is because capital stock growth started from an exceptionally low point in the early 1990s. The most positive conclusion from Figure 6.3 would be that the investment boom of the later 1990s halted the seemingly inexorable downward trend in the growth rate of the capital stock which had begun in the late 1960s. Moreover when the boom came to an end in 2000 capital stock growth plummeted more steeply than ever before.

Apart from a delayed effect of the new investment in the late 1990s coming on stream, it does not seem that investment and new technology can account for the continuing rapid productivity rise since 2000. A plausible explanation lies in the character of the earlier boom. As we saw in Chapter 3, the structure of corporate ownership and executive compensation led to widespread exaggeration of company profits (current and prospective) in order to bolster share prices. While actual company profits (measured in the national accounts) were stagnating between 1997 and 2000, reported profits rose by 70%, and then fell by more than half up to the beginning of 2001 as companies made provision against earlier exaggerations and other write-offs. This brought unprecedented pressure to try to limit the reported profit slide by cutting costs as aggressively as possible. After succumbing to the 'temptation to engage in accounting tricks during 1998–2000 to maintain the momentum of earnings growth', there followed 'sheer desperation to cut costs in response to the post-2000 collapse' (Gordon 2003: 249). The result was a slashing of employment, which continued as the mild recession turned in 2002–3 into quite a rapid recovery. Three million jobs went in manufacturing between 2000 and 2003 (as compared to 1 million in the recessions of the early 1980s and early 1990s) and proportionately as many in the much smaller information sector. 'Genuine' corporate profits (as measured in the National Accounts) dipped sharply in 2000 and 2001 both in manufacturing (with huge losses by the computer industry) and the information sector and this compounded the pressure on companies to rationalize.

However productivity continued to rise very fast in US retail, wholesale and finance, which had not been so severely affected by the recession. A comparison of US and European productivity growth found that in the late 1990s *all* the difference was accounted for by these sectors—the very ones which explained most of the US acceleration after 1995. A study of US retailing found that, rather than emerging from upgrading existing stores, productivity growth came entirely from new shops, like Walmart, entering with very high productivity and driving out less efficient competitors. A McKinsey study of US retailing also argued that new technology was not the whole story. Rapid growth in retail productivity came about through organizational improvements, the advantages of large-scale Big Box stores, and the shift to higher value goods associated with the growth in the number of high-income consumers.[4]

Whatever the precise explanation of the rapid productivity growth after 2000 it resulted in a sharp recovery in profitability (Fig. 6.4).

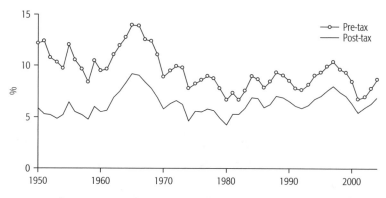

Fig. 6.4. **US Profit Rates: Non-financial Corporations, 1950–2004**
Source: Bureau of Economic Analysis. See Data Appendix.

The US pre-tax profit rate had peaked in 1997 at a higher level than had been achieved since the 1970s; given the long-run corporate tax reductions, the post-tax profit rate was higher than in any post-war year apart from a brief period in the 1960s.[5] The profit rate began to fall in 1998 well before the boom petered out. The fall was centred in manufacturing, which was being hard hit by the overvaluation of the US dollar and overcapacity in some sectors.[6] By 2004 the profit rate overall had regained its average level of the previous 30 years, and exceeded it after tax. So the savage cost-cutting, reflected in rapid productivity growth, had restored profitability considerably.

By 2004 this recovery provoked a rise in investment spending but over the whole period since 2000 private consumption accounted for most of the increase in demand, much of which flowed overseas with the ever-widening trade deficit. In a sharp reversal from the 1990s, government direct spending pumped in an extra 0.6% of GDP per year and tax cuts made up the rest of the massive fiscal boost which saw the underlying government deficit rising by nearly six percentage points of GDP over the four years. Alan Greenspan, at the Federal Reserve, also weighed in with unprecedented interest rate cuts after the stock market crash and September 11. Apparently he made only mild protests about the rising budget deficit in contrast to his dire warnings to Clinton (see Chapter 2).

The USA attracted much attention in the later 1990s as providing a model for rapid new economy growth focused on information and communication technologies from which, it was claimed, the US financial and entrepreneurial system was uniquely placed to benefit. The lesson was clear; other countries should shift their economies in the US direction (lower taxes, less regulation) as quickly as possible. As was noted in Chapter 3, some take a rather fatalistic view of the sharper booms and slumps which may flow from a very flexible financial system which can mobilize resources into new areas with great vigour. Perhaps 'creative destruction' which Schumpeter regarded as the 'essential fact' about capitalism, is more effective when booms are sharp, encouraging the most dynamic to enter the new industries, and slumps are severe, which gets rid of the weak competitors. Evidence from the UK suggests, however, that poor firms enter in booms, and the new economy period must provide many US examples. The worst firms do not seem to be dispropor-tionately affected by slumps, but under these conditions firms in general focus on rationalization at the expense of innovation.[7]

From a later vantage point the US experience indeed looks very mixed. Much of the productivity increase appeared to come from the combination of sustained consumer boom, bringing economies of scale at least in the retailing sector, plus a ferocious rationalization after 2000 when the bubble burst. Sustained by ballooning budget deficits, and relying on massive inflows of funds to finance the bal-ance of payments deficit, the overall macroeconomic pattern looks distinctly frail.

In particular the US economy, and thus the world economy as a whole, is very vulnerable to a sudden reversal of the US consumption boom. What can happen is illustrated by the earlier experience of some other countries. After financial deregulation in Sweden had brought a sharp consumer boom at the end of the 1980s, a reversal of the loose monetary policy and a severe banking crisis brought a 12 percentage point rise in the savings ratio and three years of GDP decline. As OECD notes (2002: 150) 'The larger financial exposure of households has increased the sensitivity of domestic demand to asset prices' at the same time as financial deregulation has increased the 'risk of excessive asset-price cycles'. The US economy avoided a 'hard landing' in 2001–2 largely because the government pumped in additional demand and US consumers never held back. However the vulnerability of the US economy would become very clear if the consumer boom were to weaken suddenly.

Stagnation in Japan

Japan dropped from being the most dynamic of the major OECD countries in the 1980s (growth averaging some 4% a year until 1991) to the most stagnant (some 1% growth) thereafter. The long stagnation was set in train by the collapse of gigantic bubbles in land prices, which had risen by a factor of five times between 1980 and 1990, and stock prices (up more than six times). By the early 2000s land prices were back to the 1980 level, and stock prices had also crashed. This had severe and prolonged depressing effects on bank lending and the investment of industrial firms, all of whose balance sheets were hit by asset price declines.

There were some specific features behind the bubble, including taxes which favoured land investment. It is also widely agreed that the Bank of Japan was remiss in not raising interest rates until the middle of 1989. Financial deregulation, stimulated by the need to finance big budget deficits in the late 1970s and by the internationalization of financial markets, also played a central role in the pumping up of Japanese asset markets. The following account has a familiar ring from the discussion of finance in Chapter 3:

Ceilings on bank deposit interest rates were liberalised gradually...from 1985 to 1994. Restrictions on the issuance of corporate bonds were gradually liberalised during the 1980s. As a result, large listed companies, which are traditional customers of Japanese banks, gradually shifted their funding from banks to the capital market. Banks faced a prospect of profit squeeze due to rising funding cost and a declining customer base...In view of the declining rent from the traditional business of retail deposit taking and commercial lending to large firms...most banks started to increase real estate lending. In expanding such lending, banks relied exclusively on collateral and paid little attention to the cash flow of underlying business. This was because the nominal land price in Japan had been on a rising trend since the end of World War II...Thus, financial liberalisation created a perfect environment for an asset price bubble. (Fukuo 2003: 367–8)

The collapse of the bubble ushered in a decade of stagnation. This was despite extremely expansionary macroeconomic policy. Interest rates were pushed down to 0.5% by 1995 and effectively zero by the end of the decade and the government cut taxes and raised spending, which imparted a fiscal expansion worth 1% of GDP *per year* on average between 1991 and 1999. One estimate puts the eventual bill for the Japanese taxpayer of bailing out the banks and other financial institutions at 20% of GDP.[8]

It became commonplace to blame Japanese consumers for failing to generate expansion, in comparison with the USA in particular. This is absurd. Certainly consumption has grown slowly (around 1.4% per year over the period 1991–2002), but this is because house-hold disposable income was virtually stagnant (growth of only 0.5% per year). The savings ratio (proportion of income saved) *fell* by nearly one percentage point per year, as workers strove to keep consumption growing in the face of the stagnation.[9]

The real villains of the piece seem to be exports and business investment. Japan's share of world exports fell from some 8.25% in the early 1990s to 5.5% a decade later—a fall of one-third. If Japanese exports had grown as fast as its export markets in the 1990s and early 2000s its exports would have grown nearly 4% per year faster. This would have directly contributed nearly 0.5% per year more to GDP growth with additional effects on domestic consumption and investment. Some fall in Japan's market was to be expected given the rise in the export capacity of China in particular, and the weakness of some of Japan's local markets after the Asian crisis, but the decline is much greater than can be explained simply by this. An important additional factor here was the trend appreciation in the yen which saw the real exchange rate more than 50% higher in real terms in the second half of the 1990s than it had been in the first half of the 1980s (see Fig. 3.2). Despite very poor export performance and an appreciating real exchange rate, Japan was persistently in surplus on the current account of its balance of payments by some 2–3% of GDP over this period. The explanation for this surprising result is that the feeble growth rate of GDP was pulling in imports at a comparatively slow rate. To a considerable extent export performance reflects other factors internal to the economy. If growth is rapid, imports are sucked in and the exchange rate depreciates in the long run and this generates a (roughly) equivalent rise in exports; such a rise in exports is greatly facilitated by the rapid growth of the capital stock which brings on new products and cost-reducing processes.

In the last instance, therefore, all trails lead back to business investment. In contrast to a modest rise in consumption, business investment was *no higher at all* in 2002 than it had been when the boom collapsed in 1990. There was just no rise in the level of investment to drive up demand.[10] Many features of Japanese institutions and policy have been blamed as contributing to the prolonged investment stagnation (see Saxonhouse and Stern 2003). One example is 'evergreening'—the tendency for Japanese banks to keep extending credit to firms with little prospect of repayment, apparently under pressure from government not to force clients into bankruptcy and not themselves wishing to admit to a high level of bad debts. It is claimed that this has created a penumbra of 'zombie firms' in industries like construction whose presence depresses new firm creation and deepens stagnation with 'inefficient firms crowding out new, more productive firms' (Hoshi and Kashyap 2004: 7).

It is hard to evaluate the importance of such influences on investment. Motonishi and Yoshikawa (1999) argue that reluctance to borrow has been more important in explaining weak investment over the 1990s (for large firms in particular) than reluctance of banks to lend. These authors blame lack of demand, but this tends to circularity since an important reason that demand was rising slowly was the reluctance of business to invest!

It seems very likely that the collapse of the bubble played a substantial role here and some supporting evidence comes from the behaviour of the profit rate (see Fig. 6.5). The series going back to the early 1950s is a conventional profit rate on capital employed, that is profits net of depreciation as a percentage of the replacement value of the stock of assets (buildings, machinery and inventories) calculated for the non-financial companies. Thus measured, the profit rate rose to great heights at the end of the 1960s boom, before falling back under the pressure of a very tight labour market and a rising yen, which affected manufacturing particularly. Profitability recovered a little in the 1980s, before slipping again in the 1990s as growth stagnated.

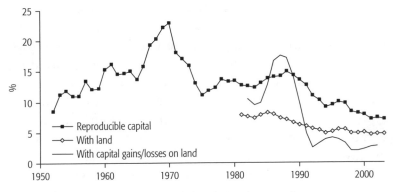

Fig. 6.5. **Japan Profit Rates: Non-financial Corporations, 1952–2003**
Source: Japan Annual Report on National Accounts. See Data Appendix.

From the early 1980s the figure shows two extended measures of profitability. The first simply includes in capital employed the value of land as well as the machinery, buildings and inventories. Land is conventionally excluded by economists because it is not 'reproducible' and is thus not part of the real cost to society of new productive capacity. However, to a capitalist sizing up the prospects of new investment, the cost of the land required (for the offices or factories) is part of the overall capital outlay which affects the profitability of the project. At the height of the land price explosion the market value of the land owned by the non-financial corporations (NFCs) exceeded the value of the machinery, buildings and inventories, thus halving the profit rate and bringing it to a very low level by the end of the boom.

The third series includes a rough estimate of capital gains or losses on holdings of land. When the land price rose sharply in the second half of the 1980s, and this is added to profits, the total rate of return from the productive investment plus the holdings of land was pushed up. At the peak, NFCs were making more in capital gains on their land holdings than from their ordinary commercial activities. No doubt this encouraged additional investments, especially in projects where land was important and thus opportunities for speculative gains seemed good. When the bubble burst, capital losses replaced capital gains and the overall rate of return slumped to a feeble 2–3%. Although nominal interest rates were very low, a slow fall in prices overall meant that the real rate of interest was substantially positive. From the point of view of the likely return on new investment, declining land prices were a distinct turn-off as they held out the prospect of capital losses in the future. From a financing point of view a fall in land prices means reduced collateral against which to borrow, making firms more reluctant to take on debt. In this way it seems likely that the financial boom and bust had an important influence on the continuing stagnation. Once it had set in, the lower rate of accumulation was strongly self-reinforcing as Japanese firms felt less pressure from their domestic competitors who were not investing at such a high rate.

There has been a tendency to blame Japan's financial system for prolonging the stagnation by its reluctance to admit the losses on 'non-performing' loans and to foreclose on bankrupt customers. If the banks had rapidly cut their losses, this would have made for a steeper recession and sharper rise in unemployment, but at the same time the excesses of the boom would have been 'cleansed' from the system more quickly, encouraging a renewed upswing before the gloom had settled in. There may be something to this argument but it requires some nerve to blame insufficient financial liberalization for Japan's problems. For it was financial liberalization, an assault on the traditional financial system, that caused the mess in the first place by fuelling the speculative behaviour which pumped up the asset bubble and brought the subsequent collapse. These 'domestic' problems were then exacerbated by the international capital flows which supported the overvaluation of the yen. However, it is a feature of hard-line free market analysis that when liberalization does not work the reason is always timidity and the solution is obvious. Complete the job.

Europe's Woes

The weak growth of the European economies in the 1990s has already been seen (Fig. 6.1). A more startling comparison begins in 1995 and focuses on output per hour worked which has slipped back seriously in Europe at the very same time as productivity growth recovered in the USA (Table 6.1).

This striking reversal of fortunes has brought European institutions and policies under the spotlight in just the same way as poor US performance in the 1970s and 1980s was the subject of soul searching there (see Chapter 4). A wide spectrum of explanations for Europe's poor growth has been offered in the literature.[11] One of the more intriguing suggestions, with strong echoes in Japan, has been that the ageing of the population and labour force has reinforced caution and an aversion to risk taking, in contrast to the youthful and dynamic USA. Amongst the more mainstream, economic explanations, at one extreme the liberalizers have argued that the whole set of European institutional arrangements between firms, banks and workers are to blame. These generated stability and predictability whilst Europe was catching up to US productivity levels but are no longer functional now that growth must be based on innovation and

Table 6.1 **Labour Productivity Growth in Business Sector, 1976–2003**

Average annual percentage changes	USA	Eurozone	Japan	USA–Euro gap	USA–Japan gap
1976–86	1.1	2.0	2.6	−0.9	−1.5
1986–95	1.2	2.1	2.2	−0.9	−1.0
1995–2003	2.5	0.8	1.5	1.7	1.0

Sources: OECD. See Data Appendix.

responsiveness to shifting global trends. A wholesale opening up to market forces is required, moving Europe in the direction of the US system.

As discussed earlier in this book, there has in fact already been a very considerable liberalization and reform in Europe. Germany reduced product market regulation more over the period 1978–98, and France nearly as much, as did the USA. Over the period 1998–2003 the EU on average, and almost every country within the EU, reduced product market regulation more than the USA, and in the cases of Italy, France and Spain very much more.[12]

A similar story applies to labour market regulation where the OECD has analysed reforms undertaken in the 1990s in response to its *Jobs Strategy*. The OECD recommended many more pieces of labour market deregulation for the Continental European countries than for the USA—for example Germany received 23 recommendations and Italy nine as compared to four for the USA. Moreover whereas the USA hardly acted on the recommendations at all, Italy and Germany were estimated by the OECD as implementing nearly half. Combining both these results, and using the OECD's weighting of the importance of the various changes, the 'volume' of labour market reform in these two countries was roughly ten times as great in the USA.[13] In the previous chapter the lack of relationship between labour market reforms and falls in unemployment was noted. Here the point is that the reforms should have boosted productivity growth in Europe.

Since Europe remains more regulated than the USA, both in terms of labour markets and product markets, it is always possible to claim that even more deregulation is required, an echo of the discussion of Japanese finance above. However, if regulation was the fundamental problem, some positive impact on labour productivity growth should have come already from the very substantial deregulation already undertaken. Deregulation should have contributed to an acceleration in productivity growth in Europe whereas actually productivity growth declined. It is hard to see how regulation, which was declining, could be the source of Europe's slowdown.

At the other extreme Keynesians blame the excessively tight policies of the European Central Bank and the Growth and Stability

Pact which have constrained demand expansion and led to a cumulative decline in confidence and business expectations. The discussion in Chapter 2 suggests that a strong influence on demand restraint is the memory of the turmoil of the 1960s and 1970s and the fear that this could return if caution was abandoned and unemployment fell too low. Although the unions are weaker and under the competitive pressures described in earlier chapters, in most of Europe they have not suffered the kind of decisive defeat inflicted on the miners in the UK by Mrs Thatcher's government.

An important finding, emphasized by Gordon (2004) and Blanchard (2004), is that most of the difference in productivity performance between Europe and the USA from the mid-1990s is located in wholesale and retail trade (see the earlier discussion of the USA). Specific influences such as restraints on developments of supermarkets have played an important role, reflecting in part different preferences over lifestyle (shopping in city centres rather than supermarkets and malls). This could be a case where a higher *level* of regulation, even if it is falling, impedes productivity acceleration in the face of new possibilities (in this case Walmart-style supermarkets). As emphasized by these authors, however, such US-style productivity growth can come at a high cost in terms of lifestyles.

One further difference helping to explain faster productivity growth in US distribution is the far faster growth of consumption. Between 1994 and 2004 US private consumption grew on average 3.8% per year. This was twice as fast as consumption growth in the Euro area, with rapidly rising flows of goods through the distributive chain bringing economies of scale in the USA.

Over and above these influences are there fundamental problems with labour costs and productivity which can explain Europe's stagnation? Earlier sections on the USA and Japan have shown the course of the profit rate on capital employed as an indicator of how propitious are the conditions for capital accumulation. Figure 6.6 presents the comparable data for UK, Germany and Italy.

The rate of profit had declined substantially in Germany from the 1960s onwards and to a somewhat lesser extent in the UK. The 1980s saw very rapid recovery in the UK, with the rationalization under Mrs Thatcher (see Chapter 2) aided by the boost to profits from North Sea Oil. In Germany the recovery was slower, but substantial by 1990. The evolution in France (not shown here) appears to be similar to that in the UK whereas in Italy there had already been some recovery in the later 1970s. In the 1990s profit trends were fairly flat apart from a fall-back in Germany just after unification.[14]

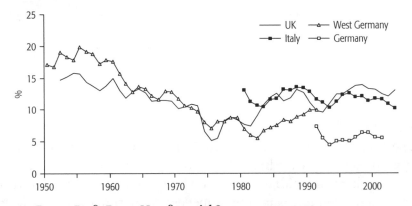

Fig. 6.6. **Europe Profit Rates: Non-financial Sector, 1950–2003**

Sources: Office of National Statistics; German National Accounts; Torrini (2005). See Data Appendix.

It is hazardous to compare such estimates of the profit rate across countries due to differing assumptions used by the national income statisticians about the rate at which capital depreciates. Nevertheless, from the available data, it appears that profit rates in Europe in the 1990s were no lower on average than in the USA—though Germany may be an important exception given the fall in profitability in the early 1990s following reunification.[15] Data for the manufacturing sector tell a rather different story. In the 1990s profits were much lower in the UK, Italy and Germany than in the USA.[16] Profitability in European manufacturing seems to have been decidedly low as compared to the US rates and compared to the rest of the economy. This must have discouraged investment, preventing manufacturing from acting as the economy's powerhouse even to the extent that it was in the USA. Furthermore, with the exception of the UK, these countries did not have such a sharp consumer boom as in the USA, so they also missed out on that stimulus to investment in the wholesale and retail sector. This adds up to feeble business investment overall.

Germany appears to exemplify this stagnant pattern and, given its pivotal position in the European economy, its lack of dynamism has infected much of the region. It is important to appreciate the sharp break in German performance associated with reunification. The German economy grew at 4% per year over the four-year period 1987–91 with a general European upswing prolonged by the pre-unification boom; business investment grew nearly twice as fast. Unemployment in West Germany fell to 4.1% and domestic inflation, though rising, was only 3.5%. Since 1991 Germany has only once exceeded 3% growth (and narrowly at that). The unification with East Germany represented an increase of around one-sixth in the population but the average productivity of its workforce turned out to be one-third of the West German level. The expected 'catch-up' to West Germany has stalled after 1995 with productivity at 60% of the Western level whilst wages are 65–75% of West German wages. Employment in the Eastern states has declined more or less continually since reunification, pushing up unemployment for the whole country by some 1%.

Adding a substantial and extremely unproductive segment to the West German economy was bound to drag down average productivity and push up average unemployment in the unified state. But the costs of unification, put at some 4–5% of West German GDP every year, have put tremendous pressure on the functioning of the western part of the economy as well. After initial rises in government deficits, the majority of these costs are paid for in higher taxation which has tended to be passed on in wage increases by the relatively strong trade unions. Germany has had an overvalued exchange rate (cost competitiveness in German manufacturing has been around 15% lower since 1995 than it was in the late 1980s). This originated in the response to unification when interest rates were forced up by the Bundesbank to contain inflationary pressure and a temporary current account deficit was considered desirable, as a means of borrowing some of the resources required for reconstructing the East. The result has been squeezed profits, especially in manufacturing as noted earlier. Since 1990 Germany has lost export market share in ten out of 14 years cutting off Germany until recently from its usual escape route out of post-war recessions via rapid export growth.[17]

There are aspects of German unification which could have been handled differently, but the fundamental problem was that the enormous costs in the West were absorbed in a haphazard and chaotic way rather than via a process of social consensus and negotiation. The old distributional struggles, which Germany had been relatively successful in containing in the 1960s and 1970s, re-emerged in a very damaging way in response to this sudden shock; the response from business was calls for financial discipline and deregulation with strong echoes from the Thatcher period. Additional pressure is being exerted by Germany's proximity, and old links, to Eastern European countries with labour costs a fraction of those in Germany and now members of the EU.

Unstable Growth?

Chapter 3 outlined a number of respects in which developments in finance have promoted instability, including the encouragement of consumption and housing booms, stock price overvaluations, major misalignments of real exchange rates and competitive pressure on financial institutions to sacrifice risk in the search for shareholder value. All of these trends would be expected to combine to make economies more vulnerable to financial crises and generally unstable, leading to greater fluctuations in output.

Table 6.2 **Global Growth Volatility, 1954–2003**

	1954–73	1974–83	1984–93	1994–2003
World of which:	4.3	5.3	4.3	3.0
15 industrial economies	2.1	2.1	1.8	1.2
91 other economies	4.7	5.9	4.7	3.3

Note: Standard deviation of annual % GDP growth.
Source: Martin and Rowthorn (2004). See Data Appendix.

Table 6.2, however, shows that the period after 1993 has been the most stable post-war decade, with the output of both advanced and less developed economies being around one third less volatile than during the 1950s and 1960s. Less volatility does not guarantee dynamism. In Japan output growth was much more stable in the 1990s when the economy was stagnating than during earlier decades of much faster growth. Nevertheless the comparative stability of out put growth is somewhat paradoxical. Possible explanations are either that greater instability deriving from the financial system has been offset by fewer problems with the supply side of the economy, particularly wage pressure, or that policy has become better at cushioning the economy from all such shocks.

We do know that throughout the OECD monetary policy in particular has become less accommodating of inflation but if any-thing this would tend to make output more variable as Central Banks squeeze hard on any signs of inflationary pressure. However wage explosions are no longer a source of instability in the most developed economies. So if commodity prices increase rapidly, which lowers real wages, this does not provoke much of a rise in money wages to restore living standards. Correspondingly governments do not squeeze so hard on demand in order to keep the lid on wages.[18]

It has become widely assumed that the US Fed will intervene actively to attempt to offset fluctuations in stock markets (as well as the market for government bonds). In 2000, near the peak of the equity bubble, comments from bank analysts of the stock market included 'we know Greenspan always comes to the defense of the stock market when it sells off' and 'if the market moves up 20 per cent over the year, then the market declines by 20 per cent, the Fed is likely to react to the 20 per cent decline and not the 20 per cent increase' (quoted Parenteau 2005, p. 143). Whilst provision of liquidity to financial markets may limit the effects of crashes, as when the US stock market fell after 2000, it may also engender overconfidence, increasing levels of risk taking, and thus greater financial fragility in the longer term—the problem of moral hazard.

Moreover there are fears that attempts to improve bank regulation may be making economies more unstable. Goodhart *et al.* (2004)

suggest that the new internationally agreed regulations ('Basel II') by incorporating more sophisticated analyses of risks could force individual banks into more cautious behaviour in bad times. This makes perfectly good sense in relation to the solvency of individual institutions. However, simultaneous attempts by many banks to meet the more demanding regulations on 'capital adequacy' could well be counter-productive for the stability of the whole system. If banks try and meet tighter capital requirements by selling assets and restricting lending in a recession, they could end up making the recession, and thus their collective position, worse. This is because if they all restricted lending the result would be reduced real investment and thus aggregate demand. Company profits would fall and the banks would be less likely to receive interest and repayments of existing loans.

It seems likely that the greater stability of total production in the economy as a whole would translate into greater stability of output and employment at the level of the firm, where it most impinges on individual workers. However Comin and Philippon (2005) document a striking increase in the volatility of output the firm level in the USA even as output in the economy overall has been fluctuating less. One aspect of this is that major firms in an industry are several times more likely to be toppled from a leading position than was the case in the 1970s. This supports the common perception that more intense product market competition has generated greater economic greater instability and insecurity. Macroeconomic stability provides some kind of cushion, in that workers who lose their jobs in one firm are more likely to find alternative work if the economy as a whole is not in recession. However this does not eliminate the costs of instability to the individuals concerned and as argued above, current macroeconomic stability is highly vulnerable to financial crises.

Prospects

This chapter has examined whether the great reversal in economic policy over the past 25 years has rekindled economic dynamism in the rich countries and how the stability of output has been affected. Excitement over the new economy boom in the USA has dissipated with the collapse of the bubble amidst a welter of scandal. The apparently impressive US recovery from the ensuing recession was only obtained by massive government intervention, fierce rationalization in workplaces, an unsustainable consumer boom and unprecedented borrowing abroad by the world's richest country. Meanwhile Japan has been stuck in a low growth quagmire for 15 years reflecting in part the after-effects of precipitate financial liberalization. Europe's economy, battered by the effects of German unification, has been growing only feebly, with mass unemployment in the large Continental economies, and with little response to repeated doses of deregulation.

The fact that output per head has been growing more slowly since 1990 than it did in the turbulent period 1973–9, never mind the Golden Age, must be a severe disappointment to those who believed that unleashing the free market would restore rapid growth. But does this constitute a 'crisis' for capitalism in the rich countries? Only by diluting the original meaning of the term which refers to 'the point in the progress of a disease when an important development or change takes place which is decisive of recovery or death' (*Oxford English Dictionary*, as quoted by Itoh 1990: 4). As argued in earlier chapters the decisive change took place in the 1980s with the implementation of traditional free market policies. Aided by the collapse of central planning and the political system which supported it, demands for greater state intervention, let alone for transformation in a socialist direction, have been beaten back. The fact that economic performance overall has been unspectacular does not imply that the system is in crisis. Capitalism as a system in the rich countries is not at present threatened by serious competitors.

Productivity per hour growing in the range 1% to 2.5% per year has been typical of the most developed capitalist economies since 1870 with the exception of European and Japanese catch-up in the 1950s and 1960s.[19] Performance over recent decades is within this 'normal' range, and memories of the Golden Age growth are too faded to still cause frustrated expectations. Nor does there seem compelling evidence for presuming that there will be a decisive shift in productivity growth from these long-run norms over the next decade or two.

From Smith, who believed that countries would reach the 'full complement of their riches', to Keynes, who asserted that capital accumulation would exhaust investment opportunities 'without great difficulty', there is a long history of economists predicting declines in the long-run growth rate of capitalist economies. One current trend acting in that direction is the rising share of employment in the service sector in general and in personal and collective services in particular, where meaningful productivity growth can only be minimal. This tends to drag down the average rate of productivity growth in the economy as a whole.[20] Such effects are slow but could reduce average labour productivity growth by up to half of 1% per year over the next 40 years. If ICT turns out to have as far-reaching effects on productivity as some analysts believe such a trend decline would not happen. A recent analysis of the centrality of the process of innovation in capitalist economies sees no compelling reasons for this process slowing down.[21] Predictions one way or the other seem futile. What is more clearly wired into the longer-run trend is a substantial decline in population growth in the rich economies and a bigger still decline in employment growth as the population ages. Thus the growth rate of GDP per head of the population will decline quite substantially in the rich countries, perhaps to little more than half a per cent per year in two or three decades.[22]

Whilst changes on the 'supply side' tend to be slow acting, economic prospects are much more dramatically affected by demand fluctuations. The genie of financial competition and expansion has been released by deregulation and financial innovation. Whilst the worst effects of the resulting financial fragility have been felt in the Asian countries hit by the crisis of 1998, it would be wrong to assume that the greater sophistication of financial markets in OECD countries insures them against financial problems. As this chapter has documented, the real economies of the USA and especially Japan have been scarred by financial excesses and the whole financial system can be threatened by the unrelenting search for 'value' though ever more complex financial trades. Regulators are trying to secure the benefits from liberalization whilst limiting the risks, but this is formidably difficult and the chances of a major financial crisis must certainly have increased. The April 2005 issue of the IMF's regular

Financial Stability Report whilst reporting a 'benign scenario' at present expressed the worry 'The combination of low risk premiums, complacency, and untested elements of risk management systems dealing with complex financial instruments could ultimately become hazardous to financial markets' (IMF 2005:1).

Potentially dwarfing in significance even the rise in density, international entanglement and fragility of financial markets is the growth of China, India and other developing countries. Until the 1980s the developing countries were economically significant for the rich economies only as suppliers of commodities and above all oil. Developing countries never constituted serious competition for more than a few Northern producers. However, as discussed in Chapter 4, these countries are now 'emerging' on to the world economic stage with great momentum. Since the mid-1990s the majority of world GDP has been produced outside the old OECD countries whilst their share is declining. The centre of capital accumulation, the driving force of the system is shifting away from the rich countries. For the North this has a number of quite contradictory effects.

First, rapid growth in the rest of the world will bring buoyant demand for exports of those goods where the rich countries maintain an advantage. This will in turn encourage capital accumulation in those industries and help to keep aggregate demand rising. This would be the South helping to sustain demand in the most developed economies, as envisaged 100 years ago by the Polish Marxist Rosa Luxemburg. In order to maintain that advantage in the face of rising competition from the South in increasingly sophisticated products, the currencies of the rich countries would have to depreciate. Living standards in the rich countries would no longer benefit so much from the import of cheap consumer goods.[23]

Secondly, there is the impact of surplus labour in China and elsewhere, significant segments of which will be highly educated but with much lower wages than in the North. Access to this cheap labour could encourage a much higher level of direct investment from the North, in effect an investment drain away from the rich countries. In effect the capital–labour ratio would decline on a world scale, by one-third or more according to one estimate, as the vast reserves of labour in those countries become inserted into the world economy. The result could be a major fall in the share of wages in the rich countries as workers find their bargaining position weakened.[24] The political consequences of such developments are hard to foresee. Growing demands for forms of protection for Northern workers from Southern competition seems very probable.

The other side of a declining wage share is obviously rising profits. However wages play a dual role in capitalism, as both cost of production and source of consumer demand, as emphasized nearly 200 years ago by Robert Malthus, better known for his pessimistic views on population. 'Excessive' wages can threaten profitability and accumulation as the account of the 1970s in Chapter 1 shows. Conversely wages growing slower than productivity threatens the buoyancy of consumer demand; with investment attracted elsewhere by Southern wages, maintaining demand in the North would then rely on increasing dollops of consumer credit or expanded government spending. Such a pattern looks unstable economically and challenging politically. To repeat the point made in Chapter 4, the development of new low cost sources of supply is not a new phenomenon. In that sense China and India are following the path of Japan and then the Asian NICs. What makes the present position different is that the population of these countries offers the potential for a far larger, and thus more disruptive, process of catch-up.

China itself could be a further major source of instability in the world economy. Its credit system is notoriously shaky, raising the possibility of a credit crisis and recession with severe impact on the North. The rate of absorption of labour could generate wage pressure and industrial conflict which the Communist Party would find it difficult to restrain. A severe recession could develop in China if interest rates were raised sharply to try and restore discipline—a rerun possibly on a grand scale of the 'overaccumulation' crisis in the OECD countries in the 1970s discussed in Chapter 1.

China's and India's appetite for energy and materials could precipitate spiralling prices, as markets try to anticipate long-run trends. The higher real costs of these inputs transfer additional real income to the producers of energy and materials who receive the higher prices for all their output. These effects would further increase pressure on the growth of living standards in the North. Nordhaus, a leading authority on the macroeconomic effects of environmental constraints, estimated that their impact on economic growth would be around 0.3% per year over the period to 2050, only slightly more than over the recent past.[25] However there is a great deal of uncertainly about such figures and, combined with the other influences discussed above, tightening environmental constraints could leave the rich countries with very low per capita growth indeed.

The fundamental point is that having beaten off the challenges of the 1970s the capitalist system in the North has not reached the 'end of history' where growth and stability are assured. Trying to work out more or less likely long-term scenarios is just peering into a highly uncertain future. A more immediate question is whether we have much choice left in the economic and social policies which our governments can implement. Are the economies of the rich countries rapidly converging under pressures from globalization on the US model with an increasingly inegalitarian income distribution, minimal welfare state and long working hours? Within the confines of capitalism are there still real choices about who gets what and who does what? The final chapter examines what has been happening to the welfare state and income distribution and speculates briefly on what might happen in the future.

7

Welfare and Income Inequality

Much of classical economics, with its [concept of the] long-run 'stationary state', had a fairly well-developed limits-to-growth argument...the argument that growth would have to stop because of limiting factors—most notably land—was definitely there.

Furthermore, the writings of our esteemed colleagues of the past are full of references to the idea that society will achieve general satiation in the distant future....With more than enough to go around, people will work less and enjoy leisure more. This vision is expressed in the writings of Marx, of Mill, of Keynes and of many others.

It can be argued that these economists underestimated the potential of technical change, or that they did not really understand human nature. Maybe that is true. But I must say it gives me some pause in trying to think about the distant future. Maybe it is we who are now overestimating the potential of technical change or it is we who do not really understand human nature. If we mainstream economic thinkers reversed ourselves so strongly over the last century, why shouldn't we reverse ourselves again over the next century?

(Martin Weitzman, Professor of Economics at Harvard, commenting in 1992 on the Limits to Growth controversy (Weitzman 1992: 54))

The period from the 1950s to the 1970s was the golden age for welfare state expansion bringing wider access to and improved quality of health, education and social services. It was no coincidence that this was also the period of growing organizational strength and influence of organized labour, since extension of the welfare state has long been at the forefront of trades union and social democratic party demands. Improved coverage of social security also contributed to reductions in income inequality in a number of OECD countries. Since then, as noted in earlier chapters, the drive for budget retrenchment has kept state spending under sustained pressure and wage inequality has increased, especially at the top end of the pay scales. This chapter reviews what has happened to welfare spending and inequality in the OECD countries since 1980. A central question is whether the heightened international competition involved in globalization is compromising the nation state's ability to fund welfare spending. Could it really be true that globalization means that 'Europe can no longer afford its welfare state'? The discussion of how the economy's output is distributed raises the further question as to whether the current emphasis on this output, as measured by GDP, really meets the needs of people when average living standards are already high. So the book concludes with a brief discussion of the pursuit of growing production and whether a redesign of the welfare state could bring about a more desirable balance of work in the formal economy and other activities.

Welfare State Spending

It is worth recalling what the welfare state is supposed to do before discussing the pressures to which its financing has been subjected. Historically, the first function of the welfare state was insurance for working people and their families against loss of earnings due to unemployment, sickness and old age. The system of compulsory social security contributions meant that the redistribution involved was primarily within the (broadly defined) working class—from those working to those out of work or sick or to the retired. The case for the state being involved in requiring such insurance was that poverty or irresponsibility would mean that some people would underinsure and risk destitution. The case for the state being involved in providing the insurance, rather than making private insurance compulsory, was cheapness of centralized administration combined with the fact many groups (chronically sick, workers in highly cyclical industries) would be unable to find affordable private insurance.

The second pillar of the welfare state is provision of education, health and other social services. Here the case for state finance out of general taxation was the egalitarian argument that all should have access to these fundamental services irrespective of family income, together with the fact that all society benefits from a healthy, well-educated population. The efficiency case for state provision of these services was that this reduced administrative costs for universal services plus the harnessing of the public service ethos that motivates many people more effectively than if they were doing the same job for a profit-making company (as noted in Chapter 2). Welfare states have developed in very different ways across the OECD countries, with varying emphasis on support through cash benefits or on direct provision of services, as discussed by Esping-Andersen (1990). However the pressures to improve provision and the problems of financing such improvements were felt across the different systems.

Pressures for improved cash transfers meant that they often increased faster than average incomes. For example, the ratio of unemployment benefits to wage incomes rose substantially to the end of the 1970s (see Fig. 5.5). Additional factors which increased social security spending were higher levels of unemployment and more people on sickness benefit. The rise in the proportion of pensioners is a further cause of higher 'demand' for welfare spending. In the provision of services like health and education there are strong social pressures for higher and higher levels of service (smaller class sizes, newly available drugs). If labour productivity was easy to increase in the public services then such improvements could be paid for out of higher productivity. However in many public services productivity is hard to raise. Smaller class sizes or more intensive nursing more or less automatically imply *lower* 'productivity' as crudely measured by pupils per teacher or patients per nurse.

The implication of minimal increases in productivity in the provision of these services is that their costs tend to rise systematically as compared to goods and services generally (the 'relative price effect') and these costs have to be covered from taxation.

Who Pays for Welfare Spending?

The strong pressures making for growing welfare spending are clear enough. However they come head to head against the age-old problem of 'where will the money come from?'

In a closed economy, with no investment or international links, an economy cannot consume more than it produces. This means that any resources devoted to public services *must* be paid for out of reduced personal consumption. Similarly, a redistribution of consuming power through the tax and benefit system must be paid for with lower consumption by those paying the higher taxes. Within this constraint an economy can afford any level of welfare spending its citizens are prepared to pay for. The fundamental issue is political support and collective discipline. The latter is important. The temptation is to try to both 'have one's cake' (better welfare services) and 'eat it' (no less personal consumption). Increases in welfare spending may be supported at elections, but that is not sufficient if workers attempt to offload the impact of the higher taxes via an increase in money wages.

The situation becomes even more difficult if an increase in benefits and thus taxation reduces the size of the cake through people choosing to work or invest less. Any resulting reduction in the total amount of production would cause a potential squeeze on welfare spending as tax revenue declined. Such disincentive effects are emphasized by conservatives. Their own design for the welfare state is strongly biased towards means-tested benefits. These have the attraction of being focussed on the poorest people, but they inevitably have to be 'withdrawn' as a person's income rises. This can lead to very high combined rates for taxation and loss of benefits on extra income. This creates much worse incentive problems for those with low incomes than more generous universal benefits. The UK pension system is a notorious example where a niggardly basic state pension is topped up by means-tested additional benefits, which cuts the incentive for modest additional personal provision for old age.

Much more noise tends to be heard about alleged disincentive effects by the higher paid who quite simply do not want to pay the tax. The American economist Arthur Okun offered the image of redistributive taxation being a 'leaky bucket' as for every dollar transferred to the poor the post-tax income of the rich would fall by more than the dollar due to their working less. The ultimate leaky bucket would be where higher tax rates yield less tax in total—the famous Laffer curve conjecture. To be set against such modest disincentive affects as may realistically arise from taxation, much welfare spending has beneficial effects on efficiency and thus contributes to higher tax revenue in the future. For example better health and education increase productivity, higher unemployment benefits can allow workers the time to find a job more appropriate to their skills. The countries with more state spending, on child care and education in particular, have fewer people entering the labour force with very poor educational attainment—in Sweden 6–8% of the population of working age had only achieved the lowest level of numeracy and literacy in 1994–5 whereas in the USA and UK the proportions were 20–23%.[1] Lindert (2003: 11) concludes from his study of the economic costs of the welfare state: 'Once we draw back from [such] extrapolations [to extreme tax rates—AG] to the historical range of policies actually tried, no expansion of taxes and transfers lowers (or raises) GDP.' This suggests that adverse incentive effects are usually not the binding constraint on welfare spending; gaining the political support for higher taxation is the issue.

Investment complicates the picture since higher welfare spending could be at the expense of capital accumulation rather than current consumption. This could occur if the spending was financed directly by increasing taxation of profits. Alternatively, if extra taxation on labour brings wage pressure and reduced profits, this has the same effect by passing on the extra tax to profits. The problem is that reduced profits jeopardize investment both because retained profits are a preferred source of finance and because expectations of the return to new investments will decline; higher taxation of profits may also be interpreted as an anti-capitalist measure presaging other threats to capital's freedom of manoeuvre and weakening confidence (see Chapter 1).

Maintaining consumption in the face of a rising share of welfare spending by a squeeze on investment could only be a short-term solution to the problem of excessive claims on national output. By slowing growth, weaker investment is likely to exacerbate distributional conflict in the future, especially if the expectations of wage earners and other sections of society are based on the experience of growing consumption. It is a fundamental problem for left-wing governments that 'making the bosses pay' by higher corporate taxation or a profits squeeze risks killing the goose that lays the golden egg of investment and growth. That is a feature of capitalism in general, not specific to its current globalized stage. As German Chancellor Helmut Schmidt, from the social democratic SPD, noted in 1976, well before globalization had been heralded: 'The profits of enterprises today are the investments of tomorrow and the investments of tomorrow are the employment of the day after' (quoted Bhadhuri 1993).

This helps to explain why corporation tax constitutes only a small proportion of tax revenue in the typical OECD country (see below). Indeed countries with more welfare expenditures do not tax incomes from capital more highly than the liberal market economies; if anything the reverse is the case. Additional tax revenue in the generous welfare states comes from extra taxation of labour incomes and of consumption.[2]

Is it possible to 'make the rich pay' for an expansion of the welfare state by stiffer taxation of high personal incomes, without jeopardizing corporate investment? In the typical high income country the top 10% of households receive around 30% of total incomes.[3] Tax systems as a whole are barely progressive.[4] Social security contributions are often capped and indirect taxation is typically regressive, counterbalancing generally progressive income taxes. Thus, as a broad figure, the top 10% typically contribute some 30% of total tax revenue. Increasing the taxation of this group by one-third would be a stiff, but far from confiscatory, increase in taxation. It would contribute an extra 10% to total tax revenue. Of course political opposition from those affected would be fierce, with threats of top earners emigrating. However self-serving such arguments, it is important not to exaggerate the extent to which the costs of welfare expansion can realistically be pushed up the income distribution. Even though a substantially more progressive tax system than currently applies in most countries would yield a very worthwhile extra contribution to total tax revenue, this would still leave the majority of taxation contributed by those with less than top incomes. This underlines the continuing degree to which the welfare state, which constitutes the major use of tax revenue, is financed by the mass of wage and salary earners and thus represents social insurance.

The discussion above has been couched in terms of higher taxes required to finance welfare spending. Exactly the same argument applies to forms of labour market regulation which in one way or another increase firms' costs. If Health and Safety Regulations reduce work speeds through adherence to safety procedures then the reduced national output must be paid for out of reduced consumption, or other welfare spending or investment. If Employment Protection Legislation reduces firms' freedom to hire and fire at will and moderates work intensity, then the effect must be lower profits or real wages, which translates into less consumption or investment or welfare spending. A cut in the working year will tend to reduce total production and annual real wages must decline if profits are not to be squeezed. Such measures may enhance productivity in other ways, by reducing labour turnover or encouraging training for example. But 'win-win' outcomes cannot usually be guaranteed; when the net effect on production is negative, this cost has to be borne by some part of national expenditure.

The general point, therefore, is that international competition, and the freedom of manoeuvre brought by globalization, do not import constraints on welfare spending where none existed before. Once underutilized resources are mobilized and the total amount of production constrained, welfare spending has to compete with the demands of personal consumption and investment. Given the need to maintain investment, the fundamental question is whether it is possible politically to persuade wage earners to accept higher taxes to pay for an extended welfare state. Globalization can only be blamed for making the welfare state unaffordable if it has severely tightened these constraints.

Constraints on the Tax Burden

Before looking at what has happened to sources of tax revenue and welfare spending over the past 25 years there are two trends encountered earlier in the book which have played a significant role in constraining tax revenues.

The generalized slowdown in labour productivity growth, discussed in the previous chapter, has implied that any increase in the tax share of GDP, required to finance increasing real costs of the welfare state, has to reduce what is already a slow growth of living standards. Real pre-tax wages have been rising at less than 1.5% per year in Europe since 1990 as compared to nearly 4.5% over the period 1960–73. Increasing the total tax share (including indirect taxes) of a worker's income from 40% to 41% say would soak up all the current rate of real wage increase leaving real take-home pay unchanged. At 1960s rates of real wage growth, however, such a tax increase would still leave workers with 3% extra to spend on consumption. It must be easier to raise the tax share when incomes are growing fast.

A second important trend bearing on redistribution is the increasing inequality of pre-tax incomes. As was noted in Chapter 5 much of the increase has been at the top end of the pay distribution, and the effect of this has been compounded by rising profits and dividends, which go disproportionately to higher income groups, as detailed later in this chapter. So, even with little or no progression in the tax system, the higher income groups are tending to contribute a greater share to total tax revenue. Thus just maintaining an existing welfare state structure implies a greater degree of redistribution. Those making a bigger contribution, and resenting it, may be able to mobilize political support against redistribution from middle income groups by agitating against those sections in society who benefit most from redistribution. There is some empirical support for this idea. Across OECD countries, greater inequality in the top half of the distribution tends to be associated with lower redistributive transfers. The study suggests that 'As the "rich" become more distant from the lower and middle classes, they find it easier to opt out of public programs and either to self-insure or buy substitutes in the private market ... they have little need for redistributive cash and new cash social benefits because they are very unlikely to benefit' (Schwarbish *et al.* 2004: 33).

The slower growth of labour productivity is certainly not the result of globalization in any straightforward way. Indeed the cheaper import prices promised by globalization, resulting for example from the expansion of low-wage Chinese exports, tend to boost the purchasing power of real incomes in the North and thus act to offset the productivity slowdown. Globalization has been implicated in the rise in income inequality. It has played a role in contributing to falling relative demand for unskilled labour, thus increasing wage differences, as discussed in the previous chapter. It has also contributed to weakening the bargaining power of trade unions, contributing to the rise in profit incomes. However it is one amongst a number of factors explaining these trends, along with skill-biased technical progress and mass unemployment.

Perhaps the most celebrated effect of globalization on taxes is 'tax competition' between countries, competing for foreign direct investment (FDI) inflows and seeking to circumvent FDI outflows. This has certainly added to the usual domestic pressures to cut corporation tax rates.[5] Amongst OECD countries there has been a substantial reduction in corporation tax rates on average and a distinct convergence of rates between countries (as indicated by the fall in the standard deviation of the rates—see Table 7.1). However the significance of this for welfare state financing is limited. Corporation tax has never been a major source of tax revenue, for reasons discussed in the previous section. As a proportion of total taxation it was on a declining trend in the later 1960s and 1970s, reflecting the profits squeeze. However it stabilized in the 1980s and, bolstered by rising profits, corporation taxes contributed the same share of OECD tax revenue (around 9%) in 2000 as in 1980.

The international organizations have campaigned hard for welfare state retrenchment, though generally in a guarded way. The OECD, in the context of the *Jobs Study*, not only warned against high benefit replacement ratios but also called for reductions in the total 'tax wedge' between employers' cost of labour and workers' net wages. This wedge comprises social security contributions by employer and worker, income taxes plus (in most formulations) indirect taxes. Thus the wedge constitutes the great bulk of the tax take. So calling for it to be cut, in the name of lowering labour costs and stimulating employment, implies a fall in welfare spending. In 2005 the OECD's paper on *Economic Policy Reforms* singled out cutting the tax wedge as one of the key measures to increase employment in as many as ten member countries, and in the case of Canada even suggested public health care costs should be reduced to fund the tax cut.

Table 7.1 **Corporation Tax Rates: OECD Countries, 1982–2001**

Percentage	Corporation Tax Rate	
	1982	2001
France	41	30
Germany	56	34
Japan	48	37
Sweden	54	23
United Kingdom	36	26
United States	39	33
OECD mean	40	29
Standard deviation	13	7

Source: Institute for Fiscal Studies. See Data Appendix.

In the light of all these pressures it might be expected that spending on the welfare state, at least as a share of GDP, would have stagnated, if not declined, with reductions taking place where the welfare state was largest and thus most 'in need' of trimming. This has not happened. As Table 7.2 indicates, social spending has kept increasing as a share of GDP, if at a slower rate than in the 1960s and 1970s. There has been some convergence between countries' spending—the standard deviation of social spending shares has moved down.[6] However, the Northern European countries, with higher

social spending in 1980 frequently reflecting strong social democratic influences, actually increased social spending *more* than the
liberal economies. An interesting exception is the Netherlands
where responsibility for payment of sickness benefits to those off
work was shifted to employers, a measure which cut government
spending by 3% of GDP. Overall, however, the convergence which
has occurred reflects the Southern European countries catching up
their Northern neighbours rather than any collapse of social spending towards US levels. This confirms the conclusion of Navarro *et al.*
(2004: 151) that the welfare systems 'have not converged during the
globalization period towards a reduced welfare state'.

Table 7.2 **Social Spending: OECD Countries, 1980–2001**

	Social Spending (% GDP)	
	1980	2001
France	21.1	28.5
Germany	23.0	27.4
Japan	10.2	16.9
Sweden	28.8	28.9
United Kingdom	17.9	21.8
United States	13.3	14.8
OECD mean	18.3	22.5
OECD std. dev.	5.8	4.6
North Europe	22.6	26.4
South Europe	14.2	22.4
Liberal economies	15.2	17.4

Source: OECD. See Data Appendix.

Why has social spending been so resistant to cuts? The most
important influence was surely the wide degree of popular support
for many of these services, especially where they are well financed
and of high quality as in the social democratic welfare states such
as Sweden. In that country a majority of people are dependent for a
majority of their incomes on employment by the state and/or
benefits paid by the state.[7] Better off salary earners are less likely to
be attracted to private provision where public education is excellent and public pensions substantial. In these countries there is a

strong political commitment to equality: 'Such political prefer-ences can prevent the most efficient outcomes from happening but a neoclassical economist can hardly criticise a nation for having inadequate preferences. There is no ethical imperative to grow faster than other nations, and seen from the perspective of the least advantaged Sweden is an extremely successful society' (Vartiainen 2001: 52).

The high share of taxation in Sweden did not prevent Swedish manufacturing from increasing productivity faster than any other industrialized country including the USA. Between 1990 and 2003 hourly labour productivity in Swedish manufacturing grew at 6% per year. This compared to 5.2% per year in the USA and only 3.2% per year in the UK, often held up as a deregulated model for Europe. Sweden also had the highest ratio of Research and Development spending to GDP in the 1990s of any OECD country, half as big again as in the UK.[8] Obviously high levels of social spending and taxation are not inconsistent with dynamism. Martin Wolf, a strong sup-porter of globalization, reaches a similar conclusion:

There is no sign that highly taxed countries in general suffer from a huge unrequited outflow of corporate capital....The conclusion is that lack of competitiveness is nowhere to be found in these highly taxed countries. Particularly important is the finding that they are not suffering a haemor-rhage of capital or of skilled people. (Wolf 2004: 260)

Globalization can even on occasion work to the benefit of the public services. The winter 1999 influenza crisis in the UK health service brought unflattering comparisons with the performance of the much better funded French system. With strong political support for the NHS, Tony Blair was bounced into suddenly promising to raise UK health spending to the EU average, implying real increases in spend-ing of 30% over five years; an example of a race to the middle.

Income Inequality

Liberalization of markets tends to bring greater inequality. At one end of the income distribution, restraints are lifted on high salaries and executive pay and dividends rise under pressure from the financial markets. At the other end of the distribution, wages may be made more flexible in the name of generating more jobs. In terms of the structure of taxation the liberalizers call for lower income tax on high incomes and a switch to regressive indirect taxes, whilst benefits may be under pressure in the name of improving incentives. If such pressures were irresistible then the impact might well be greatest in the most regulated and coordinated economies where market forces had been most repressed. This section examines what has happened to income inequality and poverty in the 1980s and 1990s.

A review of the international studies of income distribution suggests significant increases in inequality have occurred in the majority of OECD countries since 1979.[9] Spain appears to be an exception with a strong decline in inequality from the mid-1980s. In a number of countries, including Denmark and France, changes were rather small. The decade from the mid-1980s seems to have produced the strongest wave of increases in inequality, with some slackening in the later 1990s . The rise in the UK was strongest in the 1980s, the Thatcher period; New Zealand, also notorious for its degree of deregulation, saw as big an increase in inequality as the UK.[10] Sweden, with a very egalitarian starting point, also saw a substantial increase in inequality in the 1980s and 1990s. The USA maintained its position as the most unequal country with inequality increasing in both decades (see Table 7.3).

Table 7.3 also shows that there are still very large differences between countries. The ratio of incomes 10% from the top to 10% from the bottom of the distribution is nearly twice as high in the USA compared to the most egalitarian Scandinavian countries. The 90:10 ratio is also about twice as high in Mexico as in the USA. So you could say that the difference in income inequality between the USA and Scandinavia is broadly comparable to the difference between Mexico and the USA. Given that most people would regard Mexico as massively more unequal than the USA, the fact that this difference is comparable to the difference between the USA and Scandinavia underlines that even within the rich countries differences in inequality are very large indeed.[11]

The idea of a 'race to the bottom' is that those at the top tend to fall fastest as they have further to go. However the increase in inequality has been noticeably greater in the inegalitarian liberal economies than in Northern Europe. Thus, although the more redistributive countries have been unable always to preserve the rather low levels of income inequality achieved by the end of the 1970s, the subsequent rise has been generally fairly modest and differences across countries are as large as ever.

Table 7.3 **Income Inequality: OECD Countries, 1980–2000**

Ratio of post-tax incomes at 10% from top of the distribution to incomes 10% from bottom	c.1980	c.2000
France	3.5	3.4
Germany	3.1	3.3
Denmark	2.8	2.7
Sweden	2.4	3.0
United Kingdom	3.5	4.6
United States	4.7	5.4
OECD mean	3.4	3.7
OECD std. dev.	0.8	0.8
North Europe	2.9	3.1
Liberal economies	3.9	4.5

Source: Luxemburg Income Survey. See Data Appendix.

The increase in wage inequality, particularly in the top half of the pay distribution, was discussed in Chapter 5. Another important influence on inequality at the bottom end of the distribution is the proportion of workers with low pay. In the mid-1990s 20–25% of workers in the UK, Canada and USA were earning less than 65% of median earnings, whereas in Scandinavia and Belgium the proportion was 5–8%. These differences are systematically related to the institutions of the labour markets. There is a robust correlation between earnings inequality and the decentralization of wage bargaining.[12] Lack of work has obviously also been a reason for poverty; there is a rather close relation between the proportion of the working age population without work and the proportion who are poor in terms of their market incomes. Relatively generous unemployment benefits counteract this influence.

Another contributory factor to rising inequality has been a rise in the importance of property incomes in the form of dividends and interest. The rise in interest rates in the early 1980s, the boom in dividends in the 1990s as companies were under increased pressure to distribute more of their income to shareholders and finally increased profitability in a number of countries, have combined to make property incomes rather buoyant across most countries, with Japan a notable exception. The ratio of property income (dividends, interest and rent) to labour income (wages and self-employment income) rose from about 15% in the USA in 1979 to 18% in 2002 and from 7% to 12% in France.[13] Scandinavian countries have low shares of property incomes (about 8% in Norway and Finland on this measure). The true rise was certainly greater than is suggested by these statistics because inflation was much higher in 1979. Thus much of the money interest included in these figures was not real interest in 1979 in the sense of a real return in excess of inflation. By 2002 inflation was very low and most interest payments represented a real return.

Even though property incomes are more widely spread through the population in rich countries than was the case 50 years ago, they are still disproportionately held by top income groups. On average in the rich OECD countries the top one-fifth of the population received 53% of property income compared to 40% of earnings. Thus an increase in share of property incomes contributed to rising income inequality.[14]

Poverty and the Tax and Benefit System

Of particular concern within the income distribution is the extent of poverty. To make international comparisons, this is conventionally measured by the proportion of people with incomes (on a household basis adjusted for family size) which are less than a half the country's median income (see Table 7.4 below)

The liberal countries have larger proportions of their populations in poverty than the North European countries. Poverty rates are twice as high in the UK and Canada as they are in the Scandinavian countries and roughly three times as high in the USA. The fact that Finnish poverty was about one-third the US level in 2000 brings out the difference clearly, since the USA was at the end of a strong boom whilst Finland had very high unemployment. New Zealand and the UK had the biggest increases in numbers in poverty between the mid-1980s and 2000, contributing to a modest rise in the OECD total.

Table 7.4 **Poverty and Impact of the Benefit and Tax System, 2000**

	Percentage of population in poverty, 2000 or late 1990s	Tax/benefits effect in reducing poverty (% fall in numbers)	Tax/benefits effect in reducing inequality (% fall in Gini)
USA	17.0	−25	−18
UK	12.3	−61	−24
Canada	11.9	−52	−24
Australia	11.2	−55	−31
The Netherlands	8.9	−59	−40
Germany	8.2	−71	−42
Belgium	7.9	−75	−48
France	7	−70	−41
Sweden	6.4	−78	−42
Finland	5.4	−70	−40

Sources: Smeeding (2004); Forster and d'Ercole (2005). See Data Appendix.

The tax and benefit system plays a major role in accounting for differences in poverty rates, with many North European economies deploying benefits to offset 'market poverty'[15] by around three-quarters; in the USA only one-quarter of those left poor by the market are taken out of poverty by tax and benefits (Table 7.4, second column) Sweden and Germany apparently had considerably higher market poverty rates than the USA in 2000, but much lower post-benefit poverty rates since their benefit systems are so much more extensive and generous.

The final column shows the impact of taxation and benefits on income inequality as a whole as measured by the widely used Gini coefficient which reflects inequality across the whole income distribution. Tax and benefit systems achieve a much greater degree of redistribution in Northern Europe than in the liberal economies. It would be imagined that countries with a flat rate system of benefits, like the UK where state pensions or unemployment benefits are the same for everybody, would have generated more equality than countries like Sweden where such benefits are related to previous earnings. The opposite is the case however reflecting what has been termed the 'paradox of redistribution'. 'The more we target benefits at the poor and the more we are concerned with creating equality via public transfers, the less likely we are to reduce poverty and inequality' (Korpi and Palme 1998: 681). The explanation is that middle-class support for the system of benefits is much stronger when the system meets their own aspirations. For example, flat rate state pensions leads to widespread dependence on private schemes by middle income receivers and, as in the UK, the state pension is likely to erode to became a residual safety net at a pitiful level. The welfare state clearly has to adjust to the situation where many more people have some level of financial independence. In many OECD countries two-thirds or more of households own their own house and even in Germany, a laggard in this respect, home ownership is expected to rise from 40% to around 60% as enormous numbers of apartments are sold off by the companies which own them.[16]

Despite the pressures on the welfare state the impact of the tax/benefit systems in reducing inequality has remained pretty stable in the developed economies over the past 20 years. Ginis for the market income of working age households were generally reduced by similar proportions at the end of the 1990s as in the early 1980s. As Kenworthy and Pontusson (2004: 24) note, 'Although almost all European countries introduced some cutbacks in the generosity of various transfer programs in the 1980s and 1990s, in most instances they were relatively minor.' Huber and Stephens (2001: 306) come to a similar conclusion: 'Not only have the cuts in entitlements and services in all but a few cases been modest, the achievements of the welfare state in terms of income equalisation and poverty reduction have been largely preserved, despite the increases in unemployment'. They emphasize, however, that major welfare state retrenchments in the UK, under Mrs Thatcher, and in New Zealand were associated with big increases in inequality. Another example of substantial cutbacks is Japan where the proportion of an individual's medical expenses met by state medical insurance was cut from 90% to 70% over the period 1997–2003.[17]

Many would regard income inequality as especially objectionable if it is passed on within families, since an individual's position in the social and economic rankings should be as independent as possible of family circumstances. It is economically inefficient, as well as unfair on the individuals concerned, for talent to be wasted. Equality of opportunity has became a particular focus for politicians like Tony Blair who are reluctant to campaign for greater equality of outcomes for fear of losing middle-class support. However it is highly likely that unequal outcomes in the form of child poverty, lack of child care and poor schools, tend to reproduce themselves through the generations. Moreover the proportion of children living in poor families (average income less than half the median) is frequently higher than the proportions of the poor in the whole population as shown in Table 7.4. Thus in the USA around 22% of children were reckoned to be in poverty in 2000, some 16% in Italy, the UK, Ireland and New Zealand but only 2–4% in the Scandinavian countries.[18]

Position in the income distribution is just one measure of outcome and a far from perfect indicator of the extent to which a person has been able to use their talents in the most satisfying way. However being stuck in the lower reaches of the income distribution, especially in the more unequal societies, clearly imposes multiple disadvantages. Thus the extent to which position in the income distribution is passed on from parents to children is significant. As an example of the effects of family circumstances, in the UK men whose parental income had been in the bottom quarter of the income distribution were four times as likely themselves to be in the bottom quarter than the top quarter in 2000. Those with parental income in the top quarter were twice as likely to be in the top quarter themselves as in the bottom quarter.

A very careful attempt to compile internationally comparable data of the extent to which a father's position in the income hierarchy is transmitted to sons suggests the following. If father A earns double father B, in the USA A's son would tend to earn about 29% more than B's son, whereas in Scandinavian countries the difference would be about 14%. This implies there is far *less* mobility in the USA than in Scandinavia. As Figure 7.1 shows, Germany and Canada are much closer to Scandinavia than to the USA.[19] Probably the most dramatic finding is the severe decline in social mobility between people in the UK who were 30 at the end of the 1980s as compared with those who were 30 in 2000. One obvious difference between the two groups is that the former group experienced the conditions of the 1960s when children, whereas the latter group were still young in the 1980s. Between these two periods the influences limiting social mobility in the UK seem to have become much stronger. Broadly, social mobility in the UK seems to have fallen from North European to something close to US levels.

Esping-Andersen (2004) concludes from his review of the literature that, whilst minimizing child poverty through income support plays a role in improving the chances for low income children, it is far less important than public social service provision. He notes that 'Scandinavian day care is basically of uniform,

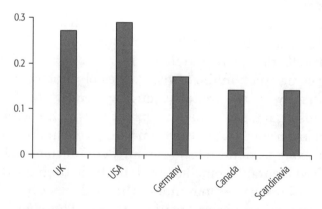

Fig. 7.1. **Correlation between Sons' and Fathers' Incomes, 2000**
Source: Blanden *et al.* (2005). See Data Appendix.

high pedagogical standards, meaning that children from disadvantaged families will benefit disproportionately. Day care in the United States is of extremely uneven quality, and children from disadvantaged families are concentrated at the low end' (Esping-Andersen 2004: 208).

The Size and Persistence of Differences

This chapter has briefly reviewed evidence on differences across the most developed economies in welfare state spending, in income inequality, in tax systems, in poverty levels and in social mobility. Two conclusions stand out. Despite the pressures on welfare state financing, the differences in distributive patterns between these economies are very large indeed, along almost every dimension considered here. Moreover the ranking of countries is pretty consistent. The Scandinavian countries show up as the most egalitarian in almost every respect, with the liberal economies, above all the UK and USA, at the other end of the scale and Continental Europe scattered between. So relatively generous welfare states, high benefits and well-funded social services combine with low wage inequality and a lesser importance for property income to generate low levels of income inequality and poverty and life chances less dependent on a child's family circumstances.

The second conclusion is that although there have been cuts in some aspects of the welfare state and increases in income inequality, these shifts have not swept away the more egalitarian patterns of distribution. The shift towards greater inequality has in fact been strongest in the more inegalitarian economies. Thus far there seems no clear tendency for the differences between countries to be eroded by a scramble to the bottom. Differences between patterns of distribution have actually become greater. This shows that, even with capitalism off the leash, it has still been possible to significantly affect the most fundamental of all economic outcomes—who gets what? The final section of this chapter, and of the book, considers whether this can continue to be the case.

Will Egalitarianism Survive?

Previous chapters have suggested that there is a prospect of real incomes growing rather slowly in the rich countries over the medium term as a result of structural change, slower population growth, environmental constraints and the unprecedented problems of adjustment if China and India grow rapidly. Moreover the latter trend will also tend to shift the distribution of income further away from wages and towards profits.

Slow growth tends to make redistribution more difficult since it involves stagnation or even cuts in the real incomes of the groups paying for the redistribution. If, in addition, profits rise faster than wages then it would be highly desirable to claw back some of the higher profits through international agreements on corporation tax rates and an assault on the inexcusable scandal of tax havens. Such agreements are particularly tricky as they require all or almost all of the major economies to sign up.[20] Realistically most revenue for redistribution will have to continue to come from tax on wage and salary earners though this may be done in a more or less progressive way.

There is one further aspect of globalization which might reduce support for the welfare state. Sinn (2002: 11) suggests that migration of groups particularly likely to be welfare recipients into generous welfare states will slowly force a progressive scaling back of such generosity to avoid being welfare magnets—a 'successive dismantling of the European welfare state is the likely outcome'. Such fears are probably much exaggerated, but the impact of migration on welfare may have longer-term significance. One study detected a tendency for countries with a larger proportion of foreign-born residents to have smaller redistributive transfers suggesting that 'more open (less homogeneous) societies are willing to spend less on social goods' (Schwarbish et al. 2004: 29). In similar vein Alesina et al. conclude from an international study of welfare states:

Racial fragmentation in the United States and the disproportionate representation of ethnic minorities amongst the poor clearly played a major role in limiting redistribution, and indeed racial cleavages seem to serve as a barrier to redistribution throughout the world. This history of American redistribution makes it quite clear that hostility to welfare derives in part from the fact that welfare spending in the United States goes disproportionately to minorities. (2001: 247)

Patterns such as these are employed by some people to buttress the idea that a redistributive welfare state is simply incompatible with an open multi-ethnic society. But, as I have argued throughout this chapter, the erosion of egalitarianism is not an irresistible consequence of any of the economic changes taking place in the world, large though these changes are. The welfare state was created by political action and has been defended by political action under the already difficult circumstances of the past three decades. Neither the industrialization of Asia nor a rising volume of migration means that political action to defend and expand the welfare state is now futile. Of course it will require plenty of ingenuity to develop the new forms of solidarity and political mobilization necessary to sustain the more global conception of egalitarianism appropriate to today.

Fortunately there is good evidence that popular support for egalitarianism is very much alive. The OECD reports results from the International Social Science Programme that in every OECD country surveyed more than 60% of respondents agreed with the statement that 'differences in income are too large' in the country in which they lived, with proportions ranging from over 60% in the USA to nearly 90% in Spain, Italy and France and 75–80% in Germany and the UK. Only in the USA do substantially less than half the respondents agree or strongly agree with the statement that 'it is the responsibility of governments to reduce inequalities' and in the UK the number is over 60%. Swedes and Norwegians believed in the early 1990s that a doctor should be paid about twice as much as an unskilled factory worker and the chairman of a large national company should earn just less than 2.5 times; in the USA legitimate income differences were felt to be six times an unskilled worker's pay for doctors and 11 times for CEOs.[21] Ideology and political history clearly engender big differences in attitudes to and patterns of distribution. The adverse shifts in income distribution which have occurred cannot be blamed as simply the inevitable, natural result of market forces; politics are as important as ever.

Going for Growth?

How the cake is divided up cannot be divorced from the issue of its growth rate. No sooner had economic growth risen to prominence as a central economic objective in the 1960s than sceptical voices were raised. These stressed variously the costs of rising pollution and congestion and physical limitations to growth as natural resources were depleted. But do we really benefit from growth in the volume of production anyway?

Social surveys have for some time asked people how happy or satisfied they are and comparisons of their answers over time suggest a striking conclusion. Over the long term, levels of personally reported well-being have not increased significantly despite the substantial long-term rise in GDP per head. Thus for Japan 'Between 1958 and 1991 its per capita income rose six fold. Nevertheless, the Japanese people report a satisfaction with life which remains largely unchanged' (Frey and Stutzer 2002: 8). In the USA since 1945, and with slower but still substantial growth, the average level of reported happiness was broadly flat and the same appears true of the UK. Although several European countries, especially Italy, show some increase in average happiness since 1975, the rise is 'small relative to the huge increase in incomes' (Layard 2005: 30).

The plot thickens because survey answers also show that, at a particular point in time, those with higher incomes in a country experience markedly higher levels of satisfaction than those with lower incomes. This seems to imply that if incomes rise on average so will average well-being.[22] There are two types of explanation for why this has not happened. It is very likely that my absolute level of income may be less important to my feeling of well-being than my income relative to those around me or to the average or to some other reference group. In that case if all incomes rise broadly together I would feel no better off once I had recognized that my relative position had not improved. Alternatively some other trend could be offsetting the effect of higher incomes.

In fact the pattern of economic growth itself may well be having other detrimental effects on a number of central important influences on our well-being. The US General Social Survey lists financial situation as second most important contributor to reported personal happiness, with family relationships first and work third. Relationships may be put under additional strain by pressures for more and more of a household's time to be spent working, especially in the USA where not only are there more and more households with all adults working but also working hours have stopped falling. This has led to what Juliet Schor (1992) termed 'the insidious cycle of work and spend'. Moreover it appears that in a number of countries including the UK, Germany and possibly the USA job satisfaction, as revealed in surveys, has tended to decline over the last 30 years. This seems surprising given the increasing skill level in the labour force, which might be supposed to make work more interesting. However many jobs for qualified workers involve a frustratingly low utilization of these skills, whilst insistent demands for greater 'flexibility' at work can lead to low job satisfaction and feelings of personal insecurity as Richard Sennett has vividly documented. Being out of work is far worse, of course, leading to a reduction in reported well-being that is far greater than can be accounted for simply by the loss of income.[23]

There are real debates about how to interpret such survey-based evidence. However, taken at face value, it does support the idea that in the rich countries workers/consumers are on a treadmill where they have to run to avoid falling behind. We would all benefit if we agreed to strive less vigorously for higher consumption, but very few of us dare for fear of falling behind the Joneses.

Further, it has been suggested that declining attachment to communities and jobs and the increasing influence of the media encourages comparisons with the rich and famous rather than those around us.[24] Since the majority are falling increasingly behind those at the top in many countries, as documented in earlier chapters, such comparisons must yield increasing dissatisfaction. They may also explain the extraordinary *Time*/CNN poll finding in 2000 that 39% of Americans believe that they are either in the wealthiest 1% or will be there 'soon'.[25]

The fundamental point, however, is that the benefits from higher productivity per hour worked, which capitalism seems capable of continuing to deliver, offers society a menu of choices. Higher output per head of the population is one option; reducing hours of work is another. As we have seen, the USA opted for growing material living standards, though these have mainly accrued to the best off in recent decades. In Europe working time per person has continued to decline and a recent study finds a 'negative relationship between hours worked across countries and life satisfaction' (Alesina *et al.* 2005: 30). Noting that the 1948 US standard of living could be reproduced in less than half the working time Schor (1992: 2) posed the issue in an arresting way: '...imagine this: every worker in the United States could now be taking off every other year from work, with pay.'

A reorientation of priorities away from growth would require a major shift for most of the left. Twentieth-century socialist thinking claimed that common ownership would improve material living standards more rapidly, as well as distributing them more fairly, than crisis-prone capitalism. But the longer-term objective of socialism was always to facilitate the development of people's lives in a more fulfilling direction. Is it possible to make serious moves in this direction even within what is still a predominantly capitalist economy?

The idea that economic growth could provide the material basis for a society with very different priorities has not been confined to socialists. Keynes in his remarkable discussion of Europe before the 1914–18 war in *The Economic Consequences of the Peace* speculated that with continued economic growth 'perhaps a day might come when there would at last be enough to go round, and when posterity could enter into the enjoyment of *our* labours. In that day overwork, overcrowding and underfeeding would come to an end and men, secure of the comforts and necessities of life, could proceed to the nobler exercises of the faculties' (Keynes 1919: 18). GDP per head in the UK is more than four times as high as when Keynes was writing. Has capitalism, having developed the productive potential of the rich countries to a degree unimaginable a century ago, laid the basis for a new balance between work and other activities? The most innovative policy suggestion to encourage moves in this direction is the proposal for a Basic Income.

Under a Basic Income scheme each person would receive a regular and unconditional cash grant from the state. It would be

unconditional in the sense of being received by everyone irrespective of other income or whether they were in work or not, and it could
be spent on whatever the recipient wished. At one level it would
replace many means-tested benefits which are becoming an increasingly important feature of some welfare states as governments
strive to both reduce poverty and restrain social security budgets.
Means-tested benefits have very well-known problems. First, take-
up amongst those in need and eligible is often low as a result of the
stigma attached to claiming and the complexity of so doing.
Secondly, means-tested benefits impose very high effective rates of
taxation as a claimant has a proportion of these benefits withdrawn
as her/his income rises, as well as paying income tax and social
security contributions. So Basic Income would involve a big saving
in costs of administering social security and would tend to increase
the incentive for those on existing benefits to take paid work, especially part-time work, which would at present leave them stuck in
the 'unemployment trap' of benefit withdrawal. Certainly marginal
tax rates across the board would have to increase to pay for Basic
Income, but for the low-paid the fact that they were no longer losing
benefits would more than compensate.[26] Even if it was introduced
at a very modest level so that the unemployed for example still
received an extra benefit whilst out of work, the fact that they would
still receive the basic income if they took a job would mean they
gained more from working for any job above a few hours a week.

Viewed in this light Basic Income would involve a recasting of
elements of the welfare state in an egalitarian direction which would
be extremely worthwhile. This is especially the case in the current
context where supporters of the welfare state have been continually
on the defensive trying, with some success as we have seen, to preserve its egalitarian effects. However to really contribute to an alternative vision the effects of the scheme must extend beyond those
currently dependent on state benefits. Basic Income does indeed
hold out the possibility of a much more fundamental reorientation
of priorities for society as a whole.

Under capitalism work does not have to involve the satisfaction of
some intrinsic need and for many people is mainly instrumental.
'Working to live' was expressed by a US automobile worker who,
being absent from work most Mondays, explained to his exasperated

manager that he worked for only four days a week 'Because I can't make a living working three days' (quoted Halberstam 1987: 495). Lack of any intrinsic interest in the work applies to many, but by no means all, low-paid jobs. Conversely professional jobs may be more varied and interesting but as noted earlier they can still engender alienating insecurities, especially in workplaces where the search for flexibility is in full swing. Provided Basic Income could be set at a reasonable level it would give workers, especially the low-paid, greater bargaining power in relation to their employers as they would have a financial cushion against the consequences of the sack or of quitting voluntarily in order to find more rewarding work. More fundamentally it would allow people the economic security to spend less time working for pay, perhaps none for the few with very austere needs, and more time for pursuing more intrinsically satisfying activities. This could include emulators of J. K. Rowling writing children's stories, political activists, rock musicians honing up their guitar technique, computer buffs contributing on line to the development of freely available 'open source' computer programs (Kogut and Metiu 2001), students, people looking after children or gardening.

Such a scheme invites two fundamental questions. Is Basic Income feasible politically, especially if those receiving it were absolutely free to do what they liked with all their time? Would people accept that even surfers, to borrow a famous example, should receive Basic Income and in effect live off the work of others? Full unconditionality from the outset may be a step too far. To justify Basic Income even at a very modest level it might be necessary to limit its distribution somewhat. Atkinson (1996) has proposed a 'Participation Income' which could cover everybody involved in a very wide range of paid work, household, retirement, educational and voluntary activities, that is the great majority of the population. This would recognize the very wide range of activities, not limited to paid work, which contribute to society. Surfers would then have to work or study part time in order to receive the payment. Eventually it could very well turn out to be more trouble and expense to exclude the fairly small minority of people who would not qualify for the Participation Income—full Basic Income would then be implemented as an administrative matter.

At first sight Basic Income seems to violate the 'paradox of redistribution' noted above whereby flat rate benefits tend to achieve less effective redistribution than benefits which rise with incomes at work and thus command the support of middle income earners. Obviously a flat rate benefit is of less significance the higher up you are in the income scale. However the option-expanding character of the Basic Income means that it fulfils a very different function from many existing state benefits. Even reasonably well-off couples, both of whom work, at first sight a group who have much to lose from the higher taxation to fund the Basic Income, could find that receiving it made it easier for one of them to work part time at certain stages in their lives. Of course many of the other dilemmas with existing welfare arrangements would still have to be confronted, such as how long somebody would need to live in a country to receive Basic Income. Clearly it is no magic wand with which to solve all society's problems.

Most fundamentally, however, for a book about the economy, where will the money come from? Alongside the personally rewarding activities which may be fostered by Basic Income, will there be enough work done to produce the goods and services which fulfil basic needs? If it relieves the necessity for the unskilled to work such long hours and if the highly qualified are deterred from overexerting themselves by the high tax rates to pay for the scheme, might not the system implode as insufficient time was devoted to conventional production? For reasons of political acceptability, Basic Income would probably have to be introduced at a relatively austere level. This would have modest effects on the labour supply as most people would still want to spend plenty of effort on formal sector activities. Whilst some low-paid workers would choose to work less, others, at presently caught in unemployment or poverty traps, would work more. But the fundamental point is that if the scheme discourages moderately the total amount of formal sector work, as well as sharing it out more equally, then these effects are wholly to the good. For many formal sector jobs as presently constituted are loaded with severe 'negative externalities'. They crowd out time for personal relationships and other activities which people find intrinsically satisfying, in contrast to the alienating aspects of much formal sector work, and much of the consumption they finance imposes a heavy toll on the environment.

Data appendix

Figure 1.1 Strikes: Days on Strike per 1,000 Industrial Workers

Series is five-year moving average of median annual strike rate for the 16 OECD countries. Note that the long run of data is only available for industrial workers excluding utilities for most countries, but including transport and communication up to 1988. Thus services and notably most public sector workers are not included. The median is used rather than the mean, which is heavily influenced by extreme values (such as May 1968).

Source: *Labour Market Trends*, April 2005, p. 163 and earlier articles in the series.

Figure 1.2 Inflation and Real Wage Increases

Inflation is measured by change in consumer price.

Real wage is index of wage earnings, with varying definitions across countries, deflated by consumer price index, five-year moving average of median changes for 13 OECD countries.

Source: IMF, International Financial Statistics (IFS) website, plus early data from annual volumes.

Figure 1.3 Manufacturing Gross Profit Share

Gross profits adjusted for self-employment incomes as share of gross value added. Figure shows unweighted average for 15 OECD counties, linked on to the series for the unweighted average for ten (including all G7) countries prior to 1970.

Sources: Author's calculations from OECD STAN Database 2003 edition, supplemented with national account sources and linked to data from Glyn (1997) for years before 1970.

Figure 1.4 Real Commodity Prices

Real oil price is crude petroleum price deflated by US consumer prices.

Real non-energy commodity prices are average of food, agricultural raw materials and metals price indices deflated by US consumer prices.

Source: IFS International Financial Statistics website.

Figure 1.5 Consumer Prices in Germany, and Italy relative to USA

Consumer price index for Germany, Italy divided by index for USA.

Source: IFS International Financial Statistics website.

Figure 1.6 Mark and Lira Exchange Rates versus Dollar

Deutschemarks and Lira per US dollar.

Source: IFS International Financial Statistics website.

Figure 1.7 Growth in Labour Productivity, Whole Economy

Output per hour worked.

Source: Groningen Growth and Development Centre and The Conference Board, Total Economy Database, January 2005, http://www.ggdc.net.

Figure 1.8 OECD Government Expenditure

Total government spending on goods and services and transfers as a percentage of GDP at current prices.

Source: OECD National Accounts website and OECD, *Economic Outlook* series for total government outlays, linked back from 1970 to series calculated from OECD National Accounts for total government spending excluding interest and transfers for G7 countries.

Figure 1.9 Share Prices compared to Average Wages

Index of share prices divided by index of average earnings and expressed as an index with 2000 = 1; average of 10 countries.

Source: Share price and wage earnings series from IMF International Financial Statistics database.

Figure 2.1 Unemployment Rates

Unemployment as a percentage of the labour force.

Source: OECD standardized unemployment rates from *Economic Outlook* for 1985–2003, linked to IMF International Financial Statistics data for earlier years. The series for Europe is an unweighted average of 15 countries whilst the Eurozone series is weighted (by labour force); since the bigger countries had higher unemployment this accounts for about 1.5 percentage points of the excess of Eurozone unemployment over the series for Europe shown here.

Figure 2.2 US Short-Term Interest Rates

Nominal interest rate is rate on Treasury Bills. Real rate is nominal rate minus inflation rate (consumer prices).

Source: IMF, *International Financial Statistics*.

Figure 2.3 Long-term Real Interest Rates

Nominal yield on long-term government bonds less the inflation rate (consumer prices).

Source: Rowthorn (1995, table 3), updated from IMF, *International Financial Statistics*, and OECD, *Economic Outlook*.

Figure 2.4 Unemployment and Strikes

Strikes refers to number of days lost per 1,000 industrial workers; source as for Figure 1.1. Unemployment rates are OECD standardized series from OECD, *Economic Outlook*.

Figure 2.5 Structural Unemployment and Unemployment Benefits

Structural unemployment rates are OECD estimates of NAIRU in OECD, *Economic Outlook*.

Unemployment Benefits are OECD calculations of net replacement ratio (benefits after tax as percentage of average earnings after tax) from OECD Benefit Replacement Ratio Database.

The net replacement ratio is preferable to the gross measure used in Table 2.1 since it takes account of post-tax income and any taxation falling on benefits.

Figure 3.1 US Financial Sector Corporate Profits

Corporate profit is return to equity owners, after payments of interest, depreciation (capital consumption) and inventory valuation adjustment, but before tax. Measure is ratio of financial sector profits to non-financial sector profits. Profits from financial *activities* are underestimated by these figures for profits of financial *companies* since some non-financial corporations have significant financial operations; however this hardly affects the trend.

Source: Bureau of Economic Analysis (BEA), National Income and Product Accounts (NIPA), table 1.14 (line 11–27)/line 27. http://www.bea.gov/bea/dn/nipaweb/TableView.

Figure 3.2 Real Exchange Rates

The real exchange rate is measured by relative unit labour cost (RULC), which includes both the impact of exchange rates and relative changes in wages and labour productivity. Comparison is with dollar wage cost changes in trading partners. A rise in the index represents real appreciation.

Source: IMF, *International Financial Statistics*.

Figure 4.1 Manufacturing Productivity Relative to USA

The series is for output per hour worked

Source: The relative productivity levels come from Groningen Growth and Development Centre, ICOP Database 1987 Benchmark (for Japan), 1997 Benchmark (for Europe), http://www.ggdc.net; linked to US Bureau of Labor Statistics hourly labour productivity series for Japan (from 1987) and for Europe from 2001 http://www.bls.gov/fls/prodsupptabletoc.htm

Figure 4.2 US$ Exchange Rate: Nominal and Real

The nominal exchange rate measures the US dollar against currencies of trading partners. The real exchange rate is measured by relative unit labour cost (see Fig. 3.2).

Source: IMF, *International Financial Statistics*.

Figure 4.3 US Current Account and Domestic Investment

Current account of the balance of payments and net non-residential fixed investment both as percentage of GDP at current prices.

Source: BEA, International Transactions, table 1 and NIPA, tables 1.1.5, 5.2.5.

Figure 4.4 Shares of World Output

Output is GDP at Purchasing Power Party (PPP) exchange rates (Maddison's version).

Source: Calculated from Maddison (2001) database. Data is extended to 2004 from IMF World Economic Outlook Database. OECD refers to 'old' OECD (i.e. excluding Korea, Mexico etc.).

Figure 4.5 Catch-up to USA in Asia—Per Capita GDP

GDP at PPP per head of the population divided by US figure for the year.

Source: Calculated from Maddison (2001) database.

Figure 4.6 Shares of World Commodity Exports

Commonly exports excludes services.

Source: World Trade Organization (WTO), *International Trade Statistics*, 2004; table II.2.

Figure 4.7 Manufacturing Wages during Catch-Up

Hourly dollar compensation of manufacturing workers.

Source: Bureau of Labour Statistics (BLS) series for http://www.ftp.bls.gov/pub/special.requests/ForeignLabor/prodsuppto8.txt

China's wages estimated from Statistical Yearbook series for annual manufacturing earnings in non-state enterprises divided by 2,500 to give an hourly wage and deflated by exchange rate for yuan from IMF International Financial Statistics to put into dollar terms.

Figure 4.8 Trade as a percentage of GDP (average of imports and exports)

These series are the Penn tables current price openness indicators (exports + imports at current prices as percentage of GDP, all at PPP prices) divided by 2. http://www.pwt.econ.upenn.edu/php_site/pwt61_form.php

Figure 5.1 Men's Employment Rate in Industry

Employment rate is ratio of employment to population of working age, 15–64.

Europe is average of France, Germany, Netherlands, Spain and the UK.

Source: OECD, Labour Force Statistics.

Figure 5.2 Women's Employment Rate in Services

As for Figure 5.1

Figure 5.3 Employment Rates, Men and Women

As for Figure 5.1.

Figure 5.4 Employment Rate Changes by Skill Groups

Low skilled refers to lowest quartile by educational qualification, middle skilled refers to average of second and third quartiles. Employment rate is ratio of employment to population of working age.

Source: Glyn (2001, table 3). Europe refers to median average annual percentage change for 11 countries for various periods spanning 1979 and 2001.

Figure 5.5 Unemployment Benefits: Ratio to Earnings

Liberal economies comprise Australia, Canada, Ireland, New Zealand, the UK and the USA. Europe is the mean of 13 Continental countries.

Source: Calculated from OECD's pre-tax replacement rate database; refers to first year of unemployment.

Figure 5.6 Wage Differentials

Top/middle refers to ratio of earnings at 90th percentile (10% from top of pay distribution) to median (half-way down).

Middle/bottom refers to ratio of earnings at median to 10th percentile (10% from bottom).

Country groups are given in the text.

Source: Calculated from the OECD's pay dispersion database. A small amount of interpolation for missing years was necessary. These calculations involve taking some liberties with the data, since OECD warns against cross-country comparisons due to different coverage across countries. The pay distributions exclude part-time workers although they are typically for hourly earnings. The series shown in the figure are mean values for the groups of countries and give a broad picture of developments.

Figure 5.7 Minimum Wages—Ratio to Average Pay

Series for OECD refers to 9 countries.

Source: Calculated from OECD, Minimum Wage Database.

Figure 5.8 Trade Union Membership as a percentage of employees

Liberal economies refers to median membership for six countries; Europe refers to 10 countries and excludes Germany. Series for Germany includes former GDR from 1991.

Source: OECD, Trade Union Membership database linked to earlier series from Nickell–Nunziata database as used in Baker *et al.* (2005).

Figure 6.1 Growth of Output per Head of the Population

Europe refers to average of 16 countries, OECD to average of 21 countries.

Source: Groningen Growth and Development Centre and the Conference Board: The Total Economy Database, http://www.ggdc.net.

Figure 6.2 Contributions to US GDP Growth: Three Long Expansions

Source: BEA NIPA, tables 1.12, 3.1.

Figure 6.3 US Capital Stock Growth: Private Business

Series is for real net capital stock; private business covers corporations and unincorporated enterprises.

Source: BEA Fixed Asset, table 4.2.

Figure 6.4 US Profit Rates: Non-financial Corporations

Profits expressed as percentage of net capital stock.

Pre-tax profits are operating surplus, calculated after capital consumption and inventory valuation adjustment (BEA NIPA, table 1.14, line 24) less business transfers (line 26). Post-tax profits subtract taxes on corporate income (line 28).

Net capital stock is average of beginning and end year net stock of fixed assets at current prices (Fixed Asset tables 4.1, line 28) plus inventories. Non-financial corporations (NFC) inventories estimated as same percentage of non-farm inventories as NFC fixed capital stock is of non-farm business capital stock (NIPA, table 5.5.7A, line 3).

Figure 6.5 Japan Profit Rates: Non-financial Corporations

Three profit rates are shown. The standard series is profits expressed as percentage of net reproducible capital stock (fixed assets and inventories).

Second series adds value of land in with capital stock. Third series includes capital gains and losses on land (estimated as change in land values in balance sheets); this series is shown as a three-year moving average centred in year in question because of sharp year to year fluctuations. To the extent that NFCs were buying land from other sectors, then capital gains are overestimated. It seems unlikely that such effects were very big.

Sources: Net operating surplus from Operating Account of Private NFCs, Annual Report on National Accounts, table 1.2.(2); stock of net fixed assets, inventories and land from (table 2.2.1(a). The profit rate on the reproducible capital series was linked back from 1970 to the business net profit rate series in Armstrong *et al.* (1991, table A2).

Figure 6.6 Europe Net Profit Rates: Non-financial Sector

UK Office of National Statistics series for net rate of return for private non-financial companies, http://www.statistics.gov.uk/statbase/tsdtables1.asp? vlnk = prof (series LRWW), linked back from 1965 to Armstrong *et al.* (1991, table A2).

Germany Net operating surplus, with adjustment for self-employment incomes, of non-agricultural business as a percentage of net capital stock. Source: German National Accounts as described in Armstrong *et al.* (1991, data appendix). Series break in 1991 represents combined effects of unification (which appear to be rather small) plus a new system of national accounts which accounts for most of the lower profit rate in the new series, for unexplained reasons. Inventories have to be estimated in the new system and some parts of the services sector are excluded.

Italy Business sector profit rate taken directly from Torrini (2005).

Figure 7.1 Correlation between Sons' and Fathers' Incomes

The measure is the 'intergenerational partial correlation' between fathers' and sons' incomes. Scandinavia is the average of estimates for Denmark, Finland, Norway and Sweden.

Source: Blanden *et al.* (2005, table 2).

Table 1.1 Labour Market Trends

Employment Protection is an index of employment protection stringeney from the Nickell–Nunziata database.

Sources: Unemployment benefit, Union membership and unemployment rate as for figures 5.8, 5.5, and 2.1.

Table 2.1 Budget Deficits

General government budget balance as a percentage of GDP at current prices.

Sources: OECD, *National Accounts, Historical Statistics, Economic Outlook.*

Table 2.2 Production and Incomes in UK Utilities

Sector covers gas, electricity and water. Labour productivity is output per worker. Real wages and real profits are calculated by deflating money wages and money profits by the consumer price deflator.

Source: National Accounts data from Office of National Statistics website. M. O'Mahoney series for employment linked to ONS workforce employees.

Table 4.1 Financing the US Balance of Payments Deficit

Calculated from BEA Balance of Payments table 1. Lines 76, (51+64), (50+63−51−64), 56.

Table 4.2 Capital Accumulation: Growth Rates of Fixed Capital Stock

Calculated from background data for Bosworth and Collins (2003), kindly supplied by Susan M. Collins, except series for USA, Europe and Japan from OECD, *Economic Outlook*, table 22 database, business capital stock. Europe data for 1960s and 1970 s are the unweighted average growth rates for 10 countries.

Table 4.3 China's Exports

Calculated from WTO, *International Trade Statistics*, 2004; table II.3–5, III.7.5, IV.26.

Table 4.4 Import Penetration of Domestic Markets for Manufactures

Import penetration is measured by value of imports as a percentage of apparent consumption (production plus imports less exports).

    Data for Europe are simple averages of the UK, Germany, France and Italy

Sources: 1913–63: Batchelor *et al.* (1980, table 3.3); 1974–2001: author's calculations from OECD, Stan Database, 1998 and 2004 editions. There are minor breaks in the series after 1950 and after 1963 and for Germany after 1989. The figure for imports from the South (comprising all sources other than Western Europe, North America, Japan and Australia/New Zealand) are derived from total imports for 2001 and share of the South in manufactured imports in 2003 from WTO International Trade, table IV.25.

Table 4.5 Foreign Direct Investment Flows

Source: UNCTAD (2004, annex table B.5).

Table 6.1 Labour Productivity Growth in Business Sector

Source: Calculated from OECD, *Economic Outlook*, June 2004, annex table 12.

Table 6.2 Global Growth Volatility

The measure of volatility is calculated as the average across countries of growth volatility within each country, with the latter measured by the standard deviation of the country's real growth rate.

Source: Martin and Rowthorn (2004, table 6).

Table 7.1 Corporation Tax Rates: OECD Countries

Measure used is effective average tax rate on new investment (including investment incentives).

Mean and standard deviation refer to 14 OECD countries.

Source: Institute for Fiscal Studies Corporation Tax Database (see Devereux *et al.* 2002).

Table 7.2 Social Spending: OECD Countries

Social expenditure includes health, social services and unemployment and pension benefits, but not education.

OECD median and standard deviation refer to 21 countries; North Europe refers to 10 countries from Scandinavia to Switzerland; South Europe refers to Greece, Spain, Portugal and Italy; Liberal Economies refer to Australia, New Zealand, Ireland, Canada, the USA and UK.

Source: OECD, Social Expenditure Database.

Table 7.3 Income Inequality: OECD Countries

90:10 ratios for household disposable income.

North Europe refers to nine countries, Liberal Economies to six countries, OECD to 19 countries.

Source: Luxemburg Income Survey website http://www.lisproject.org/techdoc.htm and Forster and d'Ercole (2005) Annex Table A.3.

Table 7.4 Poverty and Impact of the Benefit and Tax System

Numbers in poverty are those with household income adjusted for family size which is less than 50% of the median income.

Tax/benefit effects show extent to which povery is reduced or the Gini coefficient measure of overall income inequality is reduced by the effect of the tax and benefit system. The comparison is with what poverty would have been or what inequality would have been without taxes and benefits but with market incomes not affected.

Source: Smeeding (2004 figs. 8 and 9) plus Forster and d'Ercole (2005, fig. 14, annex table A7).

Notes

Preface

1. Glyn and Sutcliffe (1972), Armstrong *et al.* (1991) and Glyn *et al.* (1990).
2. Quoted in Armstrong *et al.* (1991: 85–100) where post-war reconstruction is analysed in some detail.
3. The rise of neo-liberal ideas is discussed in Harvey (2005).

Chapter 1

1. This group of countries comprises original members of the Organization for Economic Co-operation and Development. In the remainder of this book this group will also be referred to interchangeably as the OECD countries, the 'rich countries' and the 'North' (particularly when the context is relations with the less developed 'South').
2. See, for example, Bruno and Sachs (1985), Brenner (2002), Arrighi (2003), Dumenil and Levy (2004).
3. Maddison (1991, table C.5).
4. See the vivid description of these trends in Italy in Ginsburg (1990, ch. 7).
5. See Rowthorn and Wells (1987).
6. The rise in female labour force participation in urban areas was masked in the national statistics of those countries where large numbers of women had been counted as employed in agriculture (so that the shift out of agriculture initially tended to reduce women's participation). These trends are presented and discussed in more detail in Erdem and Glyn (2000).
7. Armstrong *et al.* (1991), ch. 8.
8. Calculated as the fall in median hours worked for 15 OECD countries from Maddison (1995, table J-4).
9. See Soskice (1978) for a description of the economic and policy circumstances around the strike waves and wage explosions and Ginsburg (1990) for a graphic account of the Italian developments.

10. Allsopp (1982, table 3.4).
11. Profit rate data are presented in Glyn (1997) but are available for fewer countries than those with profit share data used in Fig. 1.3.
12. Glyn and Sutcliffe (1972).
13. Armstrong *et al.* (1991, table 10.1).
14. Productivity data on US Bureau of Labor Statistics website plus additional BLS archived data for the USA.
15. Inklaar *et al.* (2003, table 6).
16. Meadows *et al.* (1972).
17. The real exchange rate is measured by cost competitiveness and is calculated from the IMF series of relative unit labour costs in a common currency (RULC). Source: IMF, *International Financial Statistics* website.
18. Nordhaus (2004, table 8).
19. There is a brief discussion of the idea of Fordism and evidence of the productivity problems encountered in the motor industry and elsewhere even before 1973 in Glyn *et al.* (1990).
20. Maddison (1995, table D).
21. Bacon and Eltis (1976) was the classic exposition of this line of argument in the UK.
22. Gorton and Schmid (2000), whose article on German co-determination is colourfully entitled 'Class struggle inside the firm', do find significant negative effects on share prices and on profits in the early 1990s where worker representatives constitute a half of the boards.

Chapter 2

1. Friedman (1968).
2. Dore *et al.* (1994).
3. In a similar vein the presentation of US policy in terms of controlling the money supply meant that politically unpopular increases in interest rates could be blamed on market pressures (Mussa 1994).
4. Blanchard and Muet (1993).
5. For example, Ball (1999).
6. The reserve army was supposed by Marx to keep the real wage in check. He argued that a sharp rise in real wages cuts into profits and thus reduces capital accumulation and the demand for labour. This reduces employment and the rise in the reserve army pushes real wages back down. The NAIRU by contrast is usually discussed in terms of holding

down money wage increases and inflation. However as we saw earlier (Fig. 1.2 and 1.3) rising inflation and squeezed profits coincided in the 1970s, indicating that the wage pressure was partly reflected in faster inflation and partly in profit squeeze. Exactly the reverse happened in the 1980s and 1990s.

7. This chart follows Blanchard and Philippon (2004) who find a significant relationship using different periods and a different strike measure. They interpret the strike measure as reflecting an underlying lack of 'trust' in industrial relations. The measure for strikes used here is the median across countries of days occupied per 1,000 workers in industry and transport (which typically is more organized and with higher strike levels than most of the service sector).

8. Over the period 1960–73 Denmark, Sweden, Norway and Finland ran budget surpluses averaging more than 3% of GDP.

9. There are differing recollections as to how gracefully Clinton acceded to bond market pressures. Robert Rubin, having moved from Wall Street to head Clinton's National Economic Council, recalls Clinton's response at the crucial meeting as ' "I get it". Deficit reduction he said had become the threshold issue ... this is what we need to get the economy back on track' (Rubin 2003: 119). An alternative account has Clinton responding to discussion of the impact of deficit reduction on interest rates: 'You mean to tell me that the success of the program and my re-election hinges on the Federal Reserve and a bunch of fucking bond traders' (Woodward 1994: 84).

10. For example, European Commission (2000: 21).

11. The *Financial Times* commented on the 2003 Bush tax cut: 'the lunatics are now in charge of the asylum ... Proposals to slash federal spending, particularly on social programs is a tricky electoral proposition, but a fiscal crisis offers the tantalising prospect of forcing such cuts through the back door' (quoted by Krugman 2004: 446).

12. Bortolotti and Siniscalco (2004) and Megginson *et al.* (2005).

13. Card and Freeman (2004, table 1.1).

14. See Green and Haskel (2004) for a recent review of UK privatization, which is relied on in the next few paragraphs.

15. Willner (2003) provides a sceptical review.

16. Reported in OECD (2003a: 36).

17. In 1979 in the UK the real rate of return on the replacement cost capital of the nationalized industries was 0.6% as compared to 8.4% in the private sector (public corporations calculated from tables 6.2, 14.3 and 14.7 of UK *National Accounts*, 1990 edition: private

non-financial companies profit rate from ONS company profitability release).

18. The most dramatic case of pre-privatization rationalization was coal mining where only 12 pits were functioning by the time of privatization in 1994 compared to 172 before the 1984-5 miners' strike (see Chapter 5), and productivity on the remaining pits had doubled (Glyn and Machin 1997).

19. This does not refer to the whole price of gas or electricity, but only to the value added by the industry to the coal and gas supplies. Data for prices of the energy and water shown in Green and Haskel (2004, fig. 2.1) suggest that the price fall took place in gas and electricity with water prices rising substantially.

20. Green and Haskel (2004: 74, 99) for these points.

21. The immediate gain for subscribing to BT shares was not untypical. Megginson and Netter (2001, table 8) report a study suggesting that UK privatizations generated an average immediate price increase over the offer price of about 40%.

22. Itoh (2005).

23. OECD (1983, table 18).

24. Nicoletti *et al.* (2001, table 12).

25. OECD (2005 fig. 4.4).

26. Joumard *et al.* (2003).

27. Domberger and Jensen (1997: 72-5).

28. HM Treasury (2003*b*: 13).

29. Grout and Stevens (2003: 230).

30. ONS (2004).

31. This is detailed in Pollock (2004, ch. 1).

32. OECD (1999).

33. Baker *et al.* (2005).

34. Agell (1999).

Chapter 3

1. US National Income and Product Accounts, tables 1.12, 2.1

2. Another illustration of the fact that income is less of a short-term constraint on consumption: the correlation between the annual change in real consumption and the annual change in real household disposable (post-tax) income fell in UK from 0.82 in the period 1948-73 to 0.56 for 1979-2003.

3. OECD *Economic Outlook*, June 2004, Annex tables 23, 58.
4. Lazonick and O'Sullivan (2000).
5. Gugler *et al.* (2004, table 2).
6. Shiller (2000: 8).
7. These data on executive compensation are from Hall and Murphy (2003), Coffee (2005), Bebchuk and Fried (2003) and Coffee (2003) respectively. The authoritative survey of research into CEO compensation and stock options noted the paucity and contradictory results of research into the impact of compensation on firm performance. It concluded that it was difficult to demonstrate that 'the increase in stock-based incentives has led CEOs to work harder, or smarter, or more in the interests of shareholders' (Murphy 1999: 2255–6). One recent study found that schemes for encouraging managers to own more of the company's shares raised share prices and were associated subsequently with higher reported profits (Core and Marker 2002). Given widespread massaging of earnings this is far from conclusive.
8. Lev (2003).
9. Healy and Palepu (2003).
10. Hansmann and Kraakmann (2001) quoted by Blair (2003).
11. Gugler *et al.* (2004), Morin (2000) and *Financial Times*, 31 Mar. 2005. Listing in New York evidently led to some overseas companies engaging in the same sort of exaggeration of earnings prevalent among US corporations (see Coffee 2005).
12. Hall and Soskice (2001), Allen (2005).
13. Gompers and Lerner (2001), Allen and Song (2003, table 6.1).
14. Federal Reserve Board: industrial production and capacity utilization series.
15. Davis *et al.* (1996 table 2.1 and fig. 2); Farber (2003 fig. 1–3); Pontiff *et al.*(1990).
16. Edison *et al.* (2003, tables 2 and 3).
17. *Financial Times*, 29 Sept. 2004; Obstfeld and Taylor (2003, table 2); Stultz (2005, fig. 1 and p. 8).
18. Except where limited by exchange controls individual companies could borrow abroad, but the country as a whole borrows abroad only if it is running a deficit on the current account of the balance of payments.
19. The standard deviation of current account balances roughly doubled between the mid-1980s and the early 2000s (Blanchard and Giavazzi 2002, fig. 1).

20. Calculated from the IMF, *International Financial Statistics* series for relative unit labour costs.

21. Changes in the real exchange rate may act in a stabilizing way if they offset adverse real trends or 'shocks'. The HM Treasury (2003*a*) has attempted to argue, not very convincingly, that this was typically true of UK swings in the real exchange rate.

22. Kaminsky (2003, table 4); Bordo *et al.* (2001, fig. 1 and p. 58).

23. Bordo *et al.* (2001, fig. 1, table 1 and p. 55).

24. Stiglitz (2002).

25. See, for example, the article 'How Hedge Funds are destabilising the markets' in the *Financial Times* (29 Sept. 2004) by Paul Woolley, the chairman of an investment management firm.

26. Derivatives are described by the legendary US investor Warren Buffett as 'Financial weapons of mass destruction, carrying dangers that, while now latent, are potentially lethal' (quoted in Stultz 2004: 3). Robert Rubin remarks that 'Throughout my career I had seen situations where derivatives put additional pressure on volatile markets' (2003: 288). He says that he was more concerned about derivatives than his then deputy Larry Summers, which is striking given the latter's earlier involvement in the academic literature critical of conventional assumptions of financial market efficiency.

27. In October 1998, shortly after the LTCM crisis, the dollar fell by 15% in a week. Conventional wisdom that the dollar would keep on rising relative to the yen, combined with higher interest rates in the USA, had generated huge speculative inflows into dollar assets, which were then reversed en masse when sentiment changed. 'The logic of mutually reinforcing sales meant that the harder they tried to swim away, the more they provoked the feeding frenzy. The sense of fear was palpable during the turbulent trading of 8 October' (Morris and Shin 1999: 58).

Chapter 4

1. The profit share in manufacturing increased from 30% at the beginning of the decade to 35% in 1999 but this rise would have been bigger without pressure from the high value of the dollar. Estimated from Bureau of Economic Analysis (BEA) Gross Product by Industry tables.

2. US Government (2002, table 7.1).

3. Godley, *et al.* (2004); Obstfeld and Rogoff (2004).

4. The proviso 'net' investment and savings is important here. Much business investment is financed by depreciation, but it is net investment which expands capacity in the economy.

5. The precise causal relationship between capital accumulation and growth is hotly contested. A recent study (Bond *et al.* 2004) argued that the econometric evidence confirms the importance of accumulation in determining growth.

6. Apparently those made redundant from the state firms are reluctant to take up jobs in the new export oriented factories: 'It is said that in the cities, especially those in state enterprises, workers are accustomed to the idea that "workers are masters" and "there is no exploitation in socialism", therefore they want jobs close to their home, with high wages, short work hours and easy work' (Imamura 2003: 59). On actual pay and working conditions see below.

7. Maddison excludes large repair costs and military investments which are not usually classified with investment. Stockbuilding was also extremely high in China and housing investment was high as well. The broad pattern of the capital stock growth figures for Korea, Japan and China shown in Table 4.2 is consistent with that shown by Maddison (1998).

8. Maddison (1998, table 3.9).

9. CSFB (2005, fig. 24, 27–9).

10. Brooks (2004).

11. Europe and Japan make up most of the 'non-USA OECD' category. Not included in the chart is the mass of oil producers, developing and middle income countries like India, which, together, have also gained share over the last decade.

12. In terms of the *absolute* level of GDP per capita, according to Maddison's measure China is at the level of Japan in the later 1950s and Korea/Taiwan in the mid-1970s. Such measures should be taken as no more than broadly indicative.

13. Sutcliffe (2004, fig. 2).

14. Qian (2003) provides a fascinating discussion of how the incentives for China's growth have evolved despite a path of reform which has defied the conventional wisdom.

15. 6 Asian countries including not-so-low-wage Korea, plus Poland, Czech Republic and Mexico.

16. Eichengreen *et al.* (2004); Boltho (2004, table 6); Ito and Yoshida (2004); Rumbaugh and Blancher (2004).

17. Lardy (2003).

18. Meng *et al.* (2004, table 2); Gough (2005).
19. *China Labor Bulletin* and *China Labor Watch*.
20. Calculated from WTO International Trade (2004, tables IV.1 and A.19).
21. This section draws on Sutcliffe and Glyn (2003).
22. World Bank (2003). The comparison between exports and GDP is frequently made in constant prices. However exports of manufactures tend to fall in price relatively to GDP since productivity growth is considerably faster in manufacturing than in the rest of the economy. Thus the share of employment engaged directly in exporting grows less rapidly than the volume comparison suggests; the current price ratio of exports to GDP reflects better the evolution of the share of employment engaged in exports.
23. These series are the Penn tables openness indicator (exports plus imports at current prices as a percentage of GDP, all at PPP prices) divided by 2.
24. Findlay and O'Rourke (2003, table 7).
25. The *Financial Times* (Beattie 2004) quotes Kenneth Rogoff, recently chief economist at the IMF, as claiming that only one-fifth of the US economy was subject to international competition Bhagwati *et al.* (2004) quote an estimate that 70% of US jobs are in service industries, requiring that the consumer and producer be in the same place, to which might be added construction which is not tradable. Even so the estimate of one-fifth seems on the low side, not least because a number of these jobs provide inputs into manufacturing.
26. Bhagwati *et al.* (2004); Amiti and Wei (2004, tables 4, 6).
27. Bairoch and Kozul Wright (1996).
28. See Epstein (2003) and Sinclair (2003).
29. Chiswick and Hatton (2003).

Chapter 5

1. Europe is represented here by the sum of Germany, UK, France, The Netherlands and Spain. This section is based on Glyn *et al.* (2004).
2. Webster (2000).
3. This is just an extension of the standard practice when looking at the pattern of wages which is to compare the top 10% and bottom 10% of the pay distribution.
4. Glyn (2001, table 2); Freeman (1995).
5. Berman *et al.* (1998); Autor *et al.* (2003).
6. Rowthorn and Coutts (2004).
7. Bhagwati *et al.* (2004); Rowthorn and Coutts (2004, table 2).

8. Goos and Manning (2003, table IX).

9. OECD (2004*a*); Pisani Ferry (2002).

10. Alesina *et al.* (2005); (Maddison 1995).

11. Belot and Van Ours (2000); OECD (2004*a*, table 2.A2.4).

12. Green (2006, ch. 7).

13. Mishel *et al.* (2005, table 2.6).

14. Piketty (2003). Data in Atkinson and Salverda (2004) suggest that the share of the top 1% in the UK behaved similarly to that in the USA whilst the Dutch pattern was similar to that of France.

15. Dolado *et al.* (1996).

16. Howell and Huebler (2005).

17. OECD (1999); Baker *et al.* (2005, fig. 3.7).

18. In addition there has been an increase in numbers of self-employed in the OECD since 1979. However self-employment has only grown from 9.8% of non-agricultural employment in 1979 to 11.9% and fallen in agriculture (see OECD 2000, table 5.1). It is striking that in the USA, thought of as the model for entrepreneurial opportunity, the share of self-employment in non-agricultural employment fell in the later 1980s and 1990s and is probably no higher than in 1973.

19. In the 'Ghent' system where unions administer benefits, high unemployment encourages membership (see Cecchi and Lucifora 2002). Note that the series shown here is for the median, which falls more than the mean as the latter reflects the rising membership in a few small countries, which is not typical.

20. This and the previous paragraph are based on OECD (2004*a*, ch. 3).

21. Kelly (2005).

22. Pencavel (2004).

23. Soskice (1994); Thelen and Kume (2005).

Chapter 6

1. Crotty (2002).

2. Vatter and Walker (2001).

3. Nordhaus (2002, tables 6, 7); Oliner and Sichel (reported in Gordon 2003, table 10).

4. Sharpe (2004); Foster *et al.* (2002); Baily (2002).

5. These comparisons refer to non-financial companies. As noted in Chapter 2 financial companies' profits were increasing exceptionally fast but calculating their profit rates is fraught with problems.

6. Brenner (2004) has detailed discussion of profitability movements.

7. Carlin *et al.* (2001) is the source of the Schumpeter quotation and the UK results.

8. Hoshi and Kashyap (2004).

9. Horioka (2004).

10. Because the *level* of investment was high in 1990 even maintaining it kept the capital stock growing by some 4% per year over the 1990s (see Table 5.1). This was considerably faster than the growth of output, contributing to further pressure on profitability.

11. See Boltho (2003), Gordon (2004) and Blanchard (2004) for example.

12. Nicoletti *et al.* (2001, table 12); OECD (2005, fig. 4.8).

13. Baker *et al.* (2005).

14. See Dumenil and Levy (2004, fig. 9.2) for France. The earlier trends are discussed in Armstrong *et al.* (1991). The gap in the two German series in 1991 is due more to a changed system of national accounts than to the immediate impact of including East Germany in the figures.

15. The data suggest average pre-tax profit rates for non-financial business over the period 1991–2001 of 5.6% for Germany, 11.2% for Italy and 12.2% for the UK as compared to 7.9% in the USA. French profit rates appear to be similar to those in the USA (Dumenil and Levy 2004, fig. 9.2).

16. Germany's manufacturing earned 5% on capital employed on average during 1991–2001, UK manufacturing 9.2%, Italy's 8.3% and US manufacturing 13.8%.

17. See Sinn (2003) and Carlin and Soskice (1997) for effects of unification.

18. The OECD notes that 'The evolution of aggregate wages suggests a trend towards wage moderation in the majority of OECD countries since the 1970s' (OECD 2004a: 129). The factors behind this trend are discussed in Chapter 5.

19. Maddison (1995, table 2.6).

20. Baumol (2001) gave these services the alarming title of 'asymptotically stagnant' because within them employment would become increasingly concentrated on activities where productivity could not increase (care workers rather than record keepers).

21. Baumol (2002).

22. Glyn (1994, fig. 3.2, 3.3).

23. Such a process whereby the 'gains from trade' for the North are reduced by development in the South is discussed by Samuelson (2004).

24. The estimate of the change in the capital-labour ratio is in Freeman (2005a). A shift to profits is floated as a possibility by Bhagwati *et al.* (2004). Commenting on the results of a simulation of the effects of

outsourcing of US service jobs Baily and Lawrence (2004: 267) write: 'It is not surprising to find that, if the US economy becomes more exposed to low cost labour, the result will be to shift the distribution of income towards capital'. The effects of such a shift on income distribution and the welfare state are taken up in the final chapter.

25. Nordhaus (1992).

Chapter 7

1. OECD (1997, table 1.20).
2. Lindert (2003, fig. 1–5).
3. Atkinson *et al.* (1995, table 6.9) shows shares of the top 10% in incomes earned in the market (i.e. excluding government transfers) in the later 1980s typically in the range 25–30%. Since then the share of the top 10% has tended to grow. Piketty and Saez (2003), using more comprehensive data but rather different definitions, estimate a share for the USA of more than 41% in 1998 for the top 10%, and a few percentage points higher still if capital gains are included.
4. Compare the income and tax estimates in tables 6.9 and 7.3 in Atkinson *et al.* (1995).
5. Rodrik (1997).
6. Adema's (2001) analysis of 'net social spending' (deducting taxation of benefits which are high in some Scandinavian countries and adding 'tax expenditures' like the US Earned Income Tax Credit) shows a considerably smaller dispersion than the gross shares shown in Table 7.2. However it is unlikely that the trends would be much different.
7. Lindbeck (1997).
8. Productivity data is from Bureau of Labor Statistics website; R&D from OECD (2002, fig. 2.2).
9. The various studies are far from unanimous about these trends (Atkinson 2003, fig. 1–9; Smeeding 2004, fig. 3 and 2002, fig. 4). Data for benchmark years for many countries are presented in Forster and d'Ercole (2005) and the Luxemburg Income Surveys website and these are used in Table 7.3.
10. Forster and d'Ercole (2005, Annex table A3) also report a surprising increase in the 90:10 ratio in Japan from 3.9 to 4.9 between 1985 and 1994.

11. Smeeding (2002, fig. 1) is the source for these comparisons. If the absolute difference in the 90:10 ratio is felt to be a better indicator, then the difference between the USA and Scandinavia (a difference of around 2.5 in the 90:10 ratio) is similar to that between Russia and the USA.

12. Smeeding (2004, fig. 10); OECD (2004 a, table 3.7).

13. Household receipts of rent, dividends and interest as percentage of employee compensation plus self-employment incomes ('Operating Surplus and Mixed Incomes') from OECD, National Accounts Volume II 2004, OECD website.

14. Forster and d'Ercole (2005, Annex table A.4). Real capital gains on assets such as equities should also be included in income distribution figures but there are no cross-country data available. Piketty and Saez (2001, table A7) show that realized nominal capital gains constituted some 18% of the receipts of the top 10% of income earners in the USA in 1998.

15. 'Market poverty' refers to the proportion of the population with incomes before tax and transfers which are less than a half of the national median income. Countries with strong welfare states will tend to have greater market poverty and inequality to the extent that, for example, pensioners are more dependent on state benefits and feel little need to save independently and thus have market income. The reductions in poverty for the whole population shown in Table 7.4 seem pretty similar to the corresponding data (Forster and Pearson 2002, fig. 3) for the working age population (i.e. excluding pensioners). The one exception appears to be Germany where market poverty was exceptionally low and the effect of taxes and benefits in reducing poverty was comparatively small.

16. Scanlon and Whitehead (2004, table 1).

17. Itoh (2005).

18. Forster and d'Ercole (2005, fig. 18).

19. Blanden et al. (2005, tables 1, 2 and 5) is the source for these data. Their ranking of countries is broadly consistent with the results of the earlier literature reviewed by Corak (2004).

20. The usual analysis of a high degree of capital mobility is that it forces countries to ensure that employers earn the going rate of return and that this will limit corporate taxation. However Bowles (2002) points out that such competition also implies that employers cannot earn more than the going post-tax 'world rate of profit'. The workforce then becomes the 'residual claimant' on production and would receive all

the benefit of greater work effort for example rather than having to share the gains with employers.

21. Forster and d'Ercole (2005, fig. 2 and 3); Svallfors (1997, table 3).
22. Layard (2005: 31; Frey and Stutzer (2002, fig. 4.3, 4.4). The data replies also suggest that the gap in terms of reported well-being is far greater comparing the bottom of the distribution and the middle than is the gap between the top and the middle. This implies that a more equal income distribution, especially reducing differences between top and bottom, will increase average happiness, which confirms a very old line of argument for egalitarianism.
23. Layard (2005: 63); Schor (1992); Green (2006, ch. 8); Sennett (1998).
24. Schor (2004).
25. Runciman (2005).
26. Van Parijs (2003) has a very clear exposition of these and related points and many references on Basic Income. Van Parijs (2001) contains a very helpful set of comments on Basic Income by a wide range of authors. See also the website: http://www.basicincome.org.

References

Adema, W. (2001), 'Net Social Expenditure 2nd edition,' OECD Labour Market & Social Policy Occasional Paper No. 52.

Agell, J. (1999), 'On the Benefits from Rigid Labour Markets: Norms, Market Failures and Social Insurance', *Economic Journal*, 109: F143–64.

Alesina, A., E. Glaeser, and B. Sacerdote (2001), 'Why Doesn't the US have a European-Style Welfare State', *Brookings Papers on Economic Activity*, 2:107–77.

————(2005), 'Work and Leisure in the US and Europe: Why So Different?' Harvard Institute of Economic Research Discussion Paper No. 2068.

——and R. Perotti (1995), 'Fiscal Expansions and Adjustments in OECD Countries', *Economic Policy*, 21: 207–48.

Allen, F. (2005) 'Corporate Governance in Emerging Economies', *Oxford Review of Economic Policy*, 21: 164–77.

——and W. Song (2003), 'Venture Capital and Corporate Governance,' in P. Cornelius and B. Kogut (eds.), *Corporate Governance and Capital Flows in a Global Economy*, New York: Oxford University Press.

Allsopp, C. (1982), 'Inflation' in A. Boltho (ed.) *The European Economy: Growth and Crisis*, Oxford: Oxford University Press.

Amiti, M. and S-J. Wei (2004), 'Fear of Service Outsourcing: Is it Justified?' NBER Working Paper 10808.

Arrighi, G. (2003), 'Tracking Global Turbulence', *New Left Review*, Mar./Apr.: 5–72.

Armstrong, P., A. Glyn, and J. Harrison (1991), *Capitalism since 1945*, Oxford: Blackwells (1st edn. published in 1984 by Fontana as *Capitalism since World War II*).

Atkinson, A. (1996), 'The Case for a Participation Income', *The Political Quarterly*, 67(1): 67–70.

——(2003), 'Economic Inequality in OECD Countries; Data and Explanations', CesIFO Discussion Paper.

Atkinson, A., L. Rainwater, and T. Smeeding (1995), *Income Distribution in OECD Countries*, Paris: OECD.

—— and W. Salverda (2004), 'Top Incomes in the United Kingdom and the Netherlands over the Twentieth Century,' Nuffield College, Oxford.

Autor, D., F. Levy, and R. Murnane (2003), 'The Skill Content of Recent Technological Change: An Empirical Investigation,' *Quarterly Journal of Economics*, 118(4): 1279–323.

Bacon, R., and W. Eltis (1976), *Britain's Economic Problem: Too Few Producers*, Basingstoke: Macmillan.

Baily, M. (2002), 'The New Economy: Post-Mortem or Second Wind', *Journal of Economic Perspectives*, 16(2): 3–22.

—— and R. Lawrence (2004), 'What Happened to the Great U.S. Job Machine: The Role of Trade and Electronic Offshoring', *Brookings Papers on Economic Activity*, 2: 211–84.

Bairoch, P., and R. Kozul-Wright (1996), 'Globalization Myths: Some Historical Reflections on Integration, Industrialisation and Growth in the World Economy', in R. Kozul-Wright and R. Rowthorn (eds.), *Multinational Corporations and the Global Economy*, Basingstoke: Macmillan.

Baker, D., A. Glyn, D. Howell, and J. Schmitt (2005), 'Labour Market Institutions and Unemployment: A Critical Assessment of the Cross-Country Evidence', in D. Howell (ed.), *Fighting Unemployment: The Limits of Free Market Orthodoxy*, New York: Oxford University Press.

Ball, L. (1999), 'Aggregate Demand and Long-Run Unemployment', *Brookings Papers on Economic Activity*, 2: 189–251.

Bank for International Settlements (1998), *Annual Report*, Basle: BIS.

——(1999), *Annual Report*, Basle: BIS.

——(2005), *Annual Report*, Basle: BIS.

Bank of England (2005), *Inflation Report*, London: Bank of England.

Batchelor, R., R. Major, R. Morgan, and A. Morgan (1980), *Industrialisation and the Basis for Trade*, Cambridge: Cambridge University Press.

Baumol, W. (2001), 'Paradoxes of the Services: Exploding Costs, Resistent Demand', in T. ten Raa and R. Schettkat (eds.), *The Growth of Service Industries: High Costs, Strong Demand*, Cheltenham: Edward Elgar.

——(2002), *The Free Market Innovation Machine: Analysing the Growth Miracle of Capitalism*, Princeton: Princeton University Press.

Beattie, A. (2004), 'Why are US economists so optimistic?' *Financial Times*, 11 Jan.

Bebchuk, L. A., and J. M. Fried (2003), 'Executive Compensation as an Agency Problem', *Journal of Economic Perspectives*, 17(3): 71–92.

Belot, M., and J. Van Ours (2000). 'Does the Recent Success of some OECD Countries in Lowering their Unemployment Rate Lie in the Clever Design of their Economic Reforms?' IZA Discussion Paper No. 147.

Berman, E., J. Bound and S. Machin (1998), 'Implications of Skill-Biased Technical Change: International Evidence', *Quarterly Journal of Economics*, 113(4): 1215–44.

Bertola, G., F. Blau, and L. Kahn (2001), 'Comparative Analysis of Labor Market Outcomes: Lessons for the US from International Experience', NBER Working Paper 8526.

Besley, T., and M. Ghatak (2003). 'Incentives, Choice and Accountability in the Provision of Public Services', *Oxford Review of Economic Policy*, 19(2): 235–49.

Bhadhuri, A. (1993), 'The Economics and Politics of Social Democracy' in P. O. Bardhan, M. Datta-Chaudhuri, and T. Krishnan (eds.) *Development and Change: Essays in Honour of K. N. Raj*, Delhi: Oxford University Press.

Bhagwati, J., A. Panagariya, and T. Srinivasan (2004), 'The Muddles over Outsourcing', *Journal of Economic Perspectives*, 18(4): 93–114.

Blair, M. (2003), 'Shareholder Value, Corporate Governance, and Corporate performance', in P. Cornelius and B. Kogut (eds.), *Corporate Governance and Capital Flows in a Global Economy*, New York: Oxford University Press.

Blanchard, O. (2004), 'The Economic Future of Europe', NBER Working Paper 10310.

—— and F. Giavazzi (2002), 'Current Account Deficits in the Euro Area: The End of the Feldstein-Horioka Puzzle?', *Brookings Papers on Economic Activity*, 2: 143–210.

—— and P.-A. Muet (1993), 'Competitiveness through Disinflation: An Assessment of the French Macroeconomic Strategy', *Economic Policy*, 16: 11–56.

—— and T. Philippon (2004), 'The Quality of Labor Relations and Unemployment', NBER Working Paper 10590.

Blanchflower, D. and A. Bryson (2003), 'The Union Wage Premium in the US and UK', LSE Centre for Economic Performance Discussion Paper No.6.

—— and A. Oswald (2004) 'Well-being over time in Britain and the USA' *Journal of Public Economics* 88: 1359–86.

Blanden, J., P. Gregg, and S. Machin (2005), 'Intergeneration Mobility in Europe and North America', Centre for Economic Performance, Apr.

Boltho, A. (2003), 'What's Wrong with Europe', *New Left Review*, 22 July/5–26 Aug.

Boltho, A. (2004), 'China—Can Rapid Economic Growth Continue?', *The Singapore Economic Review*, 49(2): 255–72.

Bond, S., A. Leblebicoglu, and F. Sciantarelli (2004), 'Capital Accumulation and Growth: A New Look at the Empirical Evidence', mimeo, Nuffield College, Oxford.

Boone, L., and N. Girouard (2002), 'The Stock Market, the Housing Market and Consumer Behaviour', *OECD Economic Studies*, 2: 175–200.

Bordo, M., B. Eichengreen, D. Klingebiel, and S. Pereia (2001), 'Is the Crisis Problem Growing More Severe', *Economic Policy*, 32: 51–82.

Bortolotti, B., and D. Siniscalco (2004), *The Challenges of Privatisation: An International Analysis*, Oxford: Oxford University Press.

Bosworth, B., and S. Collins (2003), 'The Empirics of Growth: An Update', *Brookings Papers on Economic Activity*, 2: 113–206.

Bowles, S. (2002), 'Globalisation and Redistribution: Feasible Egalitarianism in a Competitive World', in R. Freeman (ed.), *Inequality around the World*, Basingstoke: Palgrave Macmillan.

Brenner, R. (1998), 'The Economics of Global Turbulence', *New Left Review*, 1(229): 1–265.

——(2002), *The Boom and the Bubble*, London: Verso.

——(2004), 'New Boom or New Bubble', *New Left Review*, Jan./Feb.: 57–102.

Brooks, R. (2004), 'Labor Market Performance and Prospects', in E. Prasad (ed.), *China's Growth and Integration into the World Economy*, IMF Occasional Paper 232.

Bruno, M., and J. Sachs (1985), *The Economics of Worldwide Stagflation*, Oxford: Blackwell.

Card, D., and R. Freeman (2004), 'What have Two Decades of Economic Reform Delivered', in D. Card, R. Blundell, and R. Freeman, *Seeking a Premier-League Economy: The Economic Effects of British Economic Reforms, 1980–2000*, Chicago: University of Chicago Press.

——F. Kramarz, and T. Lemieux (1999), 'Changes in the Relative Structure of Wages and Employment: A Comparison of the US, Canada and France', *Canadian Journal of Economics*, 32(4): 843–77.

Carlin, W., J. Haskel, and P. Seabright (2001), 'Understanding the "Essential Fact about Capitalism": Markets, Competition and Creative Destruction', *National Institute Economic Review*, 175: 67–84.

——and D. Soskice (1997), 'Shocks to the System: The German Political Economy under Stress', *National Institute Economic Review*, 1: 57–76.

Cassidy, J. (2002), *Dot-Con*. Harmondsworth: Penguin.

Cecchi, D., and C. Lucifora (2002), 'Unions and Labour Market Institutions in Europe', *Economic Policy*, 35: 363–408.

Chan, A. (2003), 'Race to the Bottom', *China Perspectives*, Apr.: 41–9.

Chan, N., M. Getmansky, S. Haas, and A. Lo (2005), 'Systemic Risk and Hedge Funds', NBER Working Paper 11200.

Charlwood, A. (2003), 'The Anatomy of Union Decline in Britain: 1990–1998', Centre for Economic Performance Discussion Paper 601, London School of Economics.

Chiswick, B., and T. Hatton (2003), 'International Migration and the Integration of Labour Markets', M. Bordo, A. Taylor, and J. Williamson (eds.), *Globalisation in Historical Perspective*, Chicago: University of Chicago Press.

Coffee, J. (2003), 'What Caused Enron? A Capsule Social and Economic History of the 1990s', in P. Cornelius and B. Kogut (eds.), *Corporate Governance and Capital Flows in a Global Economy*, New York: Oxford University Press.

——(2005), 'A Theory of Corporate Scandals: Why the USA and Europe Differ', *Oxford Review of Economic Policy*, 21(2): 198–211.

Comin, D., and T. Philippon (2005), 'The Rise in Finn-Level Volatility: Causes and Consequences', NBER Working Paper 11388.

Corak, M. (2004), 'Do Poor Children become Poor Adults', UNICEF Innocenti Research Centre.

Core, J., and D. Marker (2002), 'Performance Consequences of Mandatory Increases in Executive Stock Ownership', *Journal of Financial Economics*, 64: 317–40.

Crotty, J. (2002), 'The Effects of "Financialisation" and Increased Competition on the Performance of Non-Financial Companies in the Neo-Liberal Era', mimeo, UMASS Amherst.

CSFB (2005), 'Understanding China's profit cycle', in *China Market Strategy*, Mar.

Davis, S., J. Haltiwanger, and S. Schuh (1996), *Job Creation and Destruction*, Cambridge, Mass.: MIT Press.

DeLong, B., and B. Eichengreen (2002), 'International Finance and Crises in Emerging Markets' in J. Frankel and P. Orszag (eds.), *American Economic Policy in the 1990s*, Cambridge, Mass.: MIT Press.

Dertouzos, M., R. Lester, and R. Solow (1989), *Made in America: Regaining the Competitive Edge*, Cambridge, Mass.: MIT Press.

Devereux, M., R. Griffith, and A. Klemm (2002), 'Corporate Income Tax Reforms and International Tax Competition', *Economic Policy*, 35: 451–95.

Dodd, R. (2005), 'Credit Derivatives Trigger Near Systemic Melt down', Derivatives Study Centre Special Brief 25, http://www.financial policy.org.

Dolado, J., F. Kramarz, S. Machin, A. Manning, D. Margoilis, and C. Teulings (1996), 'The Economic Impact of Minimum Wages in Europe', *Economic Policy*, 23: 317–72.

Domberger, S., and P. Jensen (1997), 'Contracting out by the Public Sector: Theory, Evidence, Prospects', *Oxford Review of Economic Policy*, 18(4): 67–78.

Dore, R., R. Boyer, and Z. Mars (1994), *The Return of Incomes Policy* London: Pinter Publishers.

Dumenil, G., and D. Levy (2004), *Capital Resurgent*, Cambridge, Mass.: Harvard University Press.

Dyck, A., and L. Zingales (2003), 'The Bubble and the Media', in P. Cornelius and B. Kogut (eds.), *Corporate Governance and Capital Flows in a Global Economy*, New York: Oxford University Press.

Edison, H., M. Klein, L. Rici, and T. Slok (2003), 'Capital Account Liberalisation and Economic Performance: Survey and Synthesis', at http://fletcher.tufts.edu/faculty/klein/pdfs/CALandEP_aug2204.pdf

Eichengreen, B. (2005), 'Financial Instability', in B. Lomborg (ed) *Global Crises, Global Solutions*, Cambridge, Cambridge University Press.

——Y. Rhee, and H. Tong (2004), 'The Impact of China on the Exports of Other Asian Countries', NBER Working Paper 10768.

Engels, F. (1847/1976), 'The Free Trade Congress in Brussels', in K. Marx and F. Engels, *Collected Works*, vol. 6, London: Lawrence and Wishart, 1976; 1st pub. 1847.

Epstein, G. (1981), 'Domestic Stagflation and Monetary Policy: The Federal Reserve and the Hidden Election', in T. Ferguson and J. Rogers (eds.), *The Hidden Election*, New York: Pantheon Press.

——(2003), 'The Role and Control of Multinational Corporations in the World Economy', in J. Michie (ed.), *The Handbook of Globalisation*, Cheltenham: Edward Elgar.

Erdem, E., and A. Glyn (2000), 'Employment Growth, Structural Change and Capital Accumulation', in Thijs ten Raa and Ronald Schettkat (eds.), *Services: High Costs, Strong Demand*, Cheltenham: Edward Elgar,

Esping-Andersen, G. (1990), *Three Worlds of Welfare Capitalism*, Princeton: Princeton University Press.

——(2004), 'Unequal Opportunities and Social Inheritance', in M. Corak (ed.), *Generational Income Mobility in North America and Europe*, Cambridge: Cambridge University Press.

European Commission (2000), *Public Finances in EMU 2000*, European Economy No. 3.

Farber, H. (2003), 'Job Loss in the United States 1981–2001', Princeton University Industrial Relations Section Working Paper No. 471.

Findlay, R., and K. O'Rourke (2003), 'Commodity Market Integration 1500–2000', in M. Bordo, A. Taylor and J. Williamson (eds.), *Globalisation in Historical Perspective*, Chicago: University of Chicago Press.

Fforde, J. (1983), 'Setting Monetary Objectives', *Bank of England Quarterly Bulletin*, June.

Forster, M., and M. Mira d'Ercole (2005), 'Income Distribution and Poverty in OECD Countries in the Second Half of the 1990s', OECD Social, Employment and Migration Working Papers No. 22.

—— and M. Pearson (2002), 'Income Distribution and Poverty in the OECD Area: Trends and Driving Forces', *OECD Economic Studies*, 34: 7–39

Fortin, N. (2005), 'Gender Role Attitudes and Labour Market Outcomes of Women across OECD Countries' *Oxford Review of Economic Policy*, 21(3).

Foster, L., J. Haltiwanger, and C. Krizan (2002), 'The Link between Aggregate and Micro Productivity Growth: Evidence from Retail Trade', NBER Working Paper 9120.

Frankel, J. (1994), 'Exchange Rate Policy', in M. Feldstein (ed.), *American Economic Policy in the 1980s*, Chicago: University of Chicago Press.

Freeman, R. (1995), 'The Limits of Wage Flexibility to Curing Unemployment', *Oxford Review of Economic Policy*, 11(1): 63–72.

——(2005a), 'What Really Ails Europe (and America): The Doubling of the Global Workforce', The Globalist http://www.theglobalist.com 3 June.

——(2005b), 'Does Globalisation of the Scientific/Engineering Workforce Threaten US Economic Leadership', NBER Working Paper 11457

Frey, B., and A. Stutzer (2002), *Happiness and Economics*, Princeton: Princeton University Press.

Friedman, M. (1968), 'The Role of Monetary Policy', *American Economic Review*, 58 (Mar.): 1–17.

Fukuo, M. (2003), 'Japan's Lost Decade and its Financial System', *World Economy*, 26(3): 365–84.

Ginsburg, P. (1990), *A History of Contemporary Italy*, Harmondsworth: Penguin Books.

Glyn, A. (1994), 'Northern Growth and Environmental Constraints', in V. Bhaskar and A. Glyn (eds.), *The North, the South and the Environment*, New York: St Martins Press.

——(1997), 'Does Aggregate Profitability *Really* Matter', *Cambridge Journal of Economics*, 21: 593–619.

——(2001), 'Inequalities of Employment and Wages in OECD Countries', *Oxford Bulletin of Economics and Statistics*, Special Issue 63: 697–714.

Glyn, A., A. Hughes, A. Lipietz, and A. Singh (1990), 'The Rise and Fall of the Golden Age', in S. Marglin and J. Schor (eds.), *The Golden Age of Capitalism: Lessons for the 1990s*, Oxford: Oxford University Press.

—— and S. Machin (1997), 'Colliery Closures and the Decline of the UK Coal Industry', *British Journal of Industrial Relations*, 35(2): 197–214.

Glyn, A., Salverda, W., Moeller, J., Schmitt, J., and Sollogub, M. (2004), 'Employment Differences in Services: The Role of Wages, Productivity and Demand', DEMPATEM Working Paper 12, Amsterdam Institute of Advanced Labour Studies.

——and B. Sutcliffe (1971), 'The Critical Condition of British Capital', *New Left Review*, 1(66): 3–33.

————(1972), *British Capitalism, Workers and the Profits Squeeze*, Harmondsworth: Penguin.

Godley, W., A. Izurieta, and G. Zezza (2004), 'Prospects and Policies for the US Economy', *Strategic Analysis*, Aug. Levy Economics Institute of Bard College.

Gompers, P., and J. Lerner (2001), 'The Venture Capital Revolution', *Journal of Economic Perspectives*, 15(2): 145–68.

Goodhart, C., B. Hoffmann, and M. Segoviano (2004), 'Bank Regulation and Macroeconomic Fluctuations', *Oxford Review of Economic Policy*, 20(4): 591–615.

Goodman, P., and P. Pan (2004), 'Chinese Workers pay for Wal-Mart's Low Prices', *Washington Post Foreign Service*, 8 Feb. p. A01.

Goos, M., and A. Manning (2003), 'Lousy and Lovely Jobs: The Rising Polarisation of Work in Britain', LSE Centre for Economic Performance Discussion Paper No. 604.

Gordon, P., and S. Meunier (2001), *The French Challenge*, Washington: Brookings Institution.

Gordon, R. (2003), 'Exploding Productivity Growth: Context, Causes and Implications', *Brookings Papers on Economic Activity*, 2: 207–98.

——(2004), 'Why was Europe Left at the Station when America's Productivity Locomotive Departed', at http://www.faculty-web.at.northwestern.edu/economics/gordon/P368-CEPR.pdf

Gorton, G., and F. Schmid (2000), 'Class Struggle inside the Firm: A Study of German Codetermination', NBER Working Paper 7945.

Gough, N. (2005), 'Trouble on the Line', *Time Asia Magazine*, Jan.

Green, F. (2006), *Demanding Work: The Paradox of Job Quality in the Affluent Economy*, Princeton: Princeton University Press.

Green, R., and J. Haskel (2004), 'Seeking a Premier-League Economy: The Role of Privatisation', in D. Card, R. Blundell, and R. Freeman, *Seeking a Premier-League Economy: The Economic Effects of British Economic Reforms, 1980–2000*, Chicago: University of Chicago Press.

Gregory, P. and R. Stuart (1986), *Soviet Economic Structure and Performance*, 3rd edn., New York: Harper & Row.

Grout, P., and M. Stevens (2003), 'The Assessment: Financing and Managing Public Services', *Oxford Review of Economic Policy*, 19(2): 215–34.

Gugler, K., D. Mueller, and B. Yurtoglu (2004), 'Corporate Governance and Globalisation', *Oxford Review of Economic Policy*, 20(1): 129–56.

Halberstam, D. (1987), *The Reckoning*, London: Bantam Books.

Hall, B. J., and K. J. Murphy (2003), 'The Trouble with Stock Options' *Journal of Economic Perspectives*, 17(3): 49–70.

Hall, P., and D. Soskice (2001), 'An Introduction to Varieties of Capitalism', in P. Hall and D. Soskice (eds.), *Varieties of Capitalism*, Oxford: Oxford University Press.

Hansmann, H., and R. Kraakmann (2001), 'The End of History for Corporate Law', *Georgetown University Law Review*, 89: 439–68.

Harvey, D. (2005), *A Brief History of Neoliberalism*, Oxford: Oxford University Press.

Healy, P. M., and K. G. Palepu (2003), 'The Fall of Enron' *Journal of Economic Perspectives*, 17(2): 3–26.

HM Treasury (2003a), *The Exchange Rate and Macroeconomic Adjustment*, EMU Study.

——(2003b), *Meeting the PFI Challenge*, www.hm-treasury.gov.uk./media//648B2/PFI_604.pdf.

Holmstrom, B., and S. Kaplan (2003), 'The State of US Corporate Governance: What's Right and What's Wrong', NBER Discussion Paper 9613.

Horioka, C. (2004), 'The Stagnation of Household Consumption in Japan', mimeo, NBER, Cambridge, Mass.

Hoshi, T., and A. Kashyap (2004), 'Japan's Financial Crisis and Economic Stagnation', *Journal of Economic Perspectives*, 18(1): 3–26.

Howell, D., and F. Huebler (2005), 'Wage Compression and the Unemployment Crisis', in D. Howell (ed.), *Fighting Unemployment: The Limits of Free Market Orthodoxy*, New York: Oxford University Press.

Huber, E., and J. Stephens (2001), 'The Social Democratic Welfare State', in A. Glyn (ed.), *Social Democracy in Neoliberal Times*, Oxford: Oxford University Press.

IMF (2003). 'Unemployment and Labor Market Institutions: Why Reforms Pay Off', *World Economic Outlook*, Apr.: 129–50.

——(2005), *Global Financial Stability Report*, Apr.

Imamura, H. (2003), 'Unemployment Problem and Unemployment Insurance in China', *Far Eastern Studies*, Mar. 45–67.

Inklaar, R., H. Wu, and B. van Ark (2003), 'Losing Ground: Japanese Labour Productivity and Unit Labor Costs in Manufacturing in Comparison to the US', Groningen Growth and Development Centre Research Memorandum GD-64.

Ito, H. and Y. Yoshida (2004), 'How does China compete with Japan in the US market', www.etsg.org

Itoh, M. (1990), *The World Economic Crisis and Japanese Capitalism*, Basingstoke: Macmillan.

—— (2005), 'The Japanese Economy in Structural Difficulties', Tokyo.

Iversen, T. (2001), 'The Choices for Scandinavian Social Democracy' in A. Glyn (ed.), *Social Democracy in Neoliberal Times*, Oxford: Oxford University Press.

Jenkinson, T. (2003), 'Private Finance', *Oxford Review of Economic Policy*, 19(2): 323–34.

Jensen, M. (2003), 'The Agency Costs of Overvalued Equity', *CES ifo Forum*, 14–16.

Joumard, I., P. Kongsrud, Y.-S. Nam, and R. Price (2003), 'Enhancing the Cost Effectiveness of Public Spending: Experience in OECD Economies', *OECD Economic Studies*, 37(2): 109–61.

Jürgens, U., and R. Rehbehn (2004), 'China's Changing Role in Industrial Value Chains', WZB Discussion Paper SP III 2004302, Berlin.

Kalecki, M. (1990, 1943), 'Political Aspects of Full Employment', 1st pub. *Political Quarterly*, 14: 322–31; repr. in J. Osiatynski (ed.), *Collected Works of Michal Kalecki*, Oxford: Oxford University Press, 1990.

Kaminsky, G. (2003), 'Varieties of Currency Crises', NBER Working Paper 10193.

Kelly, J. (2005), 'The Resurgence of Political Strikes in Western Europe', Birkbeck College.

Kenworthy, L., and J. Pontusson (2004), 'Rising Inequality and the Politics of Redistribution in Affluent Countries', mimeo. Cornell.

Keynes, J. (1919), *The Economic Consequences of the Peace*, London: Macmillan.

Klein, M., S. Schuh, and R. Triest (2000), 'Job Creation, Job Destruction and the Real Exchange Rate', NBER Working Paper 7466.

Kogut, B., and A. Metiu (2001), 'Open-Source Software Development and Distributed Innovation', *Oxford Review of Economic Policy*, 17(2): 248–64.

Korpi, W., and J. Palme (1998), 'The Paradox of Redistribution and Strategies of Equality', *American Sociological Review*, 63(5), 661–87.

Krugman, P. (2004), 'Greed is Bad', in *The Great Unravelling*, New York: Norton.

Lardy, N. (2003), 'Liberalisation and its role in China's Economic Growth', http://www.imf.org/external/np/apd/seminars/2003/newdelhi/lardy.pdf

Layard, R. (2005), *Happiness*, London: Allen Lane.

Lazonick, W., and M. O'Sullivan (2000), 'Maximising Shareholder Value—A New Ideology for Corporate Governance', *Economy and Society*, 29(1): 12–35.

Lev, B. (2003), 'Corporate Earnings: Fact and Fiction', *Journal of Economic Perspectives*, 17(2): 27–50.

Lindbeck, A. (1997), 'The Swedish Experiment', *Journal of Economic Literature*, 35(3): 1273–319.

Lindert, P. (2003), 'Why the Welfare State Looks like a Free Lunch'. NBER Working Paper 9869.

Lundberg, E. (1985), 'The Rise and Fall of the Swedish Model', *Journal of Economic Literature*, 23: 1–36.

Lundsgaard, J. (2002), 'Competition and Efficiency in Publicly Funded Services', *OECD Economic Studies*, No. 35: 79–126.

MacKenzie, D. (2003), 'Long-Term Capital Management and the Sociology of Arbitrage', *Economy and Society*, 32(3): 349–80.

Maddison, A. (1991), *Dynamic Forces in Capitalist Development*, Oxford: Oxford University Press.

——(1995), *Monitoring the World Economy, 1820–1992*, Paris: OECD.

——(1998), *Chinese Economic Performance in the Long Run*, Paris: OECD.

——(2001), *The World Economy: Historical Statistics*. OECD: CD rom.

Mankiw, G. (1999), Comment on Ball (1999), *Brookings Papers on Economic Activity*, 2: 237–41.

Manning, A. (2004), 'We Can Work It Out: The Impact of Technological Change on the Demand for Low-Skill Workers', LSE Centre for Economic Performance Discussion Paper 640.

Martin, B., and Rowthorn, B. (2004), 'Will Stability Last', mimeo. Cambridge.

Marx, K. (1867, 1968), *Capital, vol. I*, London: Lawrence and Wishart.

Meadows, D., D., Meadows, J., Randers and W. Behrens (1972), *The Limits to Growth*, New York: Universe Books.

Megginson, W., and J. Netter (2001), 'From State to Market: A Survey of Empirical Studies on Privatisation', *Journal of Economic Literature*, 39: 321–89.

——and C. Chahyadi (2005), 'Size and Impact of Privatisation—A Survey of Empirical Studies', CESifo DICE Report 3(1): 3–11.

Meltzer, A. (2002), 'Comment on Between Meltdown and Moral Hazard' in J. Frankel and P. Orzag (eds.), *American Economic Policy in the 1990s*, Cambridge, Mass.: MIT Press.

Meng, X., R. Gregory, and Y. Wang (2004), 'Poverty, Inequality and Growth in Urban China, 1986–2000', ANU, August.

Metcalf, D. (2004), 'British Unions: Resurgence or Perdition? An Economic Analysis', in S. Fernie and D. Metcalf (eds.), *British Unions: Resurgence or Perdition*, London: Routledge.

Milne, S. (1994), *The Enemy Within*, London: Verso.

Mishel, L., J. Bernstein, and S. Allegretto (2005), *The State of Working America 2004/2005*. Ithaca, NY: Cornell University Press.

Morin, F. (2000), 'A Transformation of the French Model of Shareholding and Management', *Economy and Society*, 29(1): 36–53.

Morris, S., and H. Shin (1999), 'Risk Management with Interdependent Choice', *Oxford Review of Economic Policy*, 15(3): 52–62.

Motonishi, T., and H. Yoshikawa (1999), 'Causes of the Long Stagnation in Japan during the 1990s: Financial or Real?' NBER Working Paper 7531.

Murphy, K., (1999), 'Executive Compensation' in O. Ashenfelter and D. Card, *Handbook of Labor Economics*. Amsterdam: Elsevier.

Mussa, M. (1994), 'Monetary Policy', in M. Feldstein (ed.), *American Economic Policy in the 1980s*, Chicago: University of Chicago Press.

Navarro, V., J. Schmitt, and J. Astudillo (2004), 'Is Globalisation Undermining the Welfare State', *Cambridge Journal of Economics*, 28: 135–52.

Nicoletti, G., A. Bassanini, E. Ernst, S. Jean, P. Santiago, and P. Swaim (2001), 'Product and Labour Market Interactions in OECD Countries', OECD Economics Department Working Paper No. 312.

Nickell, S., and B. Bell (1995), 'The Collapse in Demand for the Unskilled and Unemployment across the OECD', *Oxford Review of Economic Policy*, 11(1): 40–62.

Nordhaus, W. (1992), 'Lethal Model 2: The Limits to Growth Revisited', *Brookings Papers on Economic Activity*, 2: 1–60.

——(2002), 'Productivity Growth and the New Economy', *Brookings Papers on Economic Activity*, 2: 211–65.

——(2004), 'Retrospective on the Post-War Productivity Slowdown', *Cowles Foundation Discussion Paper* No. 1494.

Notermans, T. (1993), 'The Abdication from National Policy Autonomy', *Politics and Society* 21(2): 133–67.

Nove, A. (1977), *The Soviet Economic System*, London: George Allen & Unwin.

Obstfeld, M., and K. Rogoff (2005), 'Global Current Account Imbalances and Exchange Rate Adjustments' *Brookings Papers on Economic Activity* 1: 67–146.

—— and A. Taylor (2003), 'Globalization and Capital Markets', in M. Bordo, A. Taylor, and J. Williamson (eds.), *Globalisation in Historical Perspective*, Chicago: University of Chicago Press.

OECD (1977), *Towards Full Employment and Price Stability*, Paris: OECD.

——(1983), *Economic Survey of France*, Paris: OECD.

——(1990), *National Accounts of Member Countries*, Paris: OECD.

——(1994a), *OECD Jobs Study Evidence and Explanations, Part I: Labor Market Trends and Underlying Forces of Change. Part II: The Adjustment Potential of the Labor Market*, Paris: OECD.

——(1994b), *OECD Jobs Study: Facts, Analysis, Strategies*, Paris: OECD.

——(1997), *Literacy Skills for the Knowledge Economy*, Paris: OECD.

——(1999), *Implementing the Jobs Study*, Paris: OECD.

——(2000), *Employment Outlook*, Paris: OECD.

——(2001), *Ageing and Income*, Paris: OECD.

——(2002), *Economic* Outlook, June, Paris: OECD.

——(2003a), *Privatising State Owned Enterprises*, Paris: OECD.

——(2003b), *The Sources of Economic Growth in OECD Countries*, Paris: OECD.

——(2004a), *Employment Outlook*, Paris: OECD.

——(2004b), *Economic Outlook*, June, Paris: OECD.

——(2005), *Economic Policy Reforms*, Paris: OECD.

Ofek, E., and M.Richardson (2002), 'The Valuation and Rationality of Internet Stock Prices', *Oxford Review of Economic Policy*, 18(3): 265–87.

Office of National Statistics (various dates), *Labour Market Trends*.

——(2004), 'Jobs in the Public Sector—mid 2003', *Labour Market Trends*, 112(7).

Parenteau, R. (2005), 'The late 1990s US Bubble: Financialisation in the Extreme', in G. Epstein (ed.), *Financialisation and the World Economy*, Cheltenham: Edward Elgar.

Pencavel, J. (2004), 'The Surprising Retreat of Union Britain', in D. Card, R. Blundell, and R. Freeman, *Seeking a Premier-League Economy: The Economic Effects of British Economic Reforms, 1980–2000*, Chicago: University of Chicago Press.

Piketty, T. (2003), 'Income Inequality in France, 1901–1998', *Journal of Political Economy*, 111(5): 1004–42.

——and Saez, E. (2001), 'Income Inequality in the USA, 1913–98', NBER Working Paper 8467.

————(2003), 'Income Inequality in the United States, 1913–98', *Quarterly Journal of Economics*, 118(1): 1–39.

Pisani Ferry (2002), 'The Surprising French Employment Performance', CESifo Working Paper No 1078.

Plender, J. (2005), 'Shock of the New: A Changed Financial Landscape may be Eroding Resistance to Systemic Risk', *Financial Times*, 16 Feb.

Pollock, A. (2004), *NHS plc*, London: Verso.

Pontiff, J., A. Shleifer, and M. Weisbach (1990), 'Reversions of Excess Pension Assets after Takeovers', *Rand Journal of Economics*, 21: 600–13.

Pontusson, J. (1987), 'Radicalisation and retreat in Swedish social democracy', *New Left Review*, 1(165): 3–33.

——(1992), *The Limits of Social Democracy*, Ithaca, NY: Cornell University Press.

Porter, M. (1992), 'Capital Disadvantage: America's Failing Capital Investment System', *Harvard Business Review*, Sep.–Oct.: 65–82.

Pryor, F., and D. Schaffer (1999), *Who's Not Working and Why*, Cambridge: Cambridge University Press.

Qian, Y. (2003), 'How Reform Worked in China', in D. Rodrik (ed.), *In Search of Prosperity*, Princeton: Princeton University Press.

Rajan, R., and L. Zingales (2003), *Saving Capitalism from the Capitalists*, London: Random House.

Robinson, J. (1971), *Economic Heresies*, Basingstoke: Macmillan.

Rodrik, D. (1997), 'Trade, Social Insurance and the Limits to Globalisation', NBER Working Paper 5905.

Romer, C., and D. Romer (2002), 'The Evolution of Economic Understanding and Post-War Stabilisation Policy', NBER Working Paper 9274.

Rowthorn, R. (1995), 'Capital Formation and Unemployment', *Oxford Review of Economic Policy*, 11(1): 26–39.

—— and K. Coutts (2004), 'Deindustrialisation and the Balance of Payments in Advanced Countries', *Cambridge Journal of Economics*, 28(5): 767–90.

—— and J. Wells (1987), *Deindustrialisation and Foreign Trade*, Cambridge: Cambridge University Press.

Rubin, R. (2001), Comment on 'Fiscal Policy' in J. Frankel and P. Orszag (eds.), *American Economic Policy in the 1990s*, Cambridge, Mass.: MIT Press.

——(2003), *In An Uncertain World*, New York: Random House.

Rumbaugh, T. and N. Blancher (2004), 'International Trade and the Challenges of WTO accession', in E. Prasad (ed.), *China's Growth and Integration into the World Economy*, IMF Occasional Paper 232.

Runciman, D. (2005), Review of *Death by a Thousand Cuts: The Fight over Taxing Inherited Wealth* by Michael Graetz and Ian Shapiro, *London Review of Books*, 27(11) (2 June).

Sachs, J., and C. Wyplosz (1986), 'The Economic Consequences of President Mitterrand', *Economic Policy*, 2: 262–322.

Samuelson, P. (2004), 'Where Ricardo and Mill Rebut and Confirm Arguments of Mainstream Economists Supporting Globalisation', *Journal of Economic Perspectives*, 18(3): 135–46.

Sachdev, S. (2004), 'Paying The Cost: Public Private Partnerships and the Public Service'. Catalyst Working Paper.

Saxonhouse, G., and R. Stern (2003), 'The Bubble and the Lost Decade', *World Economy*, 26(3): 267–82.

Scanlon, K., and C. Whitehead (2004), 'Housing Tenure and Mortgage Systems: A Survey of 19 Countries', mimeo. London School of Economics.

Schor, J. (1992), *The Overworked American*, New York: Basic Books.

——(2004), 'Understanding the New Consumerism: Inequality, Emulation and the Erosion of Well Being', http://www.2.bc.edu/~schorj/

Schwarbish, T., T. Smeeding, and L. Osberg (2004), 'Income Distribution and Social Expenditures: A Cross National Perspective', http://www-cpr.maxwell.syr.edu/faculty/smeeding.

Sennett, R. (1998), *The Corrosion of Character*, New York: W. W. Norton.

Sharpe, A. (2004), 'Ten Productivity Puzzles Facing Researchers', *International Productivity Monitor* No. 9, http://www.csls.ca/ipm/ipm9.asp

Shiller, R. (2000), *Irrational Exuberance*, Princeton: Princeton University Press.

——(2003), 'From Efficient Markets Theory to Behavioural Finance', *Journal of Economic Perspectives*, 17(1): 83–104.

Shleifer, A. (2000), *Inefficient Markets*, Oxford: Oxford University Press.

Sinclair, S. (2003), 'The WTO and its GATS', in J. Michie (ed.), *The Handbook of Globalisation*, Cheltenham: Edward Elgar.

Sinn, H.-W. (2002), 'The New Systems Competition', NBER Working Paper 8747.

——(2003), 'The Laggard of Europe', CESifo Special Report 1/2003.

Smeeding, T. (2002), 'Globalisation, Inequality and the Rich Countries of the G-20', Luxembourg Income Study Working Paper No. 320.

——(2004), 'Public Policy and Economic Inequality: The United States in Comparative Perspective', Luxembourg Income Study Working Paper No. 367.

Soskice, D. (1978), 'Strike Waves and Wage Explosions, 1968–70: An Economic Interpretation', in C. Crouch and A. Pizzorno (eds.), *The Resurgence of Class Conflict in Western Europe*, Basingstoke: Macmillan.

——(1994), 'Reconciling Markets and Institutions: The German Apprenticeship System' in L. Lynch (ed.), *Training and the Private Sector*, Chicago: Chicao University Press.

Stiglitz, J. (2002), *Globalisation and its Discontents*, London: Allen Lane.

——(2004), 'Capital Market Liberalisation, Globalisation and the IMF', *Oxford Review of Economic Policy*, 20(1): 57–71.

Stultz, R. (2004), 'Sould we Fear Derivatives', NBER Working Paper 10574.

—— (2005), 'The Limits of Financial Globalisation', NBER Working Paper 11070.

Summers, L. (2002), 'Comment on Between Meltdown and Moral Hazard', in J. Frankel and P. Orzag (eds.), *American Economic Policy in the 1990s*, Cambridge, Mass.: MIT Press.

Sutcliffe, B. (2004), 'World Inequality and Globalisation', *Oxford Review of Economic Policy*, 20(11): 15–37.

—— and A. Glyn (2003), 'Measures of Globalization and their Misinterpretation' in J. Michie (ed.), *The Handbook of Globalisation*, Cheltenham: Edward Elgar.

Svallfors, S. (1997), 'Worlds of Welfare and Attitudes to Redistribution: A Comparison of Eight Western Nations', *European Sociological Review*, 13(3): 283–304.

Thelen, K., and I. Kume (2005), 'Coordination as a Political Problem in Coordinated Market Economies', forthcoming in *Governance*.

Torrini, R. (2005), 'Profit Share and Returns on Capital Stock in Italy: The Role of Privatisations behind the Rise of the 1990s', CEP LSE Discussion Paper 671.

UNCTAD (2004), *World Investment Report 2004*, Geneva: UNCTAD.

US Government (2002), *Economic Report of the President*, Washington.

Van Parijs, P. (2001), *Whats Wrong with a Free Lunch*, Boston, Beacon Press.

Van Parijs, P. (2003), 'Basic Income: A Simple and Powerful Idea for the 21st Century', in E. Wright (ed.), *Redesigning Distribution: Basic Income and Stakeholder Grants as Designs for a More Egalitarian Capitalism*, London: Verso.

Vartiainen, J. (2001), 'Understanding Swedish Social Democracy: Victims of Success', in A. Glyn (ed.), *Social Democracy in Neoliberal Times*, Oxford: Oxford University Press.

Vatter, H., and J. Walker (2001), 'Did the 1990s Inaugurate a New Economy', *Challenge*, Jan./Feb.: 90–115.

Webster, D. (2000), 'The Geographical Concentration of Labour-market Disadvantage', *Oxford Review of Economic Policy*, 16(1): 114–28.

Weitzman, M. (1992), Comment on Nordhaus (1992), *Brookings Papers on Economic Activity*, 2: 50–4.

White, W. (2004), 'Are Changes in Financial Structure Extending Safety Nets?' Bank for International Settlements Working Paper No. 145.

Willner, J. (2003), 'Privatisation: A Sceptical Analysis', in D. Parker and D. Saal (eds.), *International Handbook of Privatisation*, Cheltenham: Edward Elgar.

Wolf, M. (2004), *Why Globalisation Works*, New Haven: Yale University Press.

Wood, A. (1994), *North South Trade, Employment and Inequality*, Oxford: Oxford University Press.

Woodward, B. (1994), *The Agenda*, New York: Simon and Schuster.

Woolley, P. (2004), 'How Hedge Funds are Destabilising the Markets', *Financial Times*, 29 Sept.

World Bank (2003), *World Development Indicators*, Washington: World Bank.

Index

agriculture 3, 105
Alchian, A. 19
Alesina, A. 35, 176, 180
Armstrong, P. 3
Arthur Andersen 59–60
Asian crisis 69, 73–5, 139, 152
Atkinson, A. 182
Australia 53
Austria 109, 121–2, 123
automatic stabilizers 33

Baker, D. 47
balance of payments 10, 66, 133, 195
Bank for International Settlements
    (BIS) 69–70, 74, 85
bank regulation 149–50
banking crises 69–70
Basic Income 180–3
Belgium 169
Bell, B. 120
benefits:
    disincentive effects 47–8, 159–60
    means-tested 159–60
    and poverty 171–3, 198
    sickness 107
    unemployment 115–16, 187
    see also Basic Income; welfare state
Benn, Tony 20
Berle A. 55
Bertola, G. 120
Besley, T. 45
Blair, Tony 116, 167, 173
Blanchard, O. 145
Bretton Woods 10–11, 66
Brown, Gordon 32
budgetary consolidation 35–6
Bush, George 57
Bush, George W. 35

Canada 53, 120, 165, 169, 171, 174
capital
    accumulation 4, 13–14, 40, 52–3,
        86–90, 134, 195
    controls on 65, 69
    flows 66
    and profits 8
    venture 63–4
    see also investment
capital-labour ratio 153
Card, D. 120
Cassidy, J. 59
Central Bank, independence 32
Chan, A. 94
Chan, N. 72
China 16, 139
    exports and imports 90–6, 195
    foreign direct investment 100
    growth 87–90
    impact on the North 153
    investment 87
    labour 153–4
    profits 87–8
    share of world GDP 88
    source of instability 154
    trade unions 94–5
    wages 93–4
    yuan 95
Clinton, Bill 34, 137
Club of Rane 10
Coffee, J. 59–60, 62
Comin, D. 150
commodity prices 9–10, 185
competition:
    and instability 150
    international 8, 97–8
    and investment 130
    and privatization 39

competitive tendering 43
competitiveness, and exchange
    rates 67
consumption:
    and growth 52–4, 132, 136, 139
corporate governance 58–63
corporate scandals 59–63
corporation tax 161, 164, 176, 196
    see also taxation
creative destruction 130, 137
crisis of capitalism 2, 151
crony capitalism 75
currency crisis 68–9

deindustrialization 105, 123
DeLong, B. 75
demand 15, 53, 134, 136
Denmark 123, 168
deregulation 42, 144
    financial markets 51, 54, 65, 70,
        137–9,142–3
    labour markets 45–8, 144
    product markets 144
    see also liberalization
derivatives 71, 72
Dertouzos, M. 78, 79
disincentive effects 159–60
distribution see Gini coefficient;
    inequality; redistribution
Dodd, R. 73
dollar 67–8, 79–86

earnings see wages
Economist viii, ix, 113
Eichengreen, B. 69, 75
employment 3, 88, 105
    effects of outsourcing 99
    law-skilled 107–9, 120
    male\female 3, 106–7, 190
    manufacturing 64–5, 98, 105
    public sector 18, 44
    self-employment 3
    and structural change 104–7
employment protection legislation
    (EPL) 4–5, 46, 114–15
Enron 59–60, 63
enterprise egoism 126
environmental concerns 178–9
environmental constraints 131–2,
    154–5

equality of opportunity 173
Esping-Andersen, G. 174
Euro 67, 145
Europe
    deregulation 144
    employment 105–9
    productivity 14, 78–9, 143–5
    profits 145–6
European Central Bank 30, 144
European Union 121
    foreign direct investment 100
    Growth and Stability Pact 33, 36,
        144–5
exchange rates 12, 147, 185, 188
    Bretton Woods 10–11
    and capital flows 66
    and competitiveness 67
    real and nominal 12–13, 67–9,
        79–80
exports 96–7, 139–40

Fforde, J. 28
finance, international 65–9
financial markets:
    allocation of capital 54–5
    deregulation 51, 54, 65, 70, 137–9,
        142–3
    discipline 32–6
    instability 69–75
    international 65–9
financial press 60
financial sector 51–2
Financial Times 21, 59
Finland 53, 122–3, 170, 171
fiscal policy 28, 33–6
Ford 72–3
Fordism 14
foreign direct investment (FDI)
    100–2, 164, 196
foreign exchange reserves 85
Fortin, N. 118
France 36, 87
    deregulation 144
    employment protection 114–15
    'Franc fort' policy 28
    inequality 168, 177
    inflation 30
    nationalization 21
    pension funds 56
    privatization 41

profit rate 146
property incomes 170
savings ratio 53
strikes 5
trade union 122, 123
wages 118–19
working hours 113
Frankel, J. 81
Frey, B. 178
Friedman, M. 25, 31, 53
Fukuo, M. 139

Germany 36, 87
co-determination 18–19
deregulation 144
employment protection 114
exchange rates 147
industrial relations 126
inflation 11, 27, 29
job satisfaction 179
low-skilled labour 109
Mannesman 62
outsourcing 99
pension funds 56
poverty 171, 172
prices 185
productivity 9, 147
profit rate 145–6
reunification 147–8, 151
savings ratio 53–4
social mobility 174
strikes 5
trade unions 122
welfare state 177
working hours 113
Ghatak, M. 45
Gini coefficient 172
globalization:
and capital accumulation 86–90
definition 77
effect on USA 78–9
and welfare spending 162–4
world trade 96–9
see also exports; foreign direct
investment (FDI); imports;
international trade
GM 72–3
Golden Age 1, 78, 87, 98, 105, 126, 151
Goodhart, C. 149–50
Goodman, P. 95

Goos, M. 109
Gordon, P. 145
Gough, N. 94, 95
government:
deficits 32–6
employment 18
private procurement 42–5
spending 17, 133, 136–7, 186, 194,
196
Green, F. 114
Green, R. 114
Greenspan, Alan 34, 72, 137, 149
Gregory, P. 16
growth: 192
and distribution 176
in China 87–90
in Europe 143–8
future of 150–5
in Japan 138–43
New Economy in USA 132–8
in rich countries 130–2
in Soviet Union 16
unstable 148–50
Guardian 43

happiness 178–80
Haskel, J. 39
hedge funds 71, 72–3
Holmstrom, B. 58, 63
hours of work 5, 113–4, 180
Howell, D. 120
Hoshi, T. 140
Huber, E. 172
Huebler, F. 120

IMF 20, 121
Financial Stability Report 152–3
orthodox policies 46–7, 73–5, 85
imports:
impact on low-skilled labour 109,
110–11
manufactures 195
penetration 97–8
incomes policies 25
India 153
Indonesia 75
inequality 197
attitudes to 177
bottom of distibution 169
and liberalization 167–8

inequality (*cont.*)
  international companies 167–70
  top of distribution 169, 170
  and unemployment 119–20,
    169–70
  see also Gini coefficient;
    redistribution
inflation:
  dispersion 11, 28
  increase in 2, 5–6
  and interest rates 26–7, 29–30
  and real exchange rates 12–13
  and real wages 6, 184
  unpredictable 51
instability, macroeconomic 148–50
interest rates 186–7
  and inflation 26–7, 29–30
  rising 25–7
  and unemployment 26–7
  see also monetary policy
international competition 8, 97–8
international finance 65–9
international payments, imbalances 11
international trade 96–9, 190
  see also exports; globalization;
    imports
Intitial Public Offering (IPO) 60
investment 133, 134, 189
  and competition 130
  falling 139–40
  institutional 56–7, 58
  and productivity 13–14
  and welfare state 160–1
  see also capital
investment banks 60
investment managers 60–1
Ireland 123, 173
Italy
  deregulation 144
  employment protection 114
  happiness 178
  inflation 11
  prices 185
  profit rate 146
  savings ratio 53
  strikes 5
  trade union 122, 123
Itoh, M. 23, 151
Iversen, T. 120

Japan
  capital 80, 87
  consumption 139
  deficit 36
  exports 92, 97, 139–40
  financial deregulation 138–9, 142–3
  foreign direct investment 100
  happiness 178
  imports 91
  incomes policies 25
  industrial relations 126
  inflation 29
  investment 139–40
  outsourcing 99
  pension funds 56
  poverty 173
  productivity 9, 14, 78–9
  profits 141–2, 193
  savings ratio 139
  stability 148–9
  stagnation 138–42, 151
  trade unions 41
Jenkinson, T. 44
Jensen, M. 56
job satisfaction 179, 181–2
Jospin, Lionel 41
Jurgens, U. 95

Kalecki, M. 31
Kaminsky, G. 68
Kaplan, S. 58, 63
Kashyap, T. 140
Kenworthy, L. 172
Keynes, J M 33, 52, 64, 152, 180
Klein, M. 68
Korea 75, 87
Korpi, W. 172

labour 3–8, 39–40
  dismissals 46
  low-skilled 107–13
  productivity 9
  qualified 111–12
  surplus 153–4
labour market:
  unskilled 110, 111
  deregulation 45–8, 144
  regulation 162
  rigidities 47

Laffer curve 160
land price bubble 138–9, 140, 141–2
Lardy, N. 87
Layard, P. 178
Lev, B. 63
liberalization 51, 167–70
see also deregulation
Lindert, P. 160
Long-Term Capital Management (LTCM) 50, 70–3
Lord Chalfont 8
Louvre Accord 81
Lundberg, E. 19
Luxemburg, Rosa 153

McCraken Report 13
Macmillan, Harold 38
Maddison, A. 87
Malthus, Robert 154
management pay 58–9
Mannesman 62
Manning, A. 109
manufacturing:
  employment 98, 111, 135
  profit share 7, 184–5
Marx, Karl viii, 31, 52, 77, 88
Means G. 55
Meidner, R. 19
Mexico 168
migration 3–4, 102, 176–7
Miller, M. 50
Mitterand, François 21, 28, 41
monetary policy 27, 28, 149
  see also interest rates
Motonishi, T. 140
Multi Fibre Agreement 91
Mussa, M. 24

nationalization 20, 21, 41
Navarro, V. 166
Netherlands 17, 53, 109, 113, 114, 166
New Economy 132–8
New Zealand 121–2, 168, 171, 173
Nickell, S. 120
Non-Accelerating Inflation Rate of Unemployment (NAIRU) 30–1
Nordhaus, W. 131, 154
North-South trade 97–8, 110, 153

Norway 109, 170, 177
Nove, A. 16

OECD
  Economic Policy Reforms 165
  Jobs Strategy 144
  Jobs Study 45–6, 165
  and deregulation 45–6, 121
Ofek, E. 57
oil price hike 2, 9–10, 33
Okun, A. 160
OPEC 2, 9–10, 33
optimism 21–3
outsourcing 43, 99

Palme, J. 172
Pan, P. 95
paradox of redistribution 172, 183
Parmalat 62
Parenteau, R. 61, 77, 149
part-time work 113
Participation Income 182
pension funds 55–6, 73
Perotti, R. 35
Philippon, T. 150
Piketty, T. 118
planned economies 2, 16
Plender, J. 72
Pontusson, J. 19, 172
population growth 152
  ageing 143
Porter, M. 61
Portugal 66
poverty 198
  child 173
  international comparisons 170–5
price regulation 39
prices:
  commodity 9–10, 185
  consumer 116
  land 138–9, 140, 141–2
  stock market 21–5
private finance initiatives (PFIs) 43–4
private procurement 42–5
privatization 37–42
  gainers and losers 38, 40–1
  motivation for 38–9
  productivity effects 38–40

productivity 2, 39–40, 78, 151
  China 93
  and deregulation 144
  Germany 147
  and globalizaton 164
  and investment 13–14
  labour 9, 116, 125, 143, 185, 196
  manufacturing 188
  New Economy 133–4
  retail sector 135–6, 145
  services 3, 158–9
  slowdown 13–15
  and taxation 163, 167
profits 7, 39–40, 141, 145–6, 154, 192–3
  exaggerated 135
  financial sector 187–8
  maximization 55
  rate of 8
  restoration 130
  share of 116, 184–5
  and wages 8
property incomes 170
Pryor, F. 112

Radiohead, 104
Rajan, R. 56
Reagan, Ronald 131
redistribution:
  and growth 176
  paradox of 172, 183
  of spending power 17–18
  see also inequality; taxation
regulation 42, 152
  and firms' costs 162
Rehbehn, R. 95
relative price effect 159
replacement ratio 115–16
research publications rankings 92
Richardson, M. 57
risk-taking 70, 143
Robinson, J. 129
Rowling, J. K. 182
Rubin, Robert 34–5

Sachs, J. 28
Saez, E. 118
savings ratio 53, 139

Schaffer, D. 112
Schmidt, Helmut 161
Schor, J. 179, 180
Schumpeter, Joseph 130, 137
Schwarbish, T. 164, 176
Sennett, R. 179
services 3
  employment 106
  exports 98–9
  foreign direct investment 101
  labour demand 110, 111
shareholder value 55, 58, 63–5
Shiller, R. 57
Shleifer, A. 64
sickness benefits 107
Sinn, H.-W. 176
Smith, Adam 50, 152
social mobility 174–5, 194
social pacts 30
social welfare see welfare state
Soviet Union 2, 16
Spain 114, 144, 168, 177
stagflation 25
state see government
Stephens, J. 172
Stiglitz, J. 74–5
stock markets:
  high 56–7
  internet boom 57, 64
  prices 21–3
stock options 58–9
strikes 5, 31, 123–4, 184
  miners 8, 124, 145
  and unemployment 32, 187
  see also trade unions
Stuart, R. 16
Stutzer, A. 178
Summers, Larry 82
Sweden
  financial deregulation 137–8
  incomes policies 25
  industrial relations 126
  inequality 168, 177
  inflation 30
  low-skilled labour 109
  monetary policy 28–9
  poverty 171, 172
  savings ratio 53
  social welfare 166–7

state share in GDP 17
wage-earner funds 19
working hours 113

takeovers, hostile 58, 62, 65
tax revenue:
  constraints on 163–7
  and productivity growth 163
tax wedge 165
taxation 46, 161–2, 167
  competition between countries 164
  and poverty 171–3, 198
  see also corporation tax
technical progress 109–10
Thatcher, Margaret 27, 39, 116, 131,
  145, 168, 173
The Times 8
Toyota 62
trade unions 145
  China 94–5
  coverage 122
  declining influence 112, 121–6
  membership 4, 123, 191
  power 2, 15
  see also strikes

unemployment 4, 126, 186, 194
  and benefits 46–8, 107, 115–6, 187
  and industrial conflict 31, 187
  and inequality 169–70
  and inactivity 107
  and interest rates 26–7
  and labour market deregulation
    45–8
  and monetary policy 28
  Non-Accelerating Inflation Rate of
    Unemployment (NAIRU) 30–1
  rising 25, 104–7
unemployment benefits 46–7
  and earnings 158, 191
  replacement ratio 115–16
unions *see* trade unions
United Kingdom 194
  capitalization ratio 52
  exports 98
  happiness 178, 179
  health spending 167
  import controls 21
  incomes policies 25

  inequality 168, 177
  inflation 30
  Labour Party 20
  low pay 169
  low-skilled labour 110
  monetary policy 27
  nationalization 20
  NHS 44–5
  outsourcing 99
  pension funds 56
  poverty 171, 172, 173
  private procurment 43–5
  privatization 37–40
  productivity 167
  profit rate 145–6
  public sector employment 44
  savings ratio 53–4
  social mobility 174
  strikes 5, 8, 124
  trade unions 122–3, 123–5
  utilities 38
United States of America
  balance of payments 9, 79–86,
    82–4, 133, 195
  budget deficits 34–6
  consumption 82, 145
  corporate scandals 59–62
  current account deficit 83–4
  direct investment 9, 83, 84
  dollar 67–8, 79–86
  employment 105–7, 111–2
  exports 9, 83, 97
  Federal Reserve 25, 80, 149
  financial sector 52
  government spending 133, 136–7
  happiness 178, 179
  household consumption 53
  inequality 168, 177
  inflation 30
  interest rates 25–7, 80, 186
  international leader 2, 8–9
  investment 84, 133, 134, 189
  low pay 169
  low-skilled labour 108–9
  management pay 58, 118
  manufacturing employment 64–5
  migration policy 102
  MIT Commission on Industrial
    Productivity 78

United States of America (*cont.*)
  monetary policy 27, 149
  New Economy 132–8, 151
  outsourcing 99
  payments deficits 66–7
  pension funds 56
  poverty 171, 173
  prices 185
  productivity 9, 14–5, 78–9, 133–5, 167
  profits 81, 135–6, 192
  property incomes 170
  recession 36
  Sarbanes-Oxley Act 62–3
  savings ratio 53–4
  social mobility 174
  stock market boom 56–7
  strikes 5, 27
  trade union 121–2, 123
  wages 116, 117
  working hours 113
Updike, J. 77
urban population expansion 3–4

Vartiainen, J. 167
venture capital 63–4
Vodafone 62
Volker, P. 25–7, 80

wage bargaining 122–3, 124, 169
wages 5–6, 39–40, 116–19, 189
  in China 93–4
  differentials 117, 191
  distribution 116–19, 163
  dual role 154

  flexibility 119–21
  and inflation 184
  low 169
  management pay 58–9
  and profits 8
  and share prices 22, 186
  minimum 46, 118–19
  top end 118, 163
  and unemployment benefits 158
  union premium 124–5
  women's 118
Wall Street Journal 60
Weitzman, M. 156
welfare state:
  cuts 35–6; resistance to 165–7, 177
  function of 157–8
  and investment 160–1
  source of revenue for 159–63
  spending on 17–18, 157–9
  see also Basic Income; benefits
White, W. 70
Wolf, M. 167
Wood, A. 110
work:
  hours of 5, 113–14, 180
  insecurity 115
  intensity 114, 125
Wyplosz, C. 28

yen 67
Yoshikawa 140
yuan 95

Zapata 57
Zingales, L. 56